John Bell, Lorenz Lange

Travels from St. Petersburg, in Russia, to Diverse Parts of Asia

John Bell, Lorenz Lange

Travels from St. Petersburg, in Russia, to Diverse Parts of Asia

ISBN/EAN: 9783744795647

Printed in Europe, USA, Canada, Australia, Japan

Cover: Foto ©Andreas Hilbeck / pixelio.de

More available books at **www.hansebooks.com**

TRAVELS
FROM
ST. PETERSBURG
IN
RUSSIA,
TO
DIVERSE PARTS
OF
ASIA.
IN
TWO VOLUMES.

BY

JOHN BELL,
OF ANTERMONY.

VOLUME I.
CONTAINING

A journey to ISPAHAN in PERSIA, in the years 1715, 1716, 1717, and 1718.
Part of a journey to PEKIN in CHI-NA, through SIBERIA, in the years 1719, 1720, and 1721. With a map of the Author's two routes between MOSCO and PEKIN.

GLASGOW:
PRINTED FOR THE AUTHOR BY ROBERT AND ANDREW FOULIS
PRINTERS TO THE UNIVERSITY
M.DCC.LXIII.

Sold by R. & A FOULIS, and A. STALKER at GLASGOW; KINCAID & BELL at EDINBURGH; A. MILLER, J. NOURSE, T. BECKET & P. A de HONDT, and C. HENDERSON in LONDON; J. LEAKE, and J. FREDERICK at BATH; and T. CADELL at BRISTOL.

TO THE
GOVERNOR,
COURT OF ASSISTANTS,
AND FREEMEN
OF THE
RUSSIA-COMPANY;
AND TO THE
BRITISH FACTORIES
IN RUSSIA;

THE FOLLOWING
RELATIONS OF TRAVELS, &c.
ARE
RESPECTFULLY INSCRIBED,
AS A TESTIMONY OF GRATITUDE
FOR THE FAVOURS RECEIVED,
FROM MANY OF THEM, BY

THEIR MOST OBEDIENT,

AND VERY HUMBLE SERVANT,

ANTERMONY, the
1st of October, 1762.

THE AUTHOR.

THE SUBSCRIBERS.

A.

THE right hon. Earl of Aylesford.
George Abercromby of Tillibody, Esq;
Isaac Akerman, Esq; Fenchurch-street.
Ralph Allen, Esq; Prior-park, 2 sets.
Sir John Anstruther of Anstruther, Bart. 2 sets.
John Anderson, Esq; London.
Sir Charles Asgill, Bart. 2 sets.
Mr. Hugh Atkins, merchant, London, 4 sets.

B.

The right hon. Lord Belhaven.
The right hon Lord Bruce.
The hon. George Brown of Coalston, senator of the College of Justice.
The rev. Thomas Bagshaw, D. D.
The hon. George Baillie of Jerviswood, Esq;
William Baird of New-Baith, Esq;
Henry Baker, Esq; F. R. S.
James Barclay, Esq;
John Barclay, Esq;
David Barclay, junr. Esq;
The rev. Dr. Barclay, Fellow of Merton-coll. Oxon.
James Robinson Barclay of Kevle, Esq;
Richard Becher, Esq;
Thomas Becket, bookseller, London.
Peter Bell, senr. Esq; Glasgow.
Peter Bell, junr.
William Bell, merchant at Leith, 3 sets.
The rev. Mr. William Bell, minister at Campsey.
Mr. William Bell of Guernsey.
Archibald Bell at Manchester.
Capt. Thomas Bennet, London.
James Benson, Esq; London.
Thomas Best, Esq;
Capt. Leonard Bazer, London.
Dr. Birch, secretary to the Royal Society.
Dr. Blair.
Blount, apothecary to the Devon-hospital, Exon.
Charles Bouchier, Esq; Edmonton.
The rev. Mr. Bouchery, Swaffham.
John Bond of Grange, Esq;
The hon. Alex. Boswell of Auchinleck, senator of the College of Justice.
Boyd of Trochrig, Esq;
Sir Brook Bridges, Bart.
Isaac Hawkins Brown, Esq;
The rev. Mr. John Bradfute.
Thomas Berney Bramston of Skreens, Esq;
Alexander Brown of Ardrie.
Jacob Bryant, Esq;
James Buchanan of Drumpellier, Esq;
Arch. Buchanan of Drumnikil, Esq;
The rev. Dr. Buckler, Fellow of All-Souls, Oxon.
Mrs. Buchanan of Auchinreoch.
Merrick Burrell, Esq;
James Burnet of Mountbodo, Esq;
The rev. Mr. Bush of London.
John Byrom, M. D. Manchester.
Edward Byrom of Manchester.
Mr. Bruch.
James Bell of Kirkton, Esq;
Matthew Bell, Esq; of Newcastle.
Andrew Burnet, merchant of St. Petersburg.

C.

The right hon. Earl of Cardigan.
The right hon. Earl of Chesterfield.

The

THE SUBSCRIBERS.

The right hon. Earl Cowper.
The right hon. Countess-dowager of Carlisle.
The right rev. Bp. of Carlisle, F. R. S.
David Cadder of Inchbruch.
William Caddle, junr. of Carron.
John Cameron of Carntyn.
Mrs. Mary Campbell of Balquhane
The hon. John Campbell, junr. of Stonefield, senator of the College of Justice.
Dr. John Campbell.
Alex. Campbell, surgeon at Pool.
Daniel Campbell, Esq;
John Campbell, Esq;
Daniel Campbell of Shawfield, Esq;
Pryce Campbell, Esq;
Lieut. Col. Robert Campbell.
John Callendar of Craigforth, Esq;
John Carmichael of Castlecraig, Esq;
James Carmichael of Hales, Esq;
John Cathcart, Esq;
James Caulet, Esq;
John Cayley, merchant, St. Petersburg.
James Cheap of Sawchy, Esq;
The rev. Dr. Samuel Chandler.
Alex. Chancelour of Shielhill, Esq;
Joseph Chippendall of Manchester.
            Cholwell, Esq; of the Temple.
Richard Champion, Esq; of Bristol.
William Champion, Esq; of Bristol.
Sir James Clark of Pennycook, Bart.
Dr. Matthew Clarke.
The rev. Mr. John Clayton of Manchester.
Benjamin Coole of St. Petersburg, merchant.
Dr. John Cook of Hamilton.
Peter Collinson, F. R. S.
William Colquhoun of Garscadden Esq;
Andrew Cochrane, Esq; late provost of Glasgow.
Peter Colvil, junr. of Ochiltrie, Esq;

John Cornwall, Esq; of London.
James Corbett of Tolcross, Esq;
James Corbett, merchant in Glasgow.
Josiah Cotton, Esq; Old Jewry.
Hosea Coates, Esq; of Dublin.
Oliver Coult, Esq;
Nicholas Crisp, Esq;
Crayle Crayle, Esq;
John Cruikshank, merchant of London, 6 sets.
William Cumming, M. D. of Dorchester.
Alex. Cunningham, Esq; of Edinburgh.
Mr.   Currie.
John Campbell of Clathick, Esq;
John Campbell, Esq;
James Campbell of Ardkinlas, Esq;
Mrs. Campbell of Menzie.
Alan Cuthbertson, merchant in Glasgow.

D.

Her Grace the Dutchess of Douglas, 6 sets.
The right hon. the Earl of Dunmore.
Baron De Witz minister from Mecklenburg.
The right hon. Robert Dundas of Arniston, Lord President of the Court of Session.
Sir David Dalrymple, Bart.
Theophilus Daubuz, Esq;
Robert Davenport, merchant in Lond.
John Davie, merchant in Edinburgh.
Andrew Devisme, Esq; London.
John Deponthieu merchant, London.
John H. Demorin, merchant, St. Petersburg.
Simon Desnizkoi, from the university of Mosco, at present student at the University of Glasgow.
Robert Dingley, Esq; London.
Henry Digge, Esq;
John Dickson of Kilbucko, Esq;
The rev. John Dickenson, A. M. Wisbich.
            Dickenson, Esq; Lincoln's Inn.

Sir

THE SUBSCRIBERS.

Sir Alex. Dick of Prestonfield, Bart.
Alex. Donaldson, bookseller, Edinb.
Mrs. Duncan at Edinburgh.
The rev. Christopher Duffield of Featherstone.
George Drummond of Blairdrummond, Esq;
Alex. Duff of Hatton, Esq;
Thomas Dundas of Quarrell, Esq;
Henry Dundas, Esq; advocate, 2 sets.
The rev. Dr. Dumaresque.
Governor Dinwiddie.
John Drummond of Logie-Almond, Esq;

E.

The right hon. Earl of Elgin.
The right hon. Earl of Errol.
The hon. Charles Elphinstone of Cumbernauld, Esq;
The hon. James Erskine of Barjarg, senator of the College of Justice.
John Erskine of Carnock, Esq;
Mr. David Erskine, writer in Edinb.
Peter Eaton, Esq;
Godolphin Edwards, Esq;
George Edwards, Esq;
John Erskine of Cardross, Esq;
James Erskine, Esq; advocate.
Thomas Eyre, Esq;
Miss Nelly Edmonston, of Newton.

F.

The hon. Edward Finch, Esq;
The hon. Mrs. Finch.
        Fall, Esq; provost of Dunbar.
Peter Fearon of London.
William Fergus of Kirkintilloch.
Sir Adam Ferguson of Kilkerran, Bart.
Robert Ferguson, Esq; Austin-friars.
Thomas Forester of Denovan.
John Fordyce, Esq; merchant in Edinb.
The rev. Mr. Forester, rector of Passenham, Northamptonshire.
Robert Fordyce, merch. in Aberdeen.

Dr. William Freer, Edinburgh.
Miss Freame.
Robert Freeland of Kirkintilloch.
Joseph Freame, Esq; of London.
Moses Franco, Esq;
James Frampton of Mozeton, Esq;
George Fraser of Edinburgh.
George Fullerton, Esq; at Leith.
William Frederick, bookseller, Bath.

G.

The right hon. John Earl of Granville, Knight of the Garter, President of the Privy Council, &c. 50 sets.
The right hon. Earl of Granard.
The right hon. Earl of Glencairn.
The right rev. Bishop of Glocester.
The hon. William Grant of Preston-Grange, senator of the College of Justice.
Francis Garden, Esq; one of his Majesty's sollicitors.
Dr. Gardiner of Great Massingham, Norfolk.
Robert Gardiner of Edinburgh.
Alexander Garden of Troup, Esq;
John Gibson, broker in London.
Osgood Gee, Esq;
Phil. Gell, Esq; of Hopeton, Derbyshire.
John Garshore of Garshore, Esq;
Alex. Gibson, junr. of Durye, Esq;
Mr. John Glassford, merchant in Glasgow.
James Glen, Esq; late governor of S. Carolina.
Thomas Goldney, Esq; of Clifton.
Mrs. Ann Goldney of Clifton.
Mrs. Gordon at Glasgow.
Chamberlain Godfrey, Esq;
Joseph Godfrey, Esq;
Peter Godfrey, Esq;
Edmund Godfrey, Esq;
Thomas Godfrey, Esq;
Richard Gough, Esq;

William

THE SUBSCRIBERS.

William Gomm, junr. merchant, St. Petersburg.
John Gordon, Esq;
Charles Gough, Esq; London.
James Grieve, M. D. St. Petersburg.
Silvanus Grove, Esq;
James Groset of Breadisholm, Esq;
David Graham of Micklewood, Esq;
Sir Archibald Grant, Bart.
The rev. Mr. Andrew Gray, minister of New Kilpatrick.
The rev. Dr. Green, rector of Bell-Broughton, Worcestershire.
William Graham of Airth, Esq; 2 sets.
David Graeme of Orchill, Esq;
Henry Graeme, Esq; 2 sets.
John Galbreath of Balgare, Esq;
Library of the University of Glasgow.

H.
The right hon. Earl of Hyndford.
Countess of Hyndford.
Earl of Haddington.
Earl of Holdernesse.
Earl of Home.
The hon. James Hamilton, Esq;
Charles Hamilton of Wishaw, Esq;
Lady Hamilton of Roshall.
Henry Hamilton, Esq; Londonderry.
Robert Haldane of Glenegy, Esq;
Patrick Haldane, Esq;
Capel Hanbury, Esq;
Jonas Hanway, Esq;
Alex. Hay of Drummellier, Esq;
Will. Hay, junr. of Drummellier, Esq;
Rev. Mr. Harden.
John Hardman of Manchester.
George Hay of St. Petersburg.
George Gottfried Harenfeller of St. Petersburg.
Rev. Dr. Harrison of C. C. C. Oxford.
William Havard of London.
The hon. Dr. Hay.
John Hay of Belton, Esq;

William Heron, Esq;
James Henckell, Esq; London.
Rev. Mr. Humphrey Henchman.
Sir Robert Henderson of Fordell, Bart.
Thomas Hepburn, merchant in Edinb.
Patrick Heron of Heron, Esq;
Richard Hoare of Boreham, Esq;
William Hog and son, of Edinburgh.
William Hope Wier, Esq;
Edmund Holme of Manchester.
Charles Grave Hudson, F. R. S.
William Hudson, F. R. S.
Haldane, junr. of Lanerk, Esq;
Robert Hudson, Esq;

I.
Archibald Ingram, Esq; present Lord Provost of Glasgow.
James Jackson, merchant of St. Petersburgh.
William Johnston of London.

K.
Robert Kennedy of Aughtesardel, Esq;
James Kennedy of Kayly, Esq;
Thomas Kennedy, junr. of Denure, Esq;
Kincaid and Bell, booksellers in Edinburgh, 6 sets.
E. King, Esq; of Lincoln's Inn.
Marsden Kenyon of Manchester.
John Kincaid of Kincaid, Esq;
Mr. Geo. Kippen, merchant in Glasgow.
Henry Klausing of St. Petersburg, merchant.
Sir Wyndham Knatchbull, Bart.
Thomas Knight, Esq;

L.
The right hon. Earl of Leven.
William Lenox of Woodhead, Esq;
T. Llewellin, L. L. D.
W. J. Liebman, London.
Sir David Lindsay, Bart.
William Loch, writer, of Edinburgh.
Library

THE SUBSCRIBERS.

Library of Liverpool.
John Lockhart of Lee, Esq;
James Livingston, writer at Falkirk.
Thomas Lockhart, Esq;
Theodore Luders, Esq; counsellor of the embassy from the court of Russia.
Revd. Mr. Jonathan Lypeatt, of Boringer, Essex.
John Lenox, Esq;
Gilbert Laing, merchant in St. Petersburg.

M.

His serene highness Prince Charles of Mecklenburgh-Strelitz.
His serene highness Prince Ernest of Mecklenburgh-Strelitz.
His grace the Duke of Montrose, 6 sets.
The right hon. Earl of Marchmont.
The right hon. Earl of Macclesfield. P. R. S.
The right hon. Earl Mareschal.
The right hon. Lady Mansfield.
Righ. hon. and rev. Bishop of Meath.
The Laird of M‘Farlane.
Dr. M‘Farlane, of Edinburgh.
Dr. M‘Farlane, jun. of Edinburgh.
William M‘Farlane, Esq; of Aymouth.
Robert Mackye, Esq; of London, 4 sets.
Ebenezer M‘Culloch of Edinburgh.
Norman M‘Leod of M‘Leod, Esq;
Library of Manchester.
Robert M‘Nair of Falkirk.
Robert M‘Queen, Esq; advocate.
Arthur Maister, merchant of St. Petersburg.
George M‘Dougal of Makerston, Esq;
Sir William Maxwell of Springkell, Bart.
Sir James M‘Donald, Bart.
John Major, Esq; of London.
— Marks, Esq; of London.
Lascells Metcalf, Esq; of London.
Robert Menzies of Coulterhall, Esq;
Michael Miller, Esq; of Bristol.
John Misenor, Esq; of London.

Vol. I.

Richard Milles, Esq.
John Mills of London.
George Middleton of Seaton, Esq;
John Moor of Falkirk.
Dr. Mounsey, late director general of medicine in Russia.
Sir Roger Mostyn, Bart.
John Moor, Esq; rear-admiral.
Henry Moor, Esq; of Jamaica.
David Moncrief, Esq; deputy remembrancer of the exchequer, Scotland.
James Montgomery, Esq; one of his Majesty's sollicitors general.
James Moor, L. L. D. professor of Greek in the University of Glasgow.
William Murray of Touchadam, Esq;
Ja. Murray, Esq;
John Muirhead, Esq; of Gorbals.
The reverend Dr. Musgrave, provost of Christ's-coll. Oxford.
Henry Muilman, Esq; of London.
— Monro of Auchinbowie, Esq;
Mr. George Muirhead, professor of Humanity in the University of Glasgow.
James Mathias, Esq; of London.
James Murray of Abercairn, Esq;
Anthony Murray of Dollerie, Esq.
Alexander Munro, merchant in Glasgow.
— More of Leckie, Esq;

N.

The right hon. Lord Napier.
The rev. Mr. William Nairn, M. A. of Poole.
John Napier of Bolikinrene, Esq;
Lt. Colonel William Napier, 2 sets.
Miss Jenny Napier.
Doctor Napier of London.
Sir James Naismith of Posso, Bart.
Robert Nettleton, Esq; governor of the Russia company.
Nathaniel Newberry, merchant of London, 2 sets.
John Nourse, King's bookseller, Lond.

b — James

THE SUBSCRIBERS.

James Norman, Efq; London.
Henry Norris, Efq; London.
Wm. Northey, Efq; Grovefnor-fquare.
Lt. John Napier of Craiganet.
Houston Stewart Nicolfon of Carnock, Efq;

O.

The right hon. Earl of Orford.
Archibald Ogilvie of Rothemay, Efq;
Charles O Hara, Efq; of Dublin.
Leak Okeover of Okeover, Efq; Stafford-fhire.
George Ouchterlony, Efq. of London.
Library of C. C. C. Oxford.

P.

The right hon. Lord Chief Juftice Sir Charles Pratt.
David Paterfon of Bannockburn, Efq;
Robert Patrick, Efq; of Dublin.
Doctor Park of Kilmarnock.
Thomas Penn, Efq; of London, 6 fets.
The right hon. Lady Juliana Penn.
Mifs Penn.
Richard Penn, Efq;
Rev. Roger Pettyward, D. D.
Richard Pennant, Efq;
George Peters, Efq; of London.
Mrs. Pickard of Edmonton.
William Pickance of Liverpool.
Thomas Phipps, Efq;
Charles Pinfold, Efq;
M. de Plefcheoff, counfellor to the court of Ruffia.
Thomas Plummer, Efq;
Honourable Ifabella Powlett.
David Powell, jun. Efq;
William Palmer of London.

R.

The moft noble Marquis of Rockingham.
The right rev. Zachary, Bifhop of Rochefter.

David Rae, advocate.
Robert Ramfay, M. D. Edinburgh.
John Ramfay of Ouchtertyre, Efq;
James Robertfon, Efq;
Charles Rogers, Efq. F. R. S.
William Roberton, merchant of Glafgow.
Robert Rollo, fheriff-clerk of Clackmannan.
Lt. Colonel William Roy.
The rev. Mr. James Roy.
John Lockhart Rofs of Balnagown, Efq; 3 fets.
Andrew Reed, Efq; of London.
John Renton of Blackader, Efq;
James Reed of Briftol.
Jeremiah Redwood, Efq;
Sir Thomas Reeve, Knt.
John Van Rixtel, Efq; of London.
David Rofs, advocate.
Archibald Rofs, merchant St. Petersburg.
Dr. William Robertfon, Edinburgh.
Rufh, Efq;
Alexander Ruffel of Stirling.
Archibald Roberton, jun. of Bedlay, Efq;
Lorentz Baftian Ritter, merchant, St. Peterfburg.
Jacob Rigail, merchant, St. Peterfburg.
Mr. James Rannie, merchant in Leith.

S.

Her grace the Dutchefs dowager of Somerfet.
The right hon. the Earl of Suffolk.
The right hon. Earl of Sutherland.
The right hon. Lord Vifcount Spencer.
The right hon. Lady Vifcountefs Spencer.
Honourable George Sinclair of Woodhall, fenator of the College of Juftice.
Honourable Mrs. Southwell.
Sir William Saint Quintin, Bart.

Andrew

THE SUBSCRIBERS.

Andrew Saint Clare of Hermiston, Esq;
Robert Salisbury, Esq; of London.
Henry Saxby, Esq; of London.
Sir John Sebright, Bart.
Hugh Seton of Touch, Esq;
Roger Sedgewick, M. D. of Manchester.
Doctor Schomberg.
George L. Scott, Esq; commissioner of excise.
Henry Shiffner of Pontrylas, Esq;
Mrs. Shiffner of Pontrylas.
Walter Sharp, Esq; of London, 3 sets.
Mrs. Shaw of Chishunt.
Henry Sharp of Bermondsey, Esq;
William Sloane, Esq; of London.
Morgan Smith, Esq; of Bristol.
Charles Smith, Esq; of Bulogn.
John Smith of Buchanan.
John Smith, fellow commoner of Magdalen college, Oxford.
William Somervil, writer in Glasgow.
Joseph South, Esq;
Edward Southwell, Esq;
James Sperling, Esq; of London.
Charles Spence, Esq; London.
Harry Spencer, Esq;
John Russel Spence, Esq;
John Spencer, Esq;
Archibald Stirling of Keir, Esq;
Sir James Stirling of Glorat, Bart.
Lady Stirling of Glorat, 2 sets.
Sir William Stirling of Ardoch, Bart.
James Stirling of Calder, Esq;
Alexander Stirling, Esq; of St. Albans.
William Stirling, Esq;
Tho. Stephens, merchant in St. Petersburg.
Andrew Stalker, bookseller, Glasgow.
William Stewart, writer in Edinburgh.
Sir Archibald Stuart of Castlemilk.
John Struther, brewer in Glasgow.
George Stonehouse, Esq; of Standon, Wilts.
Dr. Charles Stuart of London, 3 sets.

Alexander Sutherland of Woodend, Esq;
Daniel Swaine of Laverington, Esq; Cambridge-shire.
The rev. Mr. James Stodart, minister of Kirkintilloch.
Swaffham Book-club.
Dr. Matthew Stuart, Prof. M. Edinb.
Samuel Swallow, Esq; consul general in Russia.
John Syme, writer to the Signet.
Walter Syme, merchant at Carron shore.
Walter Sim, merchant in Bothkennar.
William Steel, merchant in Glasgow.
Dr. Walter Stirling of Stirling.
Captain Thomas Stirling.
William Stirling of Northside, Esq;
James Saffre, merchant in St. Petersburg.
Mr. James Simson, merchant in Glasg.
Adam Smith, L.L.D. professor of Moral Philosophy in the University of Glasgow.
James Stirling, Esq; agent for the Scots-mining company at Leadhills.
Alexander Stevenson, Esq; clerk to the commissariot, Glasgow.

T.

The right hon. Lord Torphichen.
John Thornton, Esq; of London, 2 sets.
Sir Peter Thompson of Poole, Knt.
Andrew Thomson, Esq; of London.
John Thomson, Esq; of Edinburgh.
Alexander Thomson of Edinburgh.
Peter Thompson of Bermondsey, Esq;
Capt. William Thornton.
Sir Clement Trafford of Dunton-hall.
Lady Trafford of Dunton-hall.
Robert Tracy, Esq;
The rev. Dr. Tracy, fellow of All-souls, Oxford.
Henry Tuckfield.
Godfrey Thornton, merchant, St. Petersburg.

U.

Robert Urie, printer at Glasgow.

V. Mrs.

THE SUBSCRIBERS.

V.
Mrs. Vandewall of Greenwich.
Honourable James Veitch of Elliock, senator of the College of Justice.
James Vere, sen.
John Vere of Stonebyres, Esq;
Miss Vere of Stonebyres.
William Vigor of Taplow, Esq;
Mrs. Vigor of Taplow.
Benjamin Vigor, Esq;
Allen Vigor, of Manchester.
North Vigor, M. D.

W.
The right hon. Earl of Winchelsea.
The right hon. Lord Willoughby of Parham, F. R. S.
The right hon. Lady Charlotte Wentworth.
His excellency Count de Woronsoff, 3 sets.
William Wallace of Cairnhill, Esq;
John Watcot, Esq;
Dr. William Watson, F. R. S.
John Watson, merchant in St. Petersburg.
Joel Watson, Esq;
Capt. George Wauchope.
Rev. John Warden of Edinburgh.
John Weyland, Esq; of London.
Wensbry of Wisbitch.
Taylor White, Esq; of London.
George Whateby, Esq; of London.
Charles White, surgeon of Manchester, F. R. S.
Robert Whyt, surgeon at Falkirk.
Robert Willock, bookseller, London, 6 sets.
Sir Rowland Winn of Nostel, Bart.
Thomas Winn, Esq; of Aften.
John Wilkinson, Esq;
John Wills, Esq; of London.
Ralph Willet, Esq; of Marly.
Thomas Withington of Manchester.
John Wilson, writer at Glasgow.
Baron Wolff.
John Wright.
Major White.

Y.
The Right hon. Sir Wm. York, Bart.
William Young, Esq; of Standlinch, Wilts.
Robert Young, merchant at Edinburgh.

THE

PREFACE.

IN my youth I had a strong desire of seeing foreign parts; to satisfy which inclination, after having obtained, from some persons of worth, recommendatory letters to Doctor ARESKINE, chief physician and privy-counsellor to the Czar PETER the First, I embarked at LONDON, in the month of July 1714, on board the PROSPERITY of RAMSGATE, Capt. EMERSON, for ST. PETERSBURG. On my arrival there, I was received by Doctor ARESKINE in a very friendly manner; to whom I communicated

THE PREFACE.

municated my intentions of seeking an opportunity of visiting some parts of ASIA, at least those parts which border on RUSSIA. Such an opportunity soon presented itself, on occasion of an embassy, then preparing, from his Czarish Majesty to the Sophy of PERSIA.

ARTEMY PETROVICH VALENSKY, a gentleman of a family of distinction, and a captain of the guards, was appointed ambassador by his Majesty. Upon his nomination, he applied to Doctor ARESKINE to recommend a person, who had some knowledge in physic and surgery, to go, in his suite, in the embassy. As I had employed some part of my time in those studies, the Doctor recommended me; which he did in so cordial a manner, as produced to me, from the ambassador, many marks of friendship and regard, which subsisted not only during the journey, but also continued, from that time, to the end of his days. The Doctor, at the same time, recommended me to the college of foreign affairs at ST. PETERSBURG, by whom I was engaged in the service of PETER the First.

Having acquainted the reader with the manner of my entering on the travels, which are the principal subject of the following sheets, I shall take the liberty to say, that I have, through the whole, given the observations,

THE PREFACE.

servations, which then appeared to me worth remarking, without attempting to embellish them, by taking any of the liberties of exaggeration, or invention, frequently imputed to travellers.

I took notes of the subject of the following treatise, by way of diary, from time to time, during the course of my travels; intending nothing further, at that time, than to keep them as helps to my memory, that I might, as occasion offered, communicate, in conversation with my friends, what I had observed worth remarking; and that I might be capable of giving information to others, who might be desirous of it, on their being to make the same journies.

About four years ago, spending some days at the house of a Right Honourable, and most honoured, Friend, the subject of my travels took up a great part of our conversation; during which, upon his enquiring occasionally, whether I had taken any notes of the places, &c. through which I had passed in my several journies, and, upon my answering in the affirmative, he was pleased to take some pains to engage me to promise that I would collect my notes and observations, and form them into journals, as complete as the time elapsed would admit, and communicate them to the world.

It

THE PREFACE.

It was not without reluctance that I set about this work; which, had I thought it worth the public's acceptance and perusal, I would have done long ago. Such as it is, I now offer it to them; and flatter myself, (with hopes at least,) that the plainness of style, in which it is wrote, will be of no prejudice to it with candid readers, who may find in it some things new, and of which they would chuse to be informed.

In regard to the translation of Mr. de LANGE's Journal, I have given it for two reasons; first, because it continues the negociation begun by Mr. de ISMAYLOFF, in the course of which Mr. de LANGE furnishes the reader with a distinct detail of the manner of transacting affairs with the ministers of state, of their chicaneries, &c. at the court of PEKIN. Secondly, because I do not apprehend it hath ever appeared in the ENGLISH language; at least, I have made what enquiries I could, to find if it had been translated, which have been all fruitless.

As I well knew the worthiness and integrity of Mr. de LANGE, and am fully persuaded that his Journal was genuine, though perhaps obtained surreptitiously by the editor, I have closed the translation with the end of Mr. de LANGE's Journal, on his arrival at SELINGINSKY

THE PREFACE.

sky on the frontiers of SIBERIA; having omitted an addition to it, made by the editor, of the trade and monies of CHINA; concerning which, the editor, when he enters upon it, acquaints the reader that he had not the means necessary for sufficient information. For the rest, the translation is just, as may be seen by comparing it with the original.

ANTERMONY,
October 1st, 1762.

JOHN BELL.

THE CONTENTS.
VOLUME FIRST.

A Journey from ST. PETERSBURG in RUSSIA, to
    ISPAHAN in PERSIA.   Page 1

CHAP. I. From St. Petersburg to Cazan.   2

CHAP. II. Occurrences during our ſtay at Cazan; Our journey thence to Aſtrachan.   18

CHAP. III. Occurrences during our ſtay at Aſtrachan; Our journey thence to Shamachy.   36

CHAP. IV. Occurrences during our ſtay at Shamachy; Our journey thence to Tauris.   60

CHAP. V. Occurrences during our ſtay at Tauris; Our journey thence to Iſpahan.   76

CHAP. VI. Occurrences during our ſtay at Iſpahan.   97

CHAP. VII. From Iſpahan to Shamachy; Occurrences during our ſtay there.   129

CHAP. VIII. From Shamachy to St. Petersburg.   142

A Journey from ST. PETERSBURG in RUSSIA, to
    PEKIN in CHINA.   155

CHAP. I. From St. Petersburg to Tobolsky, the capital of Siberia.   157

CHAP. II. Occurrences at Tobolsky; Obſervations on the Kalmucks, &c. and journey continued to Tomsky.   184

CHAP. III. Occurrences at Tomsky; Obſervations on the Tzulimm Tartars, &c. and journey continued to Elimsky.   209

CHAP.

THE CONTENTS.

CHAP. IV. Obfervations on Iakutsky and Kamtzatsky, &c. Journey continued to Irkutsky; and occurrences there. — Page 233

CHAP. V. From Irkutsky, crofs the Lake Baykall, to Selinginsky; Some account of the Kutuchtu, &c. — 257

CHAP. VI. Occurrences at Selinginsky; Several parties of hunting; and journey continued to Saratzyn, the boundary between the Ruffian and Chinefe territories. — 283

CHAP. VII. From paffing the Saratzyn, and entering the Chinefe territories, to our arrival at the wall of China. — 308

CHAP. VIII. From the wall of China to Pekin; Our entry into that city. — 336

VOLUME SECOND.

CHAP. IX. Occurrences at Pekin, audience of the ambaffador, &c. — 1

CHAP. X. Continuation of occurrences at Pekin, &c. — 29

CHAP. XI. Occurrences at Pekin continued, the feftival held at court on the new year, &c. — 59

CHAP. XII. Some account of the prefent Emperor of China, the Chinefe wall, &c. — 87

CHAP. XIII. Our departure from Pekin; Occurrences, &c. during our journey back towards Mofco. — 118

CHAP. XIV. Our arrival at the town of Surgute; Our journey thence to Mofco; Some account of the creature called mammon. — 147

Journal of MR. DE LANGE. — 169

A Journey to DERBENT. — 323

A Journey to CONSTANTINOPLE. — 373

A JOURNEY
FROM
S^{T.} PETERSBURG
IN
RUSSIA,
TO
ISPAHAN
IN
PERSIA,
WITH
AN EMBASSY
FROM HIS
IMPERIAL MAJESTY,
PETER THE FIRST,
TO THE
SOPHY OF PERSIA,
SHACH HUSSEIN,
ANNO MDCCXV.

Vol. I.

NAMES OF THE PRINCIPAL PERSONS WHO COMPOSED THE TRAIN OF THE AMBASSADOR,

ARTEMII PETROVICH VALENSKY,

VIZ.

GREGORY CHRISTOPHER VENIGERKIND, Secretary.
JAQUES DE VILLETTE,   Captain Engineer.
MATPHE PARFILICH KARTZOFF,
ADRIAN IVANOVICH LOPUCHIN,   } Gentlemen of the Embassy.
The AUTHOR of this JOURNAL,
HYLARION, a MONK,   Priest.
VASSILE KURDEFFSKY,
ALEXIE TULKATZOFF,   } Interpreters.
DEMETRY PETRITZ,
VASSILE SHADAYOFF,
ALEXIE BUCHTARYOFF,   } Clerks, or Writers.

With many others; *viz.* A band of music, consisting of trumpets, kettle-drums, violins, hautboys, &c. carpenters, smiths, taylors, valets and footmen, amounting in all to above one hundred persons; besides a troop of twenty-five dragoons for our escort, from ASTRACHAN to ISPAHAN.

A JOURNEY FROM S^T. PETERSBURG TO ISPAHAN.

CHAPTER I.

From ST. PETERSBURG *to* CASAN.

ON the fifteenth of July, 1715, I set out from ST. PETERSBURG, in company with Messieurs VENIGERKIND, DE VILLETTE, and KURDEFFSKY. That city, which has since grown so considerable, was then in its infancy, having been founded, ten or eleven years before, by that truly great man PETER the First, to whom no undertaking seemed difficult.

ST. PETERSBURG is situated in sixty degrees north latitude, partly on the continent of INGRIA and CARELIA, and partly on different islands formed by the river NEVA which discharges itself, by four channels, into the GULF of FINLAND, a little below the city. It is defended by a strong castle, built with stone and brick, inaccessible to ships of force, there being but eight feet water on the bar. As the Czar had determined to form a city all at once, and not to trust to time for the growth of a place which he had chosen for the seat of government, he assembled inhabitants from every province of his empire, and allured strangers from most parts of EUROPE; so that the place was even well peopled, and had not the appearance of a city so lately founded.

The adjacent country is generally covered with woods, consisting of various kinds of pines, birch, alder, aspine, and other trees natural to the northern climates.

To the southward, especially along the shore towards PETERHOFF, the country in summer is very pleasant, with country-seats, corn-fields, and meadows interspersed.

The river NEVA falls out of the LADOGA Lake at SLUSSELBURG, a strong castle, about sixty verst above ST. PETERSBURG. It is a noble stream of clear, wholesome water, with this peculiar quality that

that it is seldom muddy. It contains a great variety of excellent fish, which supply the market all the year, and is navigable to the LADOGA by flat-bottomed vessels.

The woods on each side are stored with game; such as hares, which are white as snow in winter, and turn brown in summer; wild-deer, bears and wolves; the last are so bold that I have known them, in the night-time, carry off a dog from a man's foot, in crossing the river on the ice. There are also elks about the Lake of LADOGA. As for wild-fowl, few places can boast of greater variety. The chief are these; the urhaan, called in FRENCH *coq limoge;* this bird is black, with beautiful red streaks about its head and eyes. The cock is about the size of a turkey; the hen is less and of a brown colour. The heath-cock, in FRENCH *coq de bruiere,* of the same colour and marks as the former, but not so large. The partridge, which the FRENCH call *gilinot.* These three kinds perch on trees; and in winter feed on fir-tops, and on crane-berries, which they scrape from under the snow. There is also found here the common ENGLISH partridge; it is however but rare.

The tarmachan, a bird well known in the northern parts of ENGLAND, and in SCOTLAND, are here in plenty.

As soon as the ice goes off in the spring, vast flocks of water-fowl come hither from the CASPIAN Sea, and other southern regions, to hatch. These consist of swans, geese, a variety of wild-ducks, teal, &c.

Snipes and wood-cocks breed here, many of which are catched by the RUSSIANS, who are excellent fishers and sportsmen.

From ST. PETERSBURG we directed our course along the western bank of the NEVA, till we came to the brick-works. The weather being very hot we halted here a few hours, and in the evening pursued our journey to a small river which falls into the NEVA, about thirty verst above ST. PETERSBURG. At this place we let our horses go to grass, and lay in our waggons till the morning, but were much molested by the gnats and muskitos.

Next morning we continued our journey and passed a village called ISHORA, where the inhabitants speak a language, and wear a dress different from the

the RUSSIAN, though they profefs the fame GREEK religion. It is probable they are the defcendants of a colony, formerly brought hither, from fome of the provinces of LIVONIA.

Next day we came to the VOLCHOVA, a great river iffuing from a lake called ILMEN, not far diftant from the city of NOVOGOROD, which difcharges itfelf into the LADOGA. Here we left our horfes, and, putting our waggons and carriages on board barques, went up the river, ufing oars or fails, by turns, as neceffity obliged us. The banks of the VOLCHOVA are covered with many villages, and fruitful corn-fields, intermixed with natural woods. We found, as we went along, plenty of fifh, and country provifions.

The 19th, we arrived at NOVOGOROD VELIKOI, or the GREAT NOVOGOROD, fo called to diftinguifh it from many leffer towns of the fame name. This city ftands about two hundred verft fouth eaft from PETERSBURG. The VOLCHOVA runs through the middle of it, over which there is a wooden bridge defended by a fortrefs. There are many well built churches in the town; and a great number of monafteries.

steries in the neighbourhood, pleasantly situated, which form a very agreeable prospect. It was formerly a place of great note, but is now much decayed. Here is an archbishop who enjoys a very considerable revenue.

July 22d, having put our carriages on board another barque, we sailed up the river to the Lake ILMEN; and, leaving it on our right hand, entered a small river called MSTA, and at night came to BRUNITZ, a large village, thirty verst from NOVOGOROD. Here we discharged our boats; and, having procured horses, we proceeded next morning thirty verst to the village of ZAYTZOFF, from thence to KRASNYSTANKY, and then to KRESTITSKY, where we changed horses, with which we travelled to YASHILBITZA. Here begin the VALDAY-HILLS, which run to a great distance from east to west; but are only about twenty or thirty verst broad. They are mostly covered with wood. We came next to the town of VALDAY; this place is pleasantly situated at the foot of the hills, adjoining to a large lake of the same name, in the middle of which is an island, whereon stands a monastery. The country in the neighbourhood

hood is hilly, but not mountainous, exhibiting a beautiful variety of plain and rising grounds.

The next stage is ZIMOGORY, and after that VISH-NOY-VOLOTZOKE. Here is a canal of considerable extent, cut by PETER the first, which opens a communication, by water, from ST. PETERSBURG to all the places on the VOLGA, and many other parts of RUSSIA; and proves a great encouragement to trade, and very advantageous to the merchant, in such extensive tracts of land.

Next day we came to TORSHOAK, a small town.

The 29th we arrived at TWEER, a populous and trading town, defended by a castle; it is the capital of a province, and a bishop's seat. It derives its name from a rivulet in the neighbourhood, called TWEERTZA, and stands on the banks of the famous river VOLGA.

The VOLGA, known formerly by the name of RHA, has its source not far to the westward of TWEER. At a small distance from the source of the VOLGA, two other noble rivers take their rise; the DNIEPER, or BORYSTHENES, which runs into the

CHAP. I. BLACK Sea at OTZAKOF; and the DUINA, which falls
1715. into the BALTIC at RIGA.

The VOLGA, after visiting in its course to the south east many fruitful countries, discharges itself into the CASPIAN Sea, about sixty verst below ASTRACHAN; and, in all this long course, there is not a single cataract to interrupt the navigation. As to fish, no river in the world can afford greater variety, better of their kind, nor in larger quantities

Here we tasted the sterlett, a fish much and generally esteemed, it is of the sturgeon kind, but seldom grows above thirty inches long. It is found in other rivers of RUSSIA; but the VOLGA produces the best and in greatest plenty. The caviare, or spawn, is very good to eat raw, after being cleaned and dressed. I never could find a fisherman who had seen their fry.

The same day, having changed horses, we proceeded on our journey to GORODNA, a large village, on the west bank of the VOLGA. From this place is seen a charming landskip, containing a full view of the windings of that river.

From hence, after passing many villages, we came

to KLEEN a pretty large town, and the laſt ſtage to MOSCO. The country between KLEEN and MOSCO is pleaſant, having many tufts of wood, of unequal bigneſs, ſcattered among the corn-fields, that contribute to beautify the country, which had no great appearance of fertility.

About ſeven verſt from MOSCO we paſſed through a large village, called FSE-SWATZKY, inhabited by Chriſtians of the Eaſtern church, named GEORGIANS; their ancient country was GURGISTAN, now one of the northerly provinces of PERSIA; they were driven from their native country by the perſecution of the PERSIANS; and flying into RUSSIA, they there found an hoſpitable reception, many of them being employed in the ſervice of the Emperor.

From this place there is a view of the city MOSCO, and, at this diſtance, few cities in the world make a finer appearance; for it ſtands on a riſing ground, and contains many ſtately churches and monaſteries, whoſe ſteeples and cupolas are generally covered either with copper gilt, or tin plates, which ſhine like gold and ſilver in the ſun.

Auguſt 2d we arrived at the city of MOSCO. I have

have omitted the names and diftances of many inconfiderable places, through which we paffed, let it fuffice, that the diftance between ST. PETERSBURG and MOSCO is about feven hundred and thirty verft; and although the hot weather detained us long on the road, in winter the journey is eafily performed with fledges in three days.

On the 10th of Auguft, my friends, Meffieurs LANGE and GIRVAN, arrived here in their way to CHINA, on a meffage from the Czar to the Emperor of CHINA. The firft was a SWEDE, and the other a phyfician, from the county of AIR in SCOTLAND.

We ftayed in MOSCO about three weeks, having many things to prepare for fo long a journey. This city, ftanding on an eminence, as was already obferved, commands an extenfive profpect of a fine plain country, adorned with woods and clumps of trees, monafteries and gentlemens feats. The river MOSCO runs almoft through it, which, emptying itfelf into the VOLGA, preferves a communication with all the fouthern parts of RUSSIA, and even with PERSIA. From thefe advantages in fituation, this place is

very

very convenient for trade, which flourishes here to
a considerable degree.

The city is fortified with a strong brick-wall, called BELIGOROD, having embrasures and a ditch. Within this is another wall, called KITAYGOROD. This last inclofes what is called the CRIMLIN, in which is the old imperial palace, compounded of a number of buildings, added to one another at different times. Some of the apartments are very spacious; particularly that called GRANAVITAPALLATA, where audience was given to foreign ambassadors; adjoining to the palace are many edifices, where were held the courts of justice. Here also stands a lofty tower, wherein is hung the largest bell in the world, called IVAN VELEKE, weighing about ten thousand poods; which, reckoning each pood at near thirty-six pounds ENGLISH, will amount to about an hundred and sixty tun weight. Besides these, there is a cathedral church, and an arsenal, well furnished with brass cannon, mortars and other warlike stores. Beyond the brick-walls, already mentioned, there is an earthen one, of great circumference, round the whole;

whole; and without this the suburbs also are very extensive.

The great plenty of provisions in this place surprized me not a little; I found here fruits of different kinds, which I did not expect, particularly excellent melons, and arboozes, or water-melons.

August the 21st we shipped our baggage on board six small barques, adapted by their construction, either for sails or oars, as should be most convenient, and fell down the river. The ambassador only remained at MOSCO waiting for some dispatches from court. In the evening we passed KOLUMINSKA, a village pleasantly situated on the south side of the MOSCO river, near which is a large country-house, with gardens, and orchards, belonging to the court.

October 3d we came to COLUMNA, a fortified town. Next day, the wind being favourable, we hoisted sail, and, after going about three verst, entered the river OKA, into which the MOSCO falls and loses its name. The OKA rises in the UKRAIN, and runs to the southeast; it contains a great quantity of water, and is navigable very far up the country.

The 9th we arrived at PERESLAVE-RESANSKY, a large

large town to the left, situated about a verst from the river OKA, it is the seat of an archbishop, and the country around is very fruitful in corn.

The 16th we came to KASSIMOVA, formerly the residence of a TARTAR Prince, but the family is now converted to CHRISTIANITY, and retains only the old name of KASSIMOFSKY CZAREVITZ. The place is at present inconsiderable. There are still here a few MAHOMETAN TARTARS who are allowed the free exercise of their religion, and have a small oratory. I accompanied our interpreter to visit one of them, an old acquaintance of his. He was a very decent man; we saw a horse newly killed, which they intended to eat. They prefer this kind of food to beef, and invited us to share their repast, which we declined, pretending we had not time.

The 17th we left KASSIMOVA, and the 21st arrived at MURUM, a pretty large town, and a bishop's see. The country produces plenty of corn. About this place there are a few idolatrous TARTARS, who live in little dirty cottages, thinly scattered. They are a very simple and harmless people. How or when they settled here is not known.

The 22d we passed a large village, called PAULO-VO-PEREVOZ, the property of Prince TZERHASKOY. Its situation is on the south side of the river. Here the banks are much higher than above this place.

We came the 23d to NISHNA-NOVOGOROD, a great town, defended by a castle, standing on the high banks of the OKA, opposite to where it loses itself in the VOLGA, which now forms a mighty stream.

The following day we dined at the governor's, where I saw General CREUTZ, and several other SWEDISH officers, who had been taken prisoners at POLTAVA, and lived here at large.

The 25th we sailed from NISHNA, and soon entered the VOLGA. The wind being northerly we run along at a great rate; but in the night the river was suddenly filled with floating ice, which drove us on a sand bank, where we lay aground that night and all the next day; however, after much labour and fatigue, we got clear, although the floating ice still continued. At last the wind changed to the south, and the weather turned milder, which enabled us to pursue our voyage.

We next passed VASILY-GOROD, and then KOSMO-DEMINNSKO, small towns, both on the right.

November 3d we came to ZABACK-ZAR, a pretty large town, on the same hand.

In this country are caught the best and largest faulcons in the world, much esteemed for their strength and beauty; particularly by the TURKS and PERSIANS, who purchase them very dear. The RUSSIANS take few young hawks from the nest, preferring the old ones, which they man very dextrously to fly at swan, goose, crane, or heron. The TARTARS fly them at antelopes and hares. I have seen them take a wild-duck out of the water, when nothing of her could be perceived but the bill, which she was obliged to put up for air. Some of them are as white as a dove. The manner of catching them is very simple. They erect a tall pole upon a hill, free from wood, on a bank of the river, near which is placed a day-net; under the net some small birds are fastened by a cord, which the hawk-catcher pulls to make them flutter, on the appearance of the hawk, who observing his prey first perches on the pole, and when he stoops to seize the birds, the person, who is

VOL. I. C con-

concealed by the bushes, draws the net and covers him.

The 4th, we passed KAY-GOROD, and the 5th, SWIIASSKY, the first on the left and the other on the right hand. This evening we arrived before the town of CAZAN, and hauled our boats into the mouth of a small river, from which the town has its name, called CAZANKA. We intended to continue our voyage directly to ASTRACHAN; but, before we had made the necessary preparations at CAZAN, the winter set in, and on the 6th of September the VOLGA was filled with floating ice. This determined us to winter at that place. We therefore unloaded the boats, and came to the city, where we were hospitally received by the governor.

CHAPTER II.

Occurrences during our stay at CAZAN; *Our journey thence to* ASTRACHAN.

CAZAN is about seven hundred and thirty five verst from MOSCO by land, but much more by water. It is situated about five verst to the north of the

the VOLGA, on a high bank of the rivulet CAZANKA, which is navigable from this place to the river. The town is strong by situation, and defended by a castle, fortified with walls of brick. Within the citadel are the cathedral church, the palaces of the archbishop and governor, and the apartments for the courts of justice. The town is fenced with a ditch and palisades. The suburbs are inhabited chiefly by mechanics, except a street or two possessed by MAHOMETAN TARTARS, the posterity of the ancient natives. They live very decently, have the free exercise of their religion, and many other privileges. Some of them are very rich by the trade they carry on to TURKEY, PERSIA, and other places.

CAZAN was anciently the capital of a part of TARTARY, and the seat of government, where the royal family resided. It was taken from the TARTARS by Czar IVAN VASILOVIZ, in the year fifteen hundred and fifty two, in consequence whereof an extensive country to the southward, easily fell into his hands. The conquered Princes were converted to Christianity, and had lands assigned them in their own country, where the family still subsists.

CHAP. II.
1715.

The country adjacent is very pleasant and fertile; producing wheat, rye, barley, oats, and several kinds of pulse. The woods to the south and west consist of stately oaks, sufficient to supply all the navies in the world; and from hence ST. PETERSBURG is abundantly furnished with timber, for all the purposes of ship-building, by an easy conveyance, all the way by water. The woods to the north and east, which are of prodigious extent, consist of trees of all sorts.

In the spring, when the snow melts, the VOLGA overflows all the low grounds, sometimes to a great distance; the consequence is the same with that produced in EGYPT, by the inundations of the NILE; for the mud, carried down by the stream, fertilizes the country to a great degree; so that on the islands in the VOLGA, some whereof are very large, and overgrown with tall trees, I have found plenty of excellent asparagus.

Besides the sterlett there are plenty of sturgeon, and a fish about the size and near the shape of the largest salmon, which is very delicious, and, for the whiteness of its flesh, is called the white fish.

The

The woods afford abundance of game. And in CHAP. II. the spring great numbers of water-fowl come hither 1715. to hatch, from the CASPIAN sea. At CAZAN we found good beef, mutton and tame poultry, and provisions of all kinds very reasonable.

There is here a considerable manufactory of RUSSIA leather; the hides here being reckoned the best in the empire. Great quantities of this leather are exported to LEGHORN, and other parts of EUROPE, and may be considered among the staple commodities of this country. The strong smell of this leather is acquired in the dressing; for instead of oil, common in other places, they use a kind of tar, extracted by fire from the bark of the birch-tree; which ingredient the RUSSES call deuggit, and which tree is here in greater abundance than in other parts of the world; and then they dye them with logwood.

Besides the idolatrous TARTARS, formerly mentioned, there are two pretty numerous tribes called the TZERIMISH and TZOOWASH, they speak a language quite different from the MAHOMETAN TARTARS in these parts, who use a corrupted dialect of the ARABIC. The MAHOMETANS likewise have some learn-

learning; but the TZERIMISH and TZOOWASH have none. They have a tradition among them, that in former times they had a book of religion; but, as no body could read it, a cow came and swallowed it. They pay great veneration to a bull. From whence they came, is unknown; but from their complexion, it is probable they are from ASIA. They live by agriculture, and seem to be an inoffensive kind of people. Their huntsmen offer in sacrifice, to some deity, the first creature they catch. Hence some curious men have imagined these people part of the ten tribes of the JEWS, expelled by SHALMANEZER. I advance this only as a conjecture, which every reader may follow or not as he pleases.

By accident, I met with an ENGLISHMAN at this place. He was by trade a carpenter, and had been in the RUSSIAN service; but, being suspected of deserting, he was condemned to banishment, to this country, for a certain time: and, notwithstanding that was elapsed, the poor man, deprived of all means of asserting his liberty, remained still in the same situation. He bought a TZERIMISH wife, from her father, for six rubles, about thirty shillings Sterling.

ling. He brought her to visit me. She was a woman of a chearful and open countenance, and dressed in the manner of her country; of which, for its singularity, I shall give a short description.

Her hair was plaited round her head, in many locks, but that on the back part longer than the rest, at the end of which was tied a tassel of red silk, and in the middle a small round brass bell; about her head was a fillet set with small shells, instead of jewels, and hung all round with silver pence; above this was a piece of linen so artfully plaited, and done up, that it looked like a grenadier's cape; at the top was a silk tassel, with another brass bell, which gingled as she turned her head. The rest of her dress was clean though homely, and the whole seemed becoming enough.

I think the cold here is more intense than at ST. PETERSBURG, tho' it is five or six degrees farther south; in going about three miles from town, in a clear day, I had my face, fingers and toes frozen, notwithstanding I was not half an hour on the road. I applied the common cure, that is, rubbing the numbed

numbed parts with snow, which I found perfectly effectual.

December 24th our ambassador arrived from MOSCO. At the same time came an express from court, with the important news of the crown Princess (as she was commonly called) being safely delivered of a son, christened by the name of PETER. She died however soon after her delivery, universally lamented for her many rare and excellent virtues. She was of the WOLFFENBUTTLE family, and wife to ALEXY PETROVITZ, the Czarevitz. Besides this young Prince, she left a Princess called NATALIA.

At CAZAN we found two SWEDISH generals, HAMILTON and ROSEN, and many other officers of distinction, taken prisoners at POLTAVA, who were no farther confined than by having a soldier of the garrison to attend them at their lodgings; and, by the generosity of the governor, lived as easily as circumstances would allow. These gentlemen were invited to all the public diversions; and, by their polite and agreeable behaviour, contributed not a little to our passing the winter with a good deal of pleasure, in such a remote part of the world.

Upon

Upon the banks of the CAZANKA stands a monastery, very pleasantly situated. I accompanied our interpreter to visit the abbot, who received us in a very friendly manner. He would not however give the interpreter his blessing, nor admit him into the church, during divine service, unless he pulled off his wig. He, professing the communion of the GREEK church, expostulated a little with the priest, telling him that their learned bishops at MOSCO made no such scruples. The abbot replied, that it was contrary to the rules of discipline, to allow any man to enter the church with his head covered.

The time was now come when we expected to leave CAZAN. Our boats were ready in the beginning of May, but the VOLGA was still so high and rapid, that it was reckoned dangerous to proceed till the flood subsided; for the force of the stream frequently carries vessels from their course into the woods, where the water retiring, leaves them on dry land.

At last, on the 4th of June, we left CAZAN in eight barques, and rowed down the river with great velocity. In the night one of our boats was driven by the rapidity of the current, among the woods, and ftuck faft between two trees, up which the people climbed, being apprehenfive of danger. The confequence however was not fo fatal as the circumftances were alarming; for the veffel was got off next day with inconfiderable damage.

The 7th we paffed a fmall town called TETOOSK, and the 9th SINBIRSKY, pretty large, and the capital of a province of that name, both to the right. SINBIRSKY is defended by a caftle. Near this place are evident marks of camps and entrenchments, which I was told were the works of the great TARTAR general, called TIMYRAK-SACK, or LAME TIMYR, or TAMERLANE, who came to this place with a great army; but being informed of an infurrection in his own country SAMARKANT, now BUCHARIA, returned home.

The 10th we put off from SINBIRSKY with the wind contrary, which greatly retarded our progrefs. We paffed two hills, one of them exhibiting a very beautiful profpect, the other containing mines of fulphur as clear as amber. We paffed alfo a mound of fand, of confiderable bignefs, in the middle of a plain

plain, where they say was buried a famous TARTAR prince called MAMAY.

The 20th we arrived at the town of SAMARA, situated to the left, in a fine plain. The place is but small, and fortified only with a ditch and palisades, with wooden towers at proper distances, mounted with cannon, sufficient to defend it against the incursions of the TARTARS, called KARA KALPACKS, or BLACK CAPS, who inhabit the desert to the eastward of this place.

This tribe of TARTARS is not very considerable, and when their chiefs are united, which seldom happens, can scarce raise above ten or twelve thousand men, who are all mounted on horse-back; because, in their long marches to rob and plunder their neighbours, nothing but horse could be of any use. They live always in tents, with their flocks, removing from place to place, as led by inclination or necessity. Their weapons are bows and arrows, and sabres; some of them use fire-arms. While we were at SAMARA, the inhabitants were alarmed with the approach of two or three thousand of these people, who encamped about three miles distant. From
one

CHAP. II.
1716.

one of the towers I could plainly see their camp, and them riding about it. As they had not artillery the garrison was in no danger, though so weak however, that it durst not at this time attack them. The people were obliged to keep a constant watch to defend their cattle. This place is reckoned about three hundred and fifty verst distant from CAZAN.

The 21st, having provided fresh hands for the navigation of our barques, we departed from SAMARA; and, the weather being calm, rowed down the river, which is here very broad. The western bank is very high, but the eastern quite flat. The fields on both sides are very fruitful; but especially to the west, where the grass grows very high, intermixed with sage, thyme and other herbs; there are also some woods of oaks. A few hundred acres of such land would be of great value in ENGLAND, though it is here waste and uncultivated.

We came the 25th to the ISMEYOVI-GORY, or SERPENT-HILLS, so called from the windings of the river at this place; and after passing several towns, and many villages, all on the right, we landed at SARATOF.

тоf, a large town on the same side, about eight hundred and fifty verst from cazan. It is but slightly fortified with a ditch, wooden walls, and towers mounted with cannon, and defended by a garrison of regular troops and cossacks.

We dined next day with the governor, who entertained us with great variety of provisions, particularly fish, and very fine mutton.

After dinner a party of us crossed the river to visit a great horse-market, held by the KALMUCK TARTARS, we saw about five or six hundred of these people, assembled in a field, with a number of horses all running loose, except those on which the TARTARS were mounted. The buyers came from different parts of RUSSIA. The TARTARS had their tents pitched along the river side. These tents are of a conical figure; there are several long poles erected, inclining to one another, which are fixed at the top into something like a hoop, that forms the circumference of an aperture for letting out the smoak, or admitting the light; across the poles are laid some small rods, from four to six feet long, and fastened to them with thongs: this frame is covered with pieces of felt,

made

made of coarse wool and hair. These tents afford better shelter than any other kind, and are so contrived as to be set up, taken down, folded and packed up with great ease and quickness, and so light that a camel may carry five or six of them. Where the Chan or any person of character resides, they are placed in straight lines. These TARTARS are strong made, stout men, their faces broad, noses flattish, and eyes small and black, but very quick. Their dress is very simple, consisting of a loose coat of sheep-skins, tied with a girdle, a small round cap, turned up with furr, having a tassel of red silk at the top, leather or linen drawers, and boots, their heads are all shaved, except a lock behind, which is plaited and hangs down their backs.

They are armed with bows and arrows, a sabre and lance, which they manage with great dexterity, acquired by constant practice from their infancy. They are men of courage and resolution; but much afraid of cannon, which puts their horses in disorder. As they are almost always on horse-back, they are excellent riders.

The dress of the women differs little from that
of

of the men, only their gowns are somewhat longer than the coats of the men, a little ornamented, and bordered with party-coloured cloth; they wear earrings, and their hair all plaited in locks. The better sort drefs in filks in fummer. It muft be obferved, for the honour of their women, that they are very honeft and fincere, and few of them lewd; adultery is a crime fcarce ever heard of. The TARTARS make very good and faithful fervants; and the more mildly they are ufed the better they perform their duty; for their wandering unconfined manner of life naturally infpires them with fentiments of liberty, and averfion, and hatred to tyranny and oppreffion.

All their wealth is their flocks; like thofe who lived in the early ages of the world, they have camels, horfes, cows and fheep. The horfes are of a good fize for the faddle, and very hardy; as they run wild till they are fometimes fix years old, they are generally headftrong; they are fold at this fair at five to fifteen or fixteen crowns, and the ftrong well fhaped natural pacers much higher. They have few camels, but many dromedaries, who have two protuberances on their backs. Their cows are of a middle

middle size. The sheep large, having broad tails like those in TURKEY, the wool is coarse, but the mutton very fine.

In the preceeding century a KALMUCK prince, named TORGOTT-CHORLUKE, came from ALACK-UL-LA, (which signifies the spotted mountains) a country situated between SIBERIA on the north, and INDIA on the south, to the borders of RUSSIA; and brought along with him about fifty thousand families, or tents, as they sometimes reckon. In his march westward to the VOLGA, he defeated EYBALL-UTZICK, a TARTAR prince, who lived in tents beyond the river ENBO. Advancing forward he met three other TARTAR chiefs, named KITTA-HAPTZAY, MALEBASH and ETZAN, whom he also defeated. And at last settled to the east of the VOLGA, under the protection of the RUSSIANS. CHORLUKE had six sons; DANGTZINQ the oldest succeeded him in the government, or chanship.

The present Chan, named AIJUKA, is the fourth from CHORLUKE, and is much esteemed in the east for his sagacity and justice. I am informed that the reason why CHORLUKE left his own country, was a dispute

dispute about the succession to the chanship. He being engaged on the weakest side, and having unsuccessfully tried his fortune in the field, at last took the resolution of abandoning his own country altogether. These people are generally called the BLACK KALMUCKS, though they are not black, but only swarthy.

They have no money, except what they get from the RUSSIANS, and their other neighbours, in exchange for cattle; with this they buy meal sometimes but mostly cloth, silk-stuffs, and other apparel for their women. They have no mechanics, except those who make arms. They avoid all labour as the greatest slavery; their only employment is tending their flocks, managing horses, and hunting. If they are angry with a person, they wish he may live in one place, and work like a RUSSIAN. Their language contains none of those horrid oaths common enough in tongues of more enlightened nations. They believe virtue leads to happiness, and vice to misery; for when desired to do what they think wrong, they reply, in a proverb, 'Though a knife be sharp it 'cannot cut its own handle.'

Vol. I.   E   On

On long marches all their provisions consist of cheese, or rather dried curd, made up into little balls, which they drink, when pounded and mixt with water. If this kind of food fails they have always many spare horses, which they kill and eat. They broil or roast the flesh before the fire, on pieces of broken arrows, and never eat it raw, as is commonly believed, unless compelled by necessity. They have indeed large thick pieces of horse-flesh, smoked or dried in the sun, which they eat; but this cannot properly be called raw. I have tasted some of it, and thought it not amiss.

As to their religion I can say little; they are downright Heathens, and have many lamas or priests, who can read and write, and are distinguished by their yellow habits. Their high priest is called DELAY LAMA, and lives far to the eastward.

July 1st we put off from SARATOF; and the 2d, 7th and 9th passed the towns of KAMOSHINKA, CZARITZA, and TZORNO-YARR, all situated on the west bank, and fortified in the same manner as SARATOF. At the first of these places captain PERRY, an ENGLISHMAN, with many workmen, was employed in cutting

cutting a canal between the VOLGA and the DON, which would have opened a paſſage to the EUXINE ſea; but the ground being very hard, and riſing in ſome places conſiderably above the level, the enterprife was laid afide, though the diſtance was not above fifty verſt.

From TZORNO-YARR to ASTRACHAN it is not ſafe for RUSSIANS to travel on the weſtern banks of the VOLGA, on account of the CUBAN TARTARS, who are their enemies. To the eaſt however there is no danger, as the KALMUCKS are friends. On the iſlands in the VOLGA I obſerved great quantities of liquoriſh growing wild.

The 13th we arrived ſafe at ASTRACHAN, and were lodged in the citadel. This place was taken from the TARTARS, in the year 1554, by the warlike Czar IVAN VASILIOVITZ; whereby all his conqueſts on the VOLGA were ſecured, and the way prepared for farther extending the RUSSIAN dominion, to the ſouth and eaſt; which hath been ſucceſsfully attempted ſince his time.

CHAPTER III.

Occurrences during our stay at ASTRACHAN; *Our journey thence to* SHAMACHY.

ASTRACHAN is situated about sixty verst from the CASPIAN sea, on an island in the VOLGA, having the main branch of that river to the westward. It is fortified by a strong brick-wall, with embrasures, and square towers at proper distances. In the citadel are the cathedral church, governor's palace, and the public offices. There is a creek, or haven, for ships that navigate the river and the CASPIAN sea. The houses are generally built with wood, conveyed in rafts along the river; for the neighbouring country produces nothing, being all a barren desert. To the westward there is no water to be found for many miles. The islands, however, adjacent to the town are very fruitful, and produce excellent grapes, transplanted hither from PERSIA and other parts; also water-melons, esteemed the best in the world; and various kinds of musk-melons, peaches, cherries, pears, apples, and apricots.

Here

Here are several large vineyards, belonging partly to the court, and partly to private persons; there is a FRENCHMAN who superintends them. The wines are very good when drunk on the spot; but cannot bear carriage, for the least motion renders them insipid. Were it not for this circumstance RUSSIA would be able, not only to supply itself abundantly with wine, but even other parts of EUROPE. This pernicious quality is attributed to the nitrous particles of the soil where the vines grow. I have myself seen in the furrows, made for watering them, a whitish crust of salt: But the grapes, notwithstanding, are very sweet, without the least tincture of tartness.

About a mile below the town are collected great quantities of common salt. The people dig pits, into which they introduce the water; which being exhaled by the heat of the sun, the salt is left upon the bottom: after gathering, they transport it along the river, in large barques of about five or six hundred tun. The gun-powder manufactory is a little above the town; in which, and in the mines of saltpetre, near this place, are employed a great number of workmen for the service of the government.

The climate is healthy, though very hot. The weather is generally calm, during which great numbers of gnats and muskitos infest the inhabitants. These vermine indeed are sometimes dispersed by a breeze from the sea, which renders this place very pleasant. They are hatched and sheltered in the marshes toward the sea, which are so overgrown with strong tall reeds that they are altogether impassable.

The MAHOMETAN TARTARS here live without the town; and have the same privileges as in other places. I met several of their women in the street with rings in their noses, which were of different value, according to the rank of the person who wore them; some of gold, and others set with precious stones. On inquiring the reason of such a singular ornament, I was told, that it was the consequence of a religious dedication of these persons to the service of God: It is made by the parents, even while the mother is pregnant; in token whereof, as soon as the child is born, they put a ring in the right nostril, which continues there till death. I have seen some with two such rings.

ASTRACHAN is a place of considerable trade to
PERSIA,

PERSIA, CHIVA, BUCHARIA and INDIA. The people of these nations have a common caravanfery, where they live and expofe their goods to fale.

1716.

The ARMENIANS carry on the greateft part of the PERSIAN trade; for the PERSIANS themfelves feldom go out of their own country. There are a few INDIANS, or BANIANS, at this place, who have a ftreak of yellow down their forehead, made with faffron or fome other vegetable. They are a good natured, innocent kind of people, and live moftly on fruits.

The market is plentifully fupplied with provifions of all kinds; but efpecially fifh, of which no place that I know abounds with fuch variety. After the fale is over, which is ufually about ten o'clock, what remains of the common forts is thrown to the dunghill, where the hogs and poultry feed upon them; and hence it happens that their very pork and fowls tafte of fifh. It would be tedious to mention all the different kinds this place affords: I cannot however omit the carp, which for fize exceeds all of that name I ever heard of. I have feen fome of them of more than thirty pound weight, very fat and lufcious. Thofe caught in autumn are carried to MOSCO

frozen,

frozen, and fold there and in the places adjacent.

I observed also a great variety of uncommon birds, whereof I shall describe a few that seemed most extraordinary.

The first I shall mention, called by the RUSSIANS baba, is of grey colour, and larger than a swan; he has a broad bill, under which hangs a bag that may contain a quart or more; he wades near the edge of the river, and on seeing a shoal of fry, or small fishes, spreads his wings and drives them to a shallow, where he gobbles as many of them as he can into his bag, and then going ashore eats them, or carries them to his young. This bird I take to be the pelican.

The next is altogether white, except its feet which are black; it is somewhat less than a heron, and has a long broad bill. The GERMANS call this bird leffel-ganze, the RUSSIANS kolpeck.

There is another about the same size, also white; but its feet are long and red, and its bill crooked and round, and as red as coral; its wings are adorned with some bright scarlet feathers.

Besides these, I saw a kind of duck, something bigger than the common sort, called turpan; it is easily

easily tamed, and much admired for its beauty and a certain kind of noise peculiar to itself. I have eat of all these fowls; but did not much relish them, on account of the fishy taste with which they are all infected.

There are also partridges and bustards, which need no description. The KALMUCKS, who are keen sportsmen, particularly at hawking, in which they have arrived to a great perfection, kill the bustards with bows and arrows; when they see them feeding they ride in upon them at full speed, and as the bustard is a heavy bird, and mounts slowly, they have an opportunity of shooting them with broad-headed arrows.

On the banks of the VOLGA there is a species of deer of a brighter red, and somewhat larger than the fallow-deer; they have green horns, but not branched, about nine inches long, and covered with circles, rising one above another to the point, which is very sharp. This deer is very swift, and its flesh excellent; it has a high snout of gristle, which rises very near to the eyes, a circumstance which I have not observed in any other animal.

I saw also a small lively creature, called an ASTRACHAN hare, about the size of a squirrel, and of a reddish colour, remarkable for having the fore-feet very short in proportion to the hind-feet; its tail is long, with a tuft of hair at the extremity; it burrows in the earth, and being a very pretty creature, I have sometimes seen them in cages. The KALMUCKS eat them very greedily.

While we were at ASTRACHAN, an ambassador arrived there, from the Chan of CHIVA, going to ST. PETERSBURG. On his arrival he sent, according to the eastern custom, some small presents to our ambassador; they were brought by part of his retinue, and consisted of a hawking glove, a small knife, an embroidered purse, and some fruits.

CHIVA is a large territory, lying about two or three days journey eastward from the CASPIAN sea; bounded by PERSIA on the south, and BUCHARIA to the east. The capital, which bears the same name, is large and populous; and governed by a Chan, elected by the people. They are very troublesome and dangerous, both to travellers and their neighbours, being frequently employed either in robbing the former

mer, or making depredations on the latter. And though CHIVA is well fortified, its situation in so sandy and barren a desert is its best defence.

One day as I was walking through the streets of ASTRACHAN, I observed a very singular appearance; it was a pretty TARTAR lady mounted astride upon an ox; she had a ring in her nose, and a string drawn through the nose of the ox, which served instead of a bridle; she was dressed better than common, and attended by a footman; the singularity of the equipage, but particularly her extraordinary beauty, drew my attention. The MAHOMETAN must not be confounded with the KALMUCK TARTARS; the first are a well looked civilized people in comparison of the other.

Before I leave ASTRACHAN it may be proper to rectify a mistaken opinion, which I have observed frequently to occur in grave GERMAN authors, who, in treating of the remarkable things of this country, relate that there grows in this desert, or stepp, adjoining to ASTRACHAN, in some plenty, a certain shrub or plant, called in the RUSSIAN language Tartarskey barashka, *i. e.* Tartarian lamb, with the skin of which the caps of the ARMENIANS, PERSIANS, TARTARS, &c. are faced; they also write, that this Tartarskey barashka partakes of animal as well as vegetative life; that it eats up and devours all the grass and weeds within its reach. Though it may be thought, that an opinion so very absurd could find no credit with people of the meanest share of understanding, yet I have conversed with some who have seemed much inclined to believe it: So very prevalent is the prodigious and absurd with some part of mankind.

In search of this wonderful plant I walked many a mile, accompanied by TARTARS who inhabit these deserts; but all I could find out were some dry bushes, scattered here and there, which grow on a single stalk, with a bushy top, of a brownish colour; the stalk is about eighteen inches high; the top consisting of sharp prickly leaves: It is true that no grass or weeds grow within the circle of its shade, a property natural to many other plants here, and elsewhere. After further enquiry of the more sensible and experienced among the TARTARS, I found they laughed at it as a ridiculous fable.

At

At ASTRACHAN they have great quantities of lamb-skins, grey and black; some waved, others curled, all naturally, and very pretty, having a fine glofs, particularly the waved, which, at a small distance, appear like the richest watered tabby; they are much esteemed, and are much used for the lining of coats, and the turning up of caps in PERSIA, RUSSIA, and other parts. The best of these are brought from BUCHARIA, CHIVA, and the countries adjacent, and are taken out of the ewe's belly, after she hath been killed, or the lamb is killed immediately after it is lambed; for such a skin is equal in value to the sheep.

The KALMUCKS and other TARTARS, who inhabit the desert, in the neighbourhood of ASTRACHAN, have also lamb-skins, which are applied to the same purposes; but the wool of these being rougher, and more hairy, they are far inferior to those of BUCHARIA, or CHIVA, both in glofs and beauty, as also in the dressing, consequently in value; I have known one single lamb-skin of BUCHARIA sold for five or six shillings Sterling, when one of these would not yield two shillings.

On the 5th of August we quitted ASTRACHAN in

five

five veffels, three of them flat-bottomed, and of about an hundred and fifty tuns burden, with three mafts and ten guns each; the other two common barques. We failed from ASTRACHAN about noon; and at night came to an anchor at a fifhery, called UTTZUGG. Both the banks are now flat; to the weftward barren fands, and to the eaft marfhy and tall reeds abounding with vermine; fo that we neither eat nor flept in quiet, notwithftanding all the precautions we could ufe. I muft confefs this place had an afpect of horror, efpecially when it is confidered, that, befides the wild and difmal appearance of the banks, we were carried down a mighty river into a great gulf, in many places of dangerous navigation, and whofe fhores are inhabited by inhofpitable and barbarous nations; for fuch I reckon all of them, except the RUSSIANS and PERSIANS.

Next morning, at break of day, we got under fail, and about ten entered the CASPIAN fea; into which the river difcharges itfelf by feven or eight large channels, and many leffer ones; two only of thefe channels are navigable by fhips of any burden. At night we caft anchor near four hillocks of dry fand,

caft

cast up by the sea, called TZETEREY BUGORY, computed to be about thirty verst from the mouth of the VOLGA; all which distance we had not above six or seven feet water, and even this depth is very narrow; so that the passage is extremely dangerous in hard gales of wind.

The 7th early, we again set sail with a gentle breeze from the shore, which soon drove us into three fathom water, and out of sight of land; the water however still continued fresh as the river. About noon the wind shifted to the south, which obliged us to come to an anchor, where we lay for near three weeks in calms and contrary winds.

All this time we did not see a single ship, besides our own, except one RUSS vessel that came from GUILAN in PERSIA, with some ARMENIAN merchants; who made a present to the ambassador of a basket of oranges, melons, and other fruits; which was the more acceptable as our own provisions of that kind were all spent. As often as the weather would permit we got under sail, and endeavoured to reach the road of TERKY, a small fortified town, belonging to the RUSSIANS, on the northwest corner of the CAS-

PIAN

sea, where we might be supplied with provisions; but the continual calms prevented our success.

On the evening of the 26th of August the wind changed to the northwest, we hoisted all the sail we could, steering our course south south-east; and before night passed the island of TULLEN, *i. e.* of SEALS; many of which animals haunt this place. It continued to blow hard the whole night; and next morning we were in sight of the mountains called SHAFFKALL, which were distant about fifteen leagues. We proceeded the whole day, edging always a little nearer to the shore.

The 28th in the evening it fell calm, and being about six leagues off the land we cast anchor. Next day, the wind blowing fair, in the afternoon we passed the town of DERBENT. The ambassador ordered the castle to be saluted with nine guns; but it seems the people are not accustomed to make any return. It is a place considerably large, and the frontier of PERSIA in this quarter. It is fortified in the ancient manner, with a strong stone-wall, which reaches from the mountains to the shore; so that no army can pass this way, except mountaineers, or

TAR-

TARTARS, who find roads every where. DERBENT, being a place of great confequence, is provided plentifully with cannon and ammunition, and a ſtrong garriſon governed by a commandant appointed by the chan, or governor of SHAMACHY, on which province it depends. It is reported that it was built by ALEXANDER the Great. About the place there ſtill remain ſeveral monuments of antiquity; particularly large ſtones with inſcriptions in uncommon characters. South from DERBENT ſtands a very high mountain, called SHACHDAGH, the top of which is covered with ſnow the whole year round, though the vallies are exceedingly hot.

August the 30th we arrived at NIEZABATT, the place where we intended to land, on the territories of PERSIA. It lies about two days journey eaſt from DERBENT. There being no harbour, nor creek, we hauled up our ſhips upon the ſhore, which we performed with little trouble as they were all flat-bottomed.

The ſhip in which was our ſecretary, Monſieur VENIGERKIND, and ſeveral other officers, did not arrive till about three o'clock afternoon. The wind

CHAP. III. was now very high, and a great sea upon the beach, which obliged them to drop an anchor in the open road; but the wind blowing still harder, it became dangerous to ride there; the skipper therefore slipt the cable and stood out to sea. The gentlemen however did not like their situation on board, and being eager to get to land, ordered the master to run the ship ashore and they would be accountable for the consequences; which he, a HOLLANDER in the Czar's service, unwillingly complied with, under an easy sail, about two miles eastward of the place where we lay. All hands went to their assistance, but without effect; for though the ship had received no damage, yet the sea run so high that the boat could not be hoisted out to carry them to land.

In the mean time the secretary, impatient of remaining on board in such circumstances, prevailed with one of the sailors to carry him ashore on his back; which being done, he took his way alone towards the other ships; but, his cloaths being drenched in the salt-water, and the road lying through deep sands, he was soon fatigued, and therefore retired nearer to the woods, in hopes of finding a

more

more smooth and easy path. He discovered what he sought; but, instead of leading him to the ships, it carried him away from the shore and the right course, into thick incumbered woods; and in these circumstances night overtook him, utterly ignorant of the dismal and dangerous wild into which he had wandered. Thus destitute of all assistance, he climbed a tree to save himself from the wild-beasts, with which these woods abound; and in this situation continued all the night, and till noon next day; for the people in his own ship never doubted of his having safely reached our tents; while we, on the contrary, had not the least suspicion of his having come ashore. At last, however, about noon, his servant came inquiring for his master, who he told us left the ship the night before. This account filled us all with anxiety and apprehension; as we certainly concluded he would either be torn to pieces by the wild-beasts, or murdered by the savages who inhabit these coasts. Immediate order was given for all our people to repair to the woods in search of him. He was at last found wandering from path to path, without knowing one direction from another. When

he

he came to the tents he looked ghastly and wild, and related many strange stories of what he had heard in the night. All possible care was taken to alleviate his distress. During his sleep, which was very discomposed, he often started, groaned, and spoke; and, even after he awaked, he persisted in affirming that there were numbers of people round the tree, in the night, talking different languages. The imagination, no doubt, will naturally have a strong effect on any man in such uncommon circumstances; for, though the secretary was a man of penetration and sound judgment, in vain did we endeavour to undeceive him, by representing that it was nothing but the jackals which made the noise he had heard; and, that to be convinced of the truth of this affirmation, he needed only, at the approach of night, to step a little from the tents, where he would hear the same sounds repeated; all was to no purpose, since he insisted that the noise he heard was quite different from the yelpings of the jackals. He scarce ever recovered his former sagacity and soundness of mind. I must confess the situation of this gentleman moved me not a little; as he was a man of parts and learning, with whom I had contracted an intimate friendship.

Since I have mentioned the jackals, it may not be improper to give a short account of these animals. They are of a size larger than a fox, of the shape and colour of a wolf, with a short bushy tail. They dig burrows in the earth, in which they lye all day, and come out in the night to range for prey. They assemble in flocks among the woods, and frequently near towns and villages, when they make the hideous noise formerly mentioned, resembling in some measure a human voice, or the noise of the TARTARS and COSSACKS when they attack their enemies. They have fine noses; and hence the vulgar opinion has arisen that they hunt prey for the lion. They are in great plenty all over PERSIA, and esteemed harmless creatures.

As soon as we landed, the ambassador dispatched an interpreter to SHAMACHY, to notify his arrival to the governor of that place, and to desire him to send camels and horses to transport him thither. The interpreter was kindly received, and an order was immediately issued out for answering his demands.

September the 1st, the chan of SHAMACHY sent an officer of distinction to salute the ambassador; and, the next day, a present of provisions; consisting of an ox, some sheep, with fruits and confections.

About six or eight leagues to the eastward of NIEZABATT is a high rock, called BARMACH, or the FINGER, upon the shore, which a great many of the ARMENIANS visit annually to pay their devotions. They have a tradition that the prophet ELIJAH lived some years at this place.

September 2d we were a little alarmed with intelligence, that a considerable body of mountaineers had plundered some villages in our neighbourhood. We had not yet received any guard from the PERSIANS, and were therefore obliged to take every precaution possible for our defence. We armed all our own people, and all the sailors; and besides these we had twenty soldiers from the garrison of ASTRACHAN. Cannon were brought from the ships, and planted in proper places to prevent a surprise. These preparations seem to have intimidated the undisciplined savages, for they never attacked us.

Two days journey eastward from NIEZABATT stand
ABSHE-

ABSHEROON and BACKU, two confiderable towns; at the former is a good harbour, reckoned the beft in the CASPIAN fea, except that of ASTRABATT, which lies in the foutheaft corner of it. All the reft are fo dangerous that they fcarce deferve the name of harbours.

In the neighbourhood of BACKU are many fountains of naphtha; it is a fort of petroleum, of a brown colour, and inflammable nature. The PERSIANS burn it in their lamps; no rain can extinguifh it; but the fmell is difagreeable. I have feen of it as clear as rock-water.

The CASPIAN fea is of an oblong irregular figure; about one hundred and fifty leagues in length, from north to fouth, and forty or fifty leagues broad. The water is exceffively falt, except where it is fweetened by the VOLGA, which is at leaft to the diftance of ten leagues from the influx of that river.

The navigation of the CASPIAN belongs folely to the RUSSIANS; the PERSIANS and other borderers having nothing but fifhing-boats. It contains abundance of fifh; but no fhell-fifh, except a kind of cockle, the fhells of which are very pretty. In fome places

places there is a great depth of water. The PERSIANS obferve that of late the fea has retired confiderably from the fhore; which they reckon ominous, prefaging fome calamity to the kingdom. It has no tides, but fuch as are caufed by the wind; and, notwithftanding the great quantities of water daily received, it continues nearly about the fame height. DR. HALLEY has demonftrated, that, exhalation, in fo hot a climate, is fufficient to account for this phenomenon, without having recourfe to fubterraneous paffages.

The 4th, I was conducted by an ARMENIAN merchant, fome leagues from our tents, to vifit a PERSIAN. We were received in a very complaifant and friendly manner; the houfe was clean, and the floor fpread with carpets. Our entertainment confifted of coffee and boiled rice.

On the 11th arrived two Jefuits from INDIA, named VALERY and MARTINET, on their way to ROME. They petitioned the ambaffador for a paffage in one of our fhips to ASTRACHAN; which was granted. About this time many of our retinue began to be feized with different difeafes, particularly fevers, fluxes, and

and agues; which, in a few days, made such progress, CHAP. III. that, at the ambassador's table, where seldom fewer 1716. than ten dined, he and myself only were present. These distempers exhibited a most disagreeable prospect, and made us wish earnestly to leave a place that threatened our destruction. For this purpose, messengers were daily sent to the chan of SHAMACHY, to dispatch the camels, horses, and mules; some of them indeed were already come, but not near the number we needed; for our numerous sick could only be transported on litters carried by mules.

The 12th, a conductor, called maymander, arrived with a guard of PERSIAN soldiers, and some more cattle, which were still too few. This officer is appointed by the Shach or King to guide ambassadors to court, and furnish them with provisions, carriages, and lodgings, at the Shach's expence, from the time they enter the kingdom.

Having accommodated ourselves in the best manner we could, we quitted NIEZABATT on the 18th, keeping along the shore; and at night came to a small village, about three agatz from NIEZABATT. We found the houses all empty, the people having fled

fled to the woods or mountains on our approach.

The 20th we reached a village about four agatz (an agatz is reckoned to be four ENGLISH miles,) from the former, where we lodged again in empty houses; and the 21st proceeded four agatz further, to a brook of white and muddy water, where we pitched our tents. About noon, next day, we came to a fountain of pure water, under a great oak. Here we halted two hours to refresh the sick; and, after travelling four agatz further, arrived at an old caravansery. A long days-journey for people in such distress.

The caravanseries are generally large square-buildings, with a court in the middle. All round there are rooms for lodging travellers, and on one side a stable for horses. They are of different sizes and constructions, according to the bounty or ability of the founder; some are built by charitable people, others by good kings. They are situated as near fresh water as possible, and about a day's journey from one another.

As there are no inns in the east, these caravanseries in some measure supply that defect, though nothing

thing is found in them but shelter. They are however very convenient for travellers; and some of them can contain five hundred men, with their horses. There is commonly an old man, who cleans the rooms, and fetches necessaries from the next town or village.

The 23d, we halted to refresh the sick, and here we buried two of our mechanics.

The 24th, we travelled to a ruinous caravansery, about four agatz from the former. This was the first instance that occurred of remissness and inattention in the present government of PERSIA; for the King, without attending to his own affairs, allows himself to be guided entirely by those whose interest it is to deceive him. Nothing, in the judgment of a foreigner, can render any people more contemptible than the notorious neglect of such useful publick edifices. This day we received another supply of provisions from the chan.

The 26th, we travelled to a plain within a league of SHAMACHY, where we lay all night to be received into the town, the day following, in form and ceremony, according to the custom of PERSIA. At this place

place died my friend, captain JACQUES DE VILLETTE. He was a gentleman of a good family in FRANCE, and a very worthy man. And, besides the Captain, two servants died here.

CHAPTER IV.

Occurrences during our stay at SHAMACHY; *Our journey thence to* TAURIS.

THE 27th, in the morning, came the Kalentar and Dorruga, with many of the inhabitants, to pay their compliments to the ambassador. These officers are next in rank under the chan, and have the sole direction of affairs in his absence. They brought some fine horses, richly caparisoned, for the chief of the retinue. As we approached the place we were met by other officers, particularly the Divan, Begg and Ish-agassy, and magistrates, all mounted on stately horses, with rich furniture, which made a very splendid appearance. Before the ambassador's horse two young fellows tumbled all the way, with great agility. About two o'clock we entered the city.

As

As we passed along the streets, all the tops of the houses were filled with spectators. At last the ambassador arrived at the house of one of the principal officers, which was allotted entirely to him and his attendants. The houses in PERSIA are mostly flat-roofed. As there is but little rain in this country, a very small declivity is sufficient to carry off the water. I compute the distance between NIEZABATT and SHAMACHY to be about twenty five agatz, or an hundred miles.

October 1st, I had a visit from a gentleman well dressed in the PERSIAN fashion, and was not a little surprized to hear him talk good HIGH-DUTCH. After some conversation, he told me he was born at DANTZICK; that in his youth he came to PERSIA with a POLISH ambassador, who died at ISPAHAN. That, some differences arising between him and his countrymen, to end the dispute he turned MAHOMETAN, and settled in PERSIA, where he now enjoyed a small salary as a linguist. He had often repented of this rash step; but, having a wife and children at SHAMACHY, he could not abandon them.

The day following, the chan, with a numerous reti-

retinue, paid a ceremonial visit to the ambassador. The chan is a middle-aged man, of a graceful aspect, by birth a GEORGIAN, of Christian parents, but brought up at court from his infancy: And it must be confessed that his treatment of the ambassador was extremely obliging.

The 14th, the chan sent an invitation to the ambassador to go a hunting, with horses for that purpose. We marched about two or three miles to the eastward, till we came to a plain overgrown with short reeds. We sprung a number of pheasants, ten or fifteen whereof were killed by the chan's hawks, and several hares were run down by the grey-hounds, which were all sent to the ambassador's lodgings.

About this time there happened a misunderstanding between the ambassador and secretary, by the imprudence of the latter. It is customary for the Shach to make presents in money, or other things, to all ambassadors, according to the dignity of their respective masters; and though no money had yet been granted, the unlucky secretary, poor gentleman! not quite recovered, by an unseasonable and ill advised claim, pretended a right to part of the future dona-

donative. The ambaſſador, on the contrary, alledged, that the ſecretary was intituled to nothing from him, except the privilege of his table and proviſions for his ſervants. Both my ſituation in the retinue, and an indiſpoſition, prevented my intermeddling in this diſpute. I only adviſed the ſecretary to poſtpone his claim till ſome more favourable opportunity. My advice however had no effect, for the difference ſtill increaſed, till the ſecretary fell ſick, and was confined to his lodgings, where he died ſuddenly on the 5th of November.

This event was the more melancholy to me, in particular, as it was unexpected; by the death of this gentleman I was deprived of another worthy friend. He was a SAXON by birth; was candid, honeſt, and ſincere; and much eſteemed, by all his acquaintance, for his learning and capacity.

A few days after, there arrived at SHAMACHY a PERSIAN ambaſſador, who had been in FRANCE, and had returned homeward through RUSSIA. His behaviour in FRANCE, and in other places, had been little for the honour of his maſter. The miniſtry at ISPAHAN had perfect intelligence of his whole conduct.

duct, which he came to understand; and, being afraid to undergo a trial at court, went directly to the city of ERIVAN, the place of his residence when in his own country, where, as it was reported, he poisoned himself. He had treated a FRENCH engineer, whom he engaged in the service of his master, so cruelly that he died two days after coming to SHAMACHY.

The 25th, I dined with father PETER RICARD, in company with Monsieur BOURGARD a FRENCH merchant. This father hath lived as a missionary in different places of PERSIA for many years. He had studied physick, which he practised occasionally, and thereby introduced himself to an acquaintance with many families of distinction. He is a man of a grave and sober deportment, which procures him great respect. He has a small congregation at this place, consisting only of CHRISTIAN ARMENIANS, who have been converted from the communion of the EASTERN to the WESTERN CHURCH; for it is a capital crime to convert a MAHOMETAN. BOURGARD was employed by the ENGLISH factory at ISPAHAN, to buy raw silks here to be sent to ALEPPO.

The ambassador sent a present to the chan, of sables,

sables, and other rich furrs of confiderable value; and had, in return, a fine horfe, with a fadle, bridle, and other trappings, mounted with gold.

Sometime after, there arofe a difpute between the ambaffador and the Chan, about the Shach's gratuity; the firft thought the fum offered was too fmall, while the latter affirmed he had no authority for a greater allowance. The determination of this affair detained us longer than we intended to ftay; however, in the mean time, camels and horfes were ordered to be got ready. After many meffages on both fides, the Chan, unwilling to let the ambaffador depart unfatisfied, fent Monfieur BOURGARD with an offer of ten tomans (a toman is equal to three pounds Sterling,) a day, during his journey to ISPAHAN, and that fum for three days only of the time he continued at SHAMACHY. This propofal was at laft accepted, and the money paid. I fhall, before we leave this place, add a few remarks on the city and its environs.

SHAMACHY is fituated in about forty degrees north latitude. It was anciently part of MEDIA; but now the capital of an extenfive province, called SHIRVAN.

CHAP. IV.
1716.

The city stands on the declivity of a hill, inclining to the south, and rises toward the top in form of an amphitheatre. The place is large, but the houses are meanly built; excepting those of the governor, the chief magistrates, and a few rich merchants. The streets are narrow and irregular. The greater part of the inhabitants are PERSIANS. There is also a considerable number of GEORGIANS and ARMENIANS. The vulgar language is TURKISH; but the people of distinction speak PERSIAN. The air is more healthy than at places nearer to the CASPIAN sea.

Above the town, on the summit of the hill, stands an high edifice, having many windows and a gallery, in which, every day at the rising and setting of the sun, is held a kind of concert of musick, composed of long trumpets, large drums, and hautboys, which make a dreadful sound. It is reported that this custom is as ancient as the time of ALEXANDER the Great.

There are also in the city several mosques with high pillars adjoining, which the moulla or priest ascends every day at twelve o'clock to call the people

ple to prayers; for the MAHOMETANS use no bells. They have, besides, several publick baths, some for men, others for the women, to which both sexes resort daily for ablution, conformably to the law of their religion. The women go generally in companies of five or six, so concealed with a white veil that nothing of them is visible but the eyes and nose. There are several spacious caravanseries, very convenient for strangers or merchants, who there expose their commodities; for which they pay a small impost.

There is a considerable traffick at this place; particularly in raw-silk, which is produced in the neighbourhood, the greatest part whereof is purchased by the ENGLISH and DUTCH factories at ISPAHAN, and sent to ALEPPO; also cotton, which indeed is mostly sold to the natives, and consumed in stuffs for their own use. The country about SHAMACHY, besides many kinds of fruits, produces plenty of wheat, barley, and very fine grapes, from which the CHRISTIANS make very good wine; they keep it in great jars resembling the FLORENCE oil ones, which they deposite under ground in their gardens, covering them above

above with a thin stone, neatly pasted about the edges, for the better preservation of the liquor. When they give an entertainment they spread carpets round the jar, which is generally placed in a shade, and on these the guests are seated.

About two miles to the northward of the city stands a high mountain, named GUILISTAN-DAGH, where are seen the ruins of an ancient castle built of stone; it appeared not to be of eastern architecture. I could procure no information who was the founder, or by whom it was demolished. Adjoining to this mountain is another, on which are the tombs of two saints, or heroes, whither great numbers of devout people come annually to worship. I observed near these tombs several hallowed rocks covered with small shells brought hither by the worshippers. I observed likewise on the common rocks many shells imprinted and petrified, which seemed very extraordinary.

December 4th, all things being prepared for our departure, we were furnished by the conductor, or maymander, with one hundred and sixty camels, and near two hundred horses and mules, on which we
left

left SHAMACHY, travelling along the rising grounds. We halted two days at an ARMENIAN village called KALCK-ANII.

CHAP. IV.
1716.

On the 7th, we descended into a desert plain, called by the RUSSIANS MUGAN, and by the PERSIANS KURDISTAN. At mid-night we came to some wells of brackish water, where we lodged in such tents as are used by the inhabitants, which were prepared by the conductor.

We proceeded the 10th five agatz, to a little copse-wood, where was found tolerable water, and the 11th arrived at the river KURE, or CYRE, which we passed on a bridge of boats, and pitched our tents on the other side. The water of the river is sweet and wholesome.

About half a league above the bridge the river ARAXIS, now ARRAS, falls into the KURE, which together form a considerable stream that discharges itself into the CASPIAN sea, about a day's journey below the bridge, running northward all the way. But the mouth of the river is so choaked up with sand, that it is navigable by no vessel of any burden.

The river KURE divides the province of SHIRVAN
from

CHAP. IV. from KURDISTAN. The KURDY, probably so called
1716. from the name of the river, are a very ancient people, and seem to be the same whom XENOPHON in the ANABASIS calls KARDUCHI, who so strenuously opposed his passage, in his famous retreat from ARTAXERXES. They are still reckoned a brave people. Their horses are most esteemed of any in PERSIA, both for beauty and strength.

We left the KURF on the 13th, and proceeded seven agatz to CHUDA-TZOOLATZY, where the water was very brackish and muddy. The country around appeared plain as the sea.

Setting out early next morning, we travelled ten agatz, and in the evening reached a brook of tolerable water, called BOLGAR. This was the last day's journey in the plain of MUGAN. The inhabitants, the KURDY, live in tents all the year. The soil is very dry and barren, notwithstanding the cattle are in good condition, and the mutton particularly very good.

While we halted about noon, some PERSIAN sportsmen, who, by their dress, seemed persons of distinction, pitched their tents near ours. They sent
the

the ambassador a present of wild-fowl, and an antelope. The ambassador invited them to share a traveller's dinner. Three of the gentlemen accepted the invitation, but excused themselves from eating any thing, pretending they had already dined; but it is well known that the MAHOMETANS scruple to eat with CHRISTIANS; each of them however drank a dish of coffee, and an old man a dram of brandy. They had several grey-hounds, and a couple of large hawks, which were trained to fly at antelopes; the hawks cannot indeed hold so strong a creature as an antelope; but they fly about its head, and thereby retard its velocity, till the grey-hounds, or horsemen, overtake it; for the antelope far out-runs any grey-hound I ever saw. In this desert I have seen flocks of them consisting of two or three hundred.

In manning hawks to fly at antelopes, they stuff the skins of these animals with straw, and feed the hawk between their horns, placing food there for that purpose; hence they are accustomed to hover round the head, which proves the destruction of these creatures. I was informed that it is in this manner the TARTARS manage hawks to fly at foxes and

and wolves. These particulars may possibly appear immaterial; however, as they may contribute to amuse the reader, it was thought not improper to insert them.

After resting the 16th, we travelled next day four agatz, to the foot of a very high mountain, where we found a few poor cottages deserted by their inhabitants on our approach. The water was in plenty and good. The weather was very cold, and no firewood could be got, except a little we brought along with us. One of our people straggling too near the rocks was dangerously wounded with a stone, thrown by some of these cottagers who had retired thither. On these rocks I saw a creature like a goat, called by the GERMANS Stein-buck; it is much bigger than the common kind of these animals, and its horns are of a prodigious size.

The 18th, we advanced five agatz farther; and the 19th, seven agatz to a large village, called KATCHOO-CHANA, where the chan of MUGAN has a good house. The weather being cold and frosty we continued here all the 20th.

The 21st we travelled five agatz, to a village under

der a great mountain, where was a water-mill for grinding corn, the first machine of that sort I saw in PERSIA.

The 22d we came to a small town called AGGAR. The kalentar ordered the citizens to arm and oppose our entry; and, notwithstanding the remonstrances of our conductor, he persisted unalterable in his purpose, affirming he had no order to admit such a body of armed men. He did not however refuse us provisions, wood and water, for money. We were therefore obliged to content ourselves with these, and lodge in our tents on an open field, in cold weather.

Next day we proceeded two or three agatz, to a large populous village, where the people, in imitation of those at AGGAR, assembled in arms, and barricadoed all their entries, refusing us admittance; they beat our quarter-master, a PERSIAN officer belonging to the conductor, for offering to force his way into the place. We therefore lodged again in the open air. They sent out some fire wood, and whatever else they could spare. I must confess I could scarce blame these people for their behaviour;

CHAP IV.
1716.

because, had we been admitted, the inhabitants must all have left their own houses: and where could a parcel of poor women and children have found shelter in such extremity of cold.

The 24th we continued our journey betwixt two great mountains, where the north wind was very piercing. We passed an old ruinous caravansery, and arrived in the evening at an empty village, which the natives had forsook the day before. All next day we halted, being CHRISTMASS.

The 26th we marched forward four agatz, to another village. The inhabitants were so hospitable as to afford us lodging; but charged dear for every thing we needed, especially wood, which was bought at the rate of three-pence for seven pounds.

On the 27th we travelled over exceeding high mountains, from whence, I was told by an ARMENIAN merchant in our company, might be seen, in a clear day, the top of the famous mount ARARAT, called by the PERSIANS AGGRY, by the ARMENIANS MESSIN; the summit is constantly covered with snow, and often with a cloud. It is the highest of all that

chain

chain of mountains in ARMENIA, on which we then stood.

How far my information might be true I cannot determine; but certain it is, that when the ARMENIANS see this mountain they make a sign of the cross, and say their prayers, as is their custom, when they approach any place which they esteem sacred.

In the evening we arrived at the city of TAURIS, TERRIS, or TEBRIS, as it is pronounced by some. The ambassador was met, about half a mile from the place, by the kalentar, and chief officers, who, after the common salutations, conducted him to his lodgings. Our baggage was deposited in a large caravansery in the neighbourhood.

CHAPTER V.

Occurrences during our stay at TAURIS; *Our journey thence to* ISPAHAN.

TAURIS is a large and populous city, the capital of the province of that name, and the residence of the chan. It is situated in a fruitful plain, encompassed by the high rocks of mount TAURIS, about ten days journey from SHAMACHY, and twenty five from ISPAHAN. I mean to a caravan. It is supposed to be the ancient metropolis of MEDIA. It is still of considerable extent; but not near what it has been. There are yet to be seen many curious remains of ancient grandeur; particularly an old temple converted into a mosque, now neglected and ruinous. The roof is supported by many stately pillars of porphyry, almost entire, some whereof are of a greenish colour, with other colours and veins of gold interspersed. The proportions seemed to be regular, and the workmanship very fine and curious. In short, I am unable to describe the symmetry and beauty of these pillars; and wonder how they have escaped the

fury

fury of so many barbarians. It is no less surprising where were got such massy pieces of marble, seeing nothing like them is now to be found in this country. These particulars demonstrate the ancient grandeur and riches of this place. It is, however, a deplorable truth, that this country, in general, hath undergone so many revolutions, since the time of ALEXANDER the Great, her first conqueror, that, a few places excepted, the present names, and descriptions of cities and provinces, bear almost no resemblance to those of antiquity; so that one can scarce imagine them accounts of the same places: To such a degree hath time and barbarous invaders changed the appearances of things. Fire and sword have raged to destroy magnificent cities; stately temples and palaces are demolished; whole provinces depopulated; and fruitful fields converted into a desert, by diverting the springs, or turning the rivers, that watered them, into other channels: Such are the consequences of lawless ambition on the finest productions of nature and art. The last is a circumstance to which few countries are so much exposed as PERSIA; for in the inland part of it, there is almost no rain, which obliges

bliges the inhabitants to water all their vegetables from springs and brooks. They often convey even rivers several leagues, in channels under ground, for this purpose. The dew indeed is very plentiful; but would be insufficient of itself for the purposes of vegetation.

The streets of TAURIS are narrow and irregular. The houses are built with bricks made of mud, mixed with chopped straw, and dried in the sun; the governor's palace indeed, and a few more houses, are built of stone, and make a good appearance. The roofs are generally flat, and covered with a terrace. The walls are white-washed on the inside, and look very white and clean. The floors of every house are spread with carpets, or mats, according to the circumstances of the inhabitants. The people of distinction have great halls of audience, in their outer courts, arched with square bricks, which are plaistered and painted with flowers; this is done at a small expence, and makes a very fine show.

There are several well built mosques, with stately minorets, or pillars, which the moulla ascends to call the people to prayers; also an high building for the

the mufick, that plays evening and morning, as mentioned at SHAMACHY. There are also some large caravanseries; so that no stranger can be at a loss for lodging at a small expence. The city is quite open, having no castle, or fortification to defend it. Indeed one would imagine the desert mountains, scarcity of water, and other obstructions, would be a sufficient defence against all invasions; the fury of the TURKS, however, in their wars with PERSIA surmounted all these obstacles.

TAURIS is supplied with water from a brook, called SHANKUY, which runs through the city, and some springs in the neighbourhood. The inhabitants are mostly PERSIANS; though there are among them many ARMENIANS. They have a considerable commerce in raw-silk, and manufactories of carpets, and silk and cotton stuffs. They have great crops of wheat and barley, when at the trouble and expence of watering the fields; but their principal support is rice, brought from the province of GUILAN, where it grows very plentifully; for this kind of grain, which of all other thrives best on wet land, agrees wonderfully with that rich moist soil near the CASPIAN sea.

CHAP. V.
1716.

The Capuchin miffionaries have a convent at this place, for the ufe of the ARMENIANS of the ROMAN CATHOLICK profeffion; which is fuperintended by two fathers of that order.

About a league from the city, on the road to IS-PAHAN, are feen, the ruins of a bridge, on the top of a hill, where, I believe, no water has run fince the deluge. It is faid that it was built by a whimfical prieft, in order to introduce himfelf to the King, SHACH ABBAS, who could not avoid taking notice, when he paffed that way, of fuch an extraordinary appearance.

About four or five leagues from TAURIS, in a plain called ROOMY, there are feveral fprings of water that petrify wood, and, I have been informed, even reptiles; fuch as lizards. One thing is certain, that, after a ftagnation of this water, for a certain time, there is a fubftance like marble found at the bottom, which the PERSIANS cut into any breadth, or length, at pleafure. I have feen of it two or three inches thick. It is eafily polifhed, and is diaphanous, but not tranfparent. After fawing it into flabs, they fix them for windows in their bagnios and private apartments

ments. Perhaps, it is not improbable, the large pillars, formerly mentioned, might be hewn out of this kind of marble.

During our stay at TAURIS, little material happened. The weather continued very cold, which, together with want of horses and camels, detained us longer than we expected. I could not but pity the poor people of this place; the cold was so excessive, and bread, and other necessaries so dear, that, I was informed, many of them perished in the streets.

January 2d, 1717, Monsieur RICARD, a FRENCH Jesuit, arrived, in his way to ISPAHAN, with some letters from ROME to the Sophy. He sent Monsieur DUFFUS, one of his retinue, with his compliments to our ambassador.

The Chan being absent, the Vizir, who is his lieutenant, came the 6th, in great state, to visit the ambassador; who, on the 11th, returned the compliment, attended with all his retinue. He was received in a magnificent hall, spread with fine carpets. There was a seat placed for the ambassador; but the rest of the company sat crofs-legged on the carpets, in the PERSIAN manner.

CHAP. V.
1717.

The 20th there was a great fall of snow, which very much softened the cold piercing northerly winds.

The 23d, having, with great difficulty, procured horses and camels, we left TAURIS, and travelled two agatz through deep snow, which incommoded us not a little; particularly on account of the camels, who cannot bear deep roads.

The 24th and 25th, the roads were impassable. I saw here a male camel trample one of his keepers under his feet. For at this season, when the females are rutting, the males are very furious and ungovernable, and must be managed with great caution.

The 26th, we travelled two agatz, to a spacious well built caravansery, founded by SHACH SEPHY, sufficient to contain some hundreds of men and horses. Here we halted some time, and proceeded in the afternoon five agatz farther. In this day's journey you have the choice of two roads, both leading to ISPAHAN; one through the cities of ARDEVILLE and CASBIN; and the other by ZENGAN and SULTANY; the last whereof we choosed, being somewhat shorter.

ARDEVILLE is reported to be a very fine place;

and

and is famous for the monuments of SHACH SEPHY the first, and other PERSIAN princes and heroes, esteemed for their virtue and piety. A great many devout people come, from all parts of the country, to worship at these tombs, where a considerable charity is daily distributed to the poor pilgrims; to support which, there is a fund settled by the King, with proper officers appointed to superintend the management of it, and prevent frauds. I wanted much to visit this place, but found it impracticable.

The 27th, we advanced three agatz, through deep snow, to a caravansery built of bricks. We were at no loss for water while the snow lay upon the ground. The next day we reached a large village, called KARA-CHINA inhabited by PERSIANS and ARMENIANS. About a mile from the place we were met by an ARMENIAN priest, attended by a company of country people, who came to welcome us as fellow Christians. One of them carried a painted crucifix, raised on a long pole; others played on flutes and hautboys, and other musical instruments; to which one or two persons kept time, by beating two thin brass plates against each other; and many of them

them sung hymns and pfalms. In this manner they accompanied us to our lodgings, where we were better accommodated than we had been hitherto. We received from thefe people, in particular, very good wine and grapes, which they preferve, through the winter, by hanging them in dry and open places.

About this time many of our people had fore eyes, and fwelled faces, caufed by the ftrong reflexion of the fun-beams from the fnow. The PERSIANS themfelves are liable to the fame diforders. As a remedy, they wear a fillet of net-work, made of black horfe hair, over their eyes; which I found, by experience, altogether effectual.

The 31ft, we fet out early, and travelled four agatz to TURKOMA, a large village. The fnow continued very deep. Here we were obliged to wait for our camels, fome of which did not arrive till next day.

February 2d, we travelled eight agatz to a little town called MIANNA, where is a caravanfery for horfes only. Here we buried another of our people.

The 4th, after two hours march, we paffed a river, over which is a fine ftone-bridge, ftanding under

der an high mountain called KAPLANTON. Leaving that place, we saw, on the left hand, the ruins of an old fortification. We repassed the river on another stone-bridge; thence to a caravansery, called TZAMATURA, and at night reached another, called SARTZAM, being eight agatz from MIANNA. Here we halted till our camels arrived; the greatest part whereof came not before next day. We perceived the depth of the snow to lessen daily, as we advanced to the south.

The 7th, we travelled five agatz to a small town named ZENGAN, where we lodged in a good caravansery. The Sultan, or chief magistrate, waited on us, and gave us a friendly and hospitable reception. He has under his jurisdiction, both this place and SULTANY; at each he resides half the year by turns.

Here we met a RUSSIAN merchant, who had about fifteen or twenty camels loaden with various kinds of merchandise, going to BUCHARIA.

We halted two days, on account of the deep snow in this neighbourhood; and the 10th, after travelling six agatz, came to SULTANY. This place is at pre-

CHAP. V.
1717.

present small and inconsiderable, though it appears to have been a great and famous city in former times. There are still to be seen several stately mosques and minorets; one of these mosques is the tomb of a PERSIAN prince, called CHUDABENDIE, which has a brass gate of lattice work, seemingly of great antiquity. In the same mosque is the tomb of SULTAN BAJAZAT, son to CHUDABENDIE.

On the 12th, we travelled four agatz to a village where we staid all night; and the 13th, three agatz to another, through deep snow, which prevented our proceeding next day.

The 15th, we travelled five agatz, and the 16th four, to a large village, called GUIGA ZAYN. At this place a RUSSIAN youth applied to the ambassador for freedom and protection. He had been carried away by the TARTARS, from some of the southern provinces of RUSSIA, and was sold some years before in PERSIA. He was forced to turn MAHOMETAN; had almost forgot his mother tongue; and was obliged to explain himself by an interpreter. The ambassador afforded him the protection he sought. His master claimed either his slave or the money he had

had paid for him; neither of which demands could be granted.

The 18th, we arrived at SEXABBATT, a village four agatz from the former, where we quartered that night, and rested all the next day.

The 20th, we advanced three agatz to ARAZANT, a small village. This district being much pestered with strong gangs of high-way men, we marched with great circumspection, and in the night the baggage was guarded, both by our own people and the conductor's soldiers.

The 21st, after a journey of three hours, we came to an old caravansery, called IDJOOP, where we rested; then advanced four agatz to another, called KOCKERA, situated in an extensive plain. The snow was now altogether gone, and the water at this place very bad. In an upper room of this caravansery, I saw the names of many EUROPEANS cut on the wall, in different languages: among which was that of OLEARIUS, secretary to the HOLSTEIN ambassadors, who published a very exact account of that fruitless embassy.

The 22d of February, we set out very early, and
in

CHAP. V. in three hours reached DENGGIE, a caravanſery,
1717. where we halted for refreſhment; and at night arrived at SABA, or SAVA, ſeven agatz from KOCKERA.

SABA appears, from many ruins, to have been a place of great note; it ſtands in a fruitful and extenſive plain, which produces all ſorts of fruit natural to the climate; particularly pomegranates, the largeſt I have ſeen. The trees were now in full bloom, and had a very fine appearance. Some years ago this place was almoſt ruined by a deluge; it has been repairing ever ſince, but is ſtill far from its former condition.

The 24th, our road lay through a deſert and barren plain, abounding with ſaltpetre. We travelled ſix agatz to JEFFRABATT, a new caravanſery; and the 25th, five agatz to the town of KOOM.

About two leagues from KOOM we ſaw a round hill to the left, call'd in TURKISH, GEDEEN-GEDMAZE, which ſignifies, that, whoever goes up never returns; which, the PERSIANS ſay, was the fate of a page ſent up by SHACH ABBASS with a lighted torch in his hand: however this be, it is certainly no eaſy matter to aſcend this place; becauſe the whole hill conſiſts of of sand, which is shifted from place to place by the wind, and must soon tire whoever attempts to climb it.

Koom is reckoned among the chief towns in PERSIA, and is the residence of a Chan. It is situated in a fertile plain, well watered by a pretty large river, over which is a fine stone-bridge. In the town is a spacious caravansery, and several well built mosques and minorets; one of these mosques is highly esteemed by the PERSIANS, because of the sepulchre of SHACH SEPHY and his son SHACH ABBASS the second, and that of SIDY FATHIMA, granddaughter to their prophet MAHOMET. These tombs are much frequented by pilgrims, from all parts of PERSIA, who resort thither once a year to pay their devotions; and are supported by a fund appropriated to that purpose.

Before you reach the mosque, you pass through three neat courts; and in the middle of the fourth, where the mosque stands, there is a large bason of clear water. Above the gate are ingraved in gilt-letters, the names of the deceased princes, with some verses in their praise. The monument of SIDY FA-THIMA

THIMA stands in the front of the building, encompassed with a grate-work of pure silver, very valuable. To each of the princes are consecrated magnificent apartments, where the priests read the Koran night and day.

This is also a place of refuge for debtors, and unfortunate people, who are maintained at the publick expence. Adjoining to the mosque is a large hall, where alms is daily distributed to the poor. Few CHRISTIANS are admitted into this sacred place. The ambassador, however with a few of the retinue, obtained this favour. KOOM is famous for manufacturing the best blades, in all PERSIA, for sabres and poinards.

The 27th, we travelled from KOOM, five agatz to KASSIM-ABBAT, a considerable village, where we lodged. The weather now began to be so hot that we could travel only in the morning and evening.

On the 28th, after travelling six agatz, we came to SINNBZYN, another village. Here our huntsman caught a porcupine, and brought it home alive.

March 1st, we arrived at a place called KASHAN, six agatz from the former. At some distance we

were

were met by the doroga, or judge, attended by about fifty horsemen. He came to salute the ambassador, and conducted him to his lodgings. The house belonged to the Shach, and was pleasantly situated in the middle of a fine garden, planted with various kinds of fruit trees.

KASHAN is a large and populous city; it is situated in a fertile plain, which secures plenty of all necessaries, and contains several well built mosques and caravanseries. The market place is well furnished with merchandise of different kinds. The common manufactures of PERSIA are found here; *viz.* silk and cotton stuffs, carpets, besides some other articles, which make this a place of considerable trade.

This city is much pestered with scorpions, especially the black kind, reckoned the most venomous. Their sting proves mortal in a few days, nay, even hours, if proper remedies be not applied. The cure used by the PERSIANS, is to anoint the wound with the oil of these animals, extracted by frying. Of this oil they have generally a quantity in reserve. If it is wanting, they bruise any scorpion and apply it to the part affected. Either of these remedies,

CHAP. V.
1717.

taken in due time, seldom fail of success. The PERSIANS have such a dread of these creatures, that, when provoked by any person, they wish a KASHAN scorpion may sting him. They are the more terrible, as few houses are free from them; for most of the floors being of earth, and covered with carpets or mats, below these the scorpions find or make holes for themselves, where they lurk unseen. They do not indeed often hurt, unless touched suddenly. It is advisable for all travellers to examine diligently the place where they are to sleep, before they go to bed. As the scorpion is well known, it will be unnecessary to say any more of it.

The 5th, we reached BUZADBATT, five agatz from KASHAN. The weather was very hot. At this place I saw a creature called the stellio, or tarantula, and by the PERSIANS inkureck; it is in shape and size somewhat like a large spider, but overgrown with hair. I was informed that it neither stings nor bites, but drops its venom upon the skin, which is of such a nature that it immediately penetrates into the body, and causes dreadful symptoms; such as giddiness of the head, a violent pain in the stomach,

and

and a lethargick stupifaction. The remedy, as in the former case, is the application of the same animal, when bruised, to the part, by which the poison is extracted. They also make the patient drink abundance of sweet milk, after which he is put in a kind of tray, suspended by ropes fixed in the four corners, it is turned round till the ropes are twisted hard together, and, when let go at once, the untwining causes the basket to turn round, with a quick motion, which forces the patient to vomit.

They also make them dance to musical instruments, which the sick person sometimes does of his own accord, till he drops down upon the spot. One of these terrible creatures happened to fall out of the cieling upon my hand, as I was going one night to bed; I shook it off instantaneously without receiving the least harm. Every thing near was moved, and searched for it, but to no purpose, there being many holes in the floor. It may easily be imagined that apprehension would prevent my sleeping much that night.

The 6th, we travelled five or six agatz to KALTABBATT; and the next day five, to NATTANEE, a
small

CHAP. V. small town situated under some high mountains.
1717. Here the Shach has a pretty little palace, with gardens, fountains of fine water, and cascades. We lodged in the palace. The jackals were so bold that they howled under the windows all the night long, and carried off some of our poultry. On the top of a mountain, near this place, stands a high tower, built by SHACH ABBASS, which is seen at a great distance.

The 8th, we left NATTANEE, and in three hours passed a fine house, with gardens, built by SHACH ABBASS, and situated by itself in a pleasant plain. About three hours after, we came to TUTRIN, an old caravansery, where we lodged. The heat increased daily as we advanced to the south. The 9th, we reached RUCK, eight agatz distant from TUTRIN, and four hours journey from the city of ISPAHAN.

The 10th, being the vernal equinox, when the new year commences among the PERSIANS, we halted all day. In the evening thirty fine horses, with rich furniture, were sent from the Shach's stables to the ambassador; some of the bridles were ornamented with

with gold, others with silver. Two lions were brought by a PERSIAN to be shown to the ambassador. They were led into a court-yard, and let loose upon a goat; but, instead of the goat, they ran at some of our people, who narrowly escaped by getting into a house and shutting the doors. It seems the sight of so many strangers had frightened them, for the keeper himself with difficulty chained them, and one of them even bit his hand.

The 11th, we advanced two agatz, to DAVILETT-ABRATT a village.

On the morning of the 13th the Maymander Basha, or chief conductor, arrived with many attendants. In the evening we mounted, and, being accompanied with a numerous train of courtiers, and other people, we travelled two agatz to the suburbs of the city, where we lodged in a palace, called TUCHTZY, belonging to the Shach.

The 14th, in the morning, came a number of horses sufficient for the ambassador and all his train; this being the day appointed for our publick entry.

About noon the maymander basha returned to conduct the ambassador to his lodgings in the city,

CHAP. V. he was attended by many perſons of diſtinction.
1717. After noon, we mounted and entered the city. We paſſed through many ſtreets crouded with ſpectators, as were alſo the tops of the houſes. It was ſaid that the Sophy himſelf was at a window, incognito, with ſome of his ladies. Curioſity had cauſed ſuch a croud, that, had not the way been cleared by the PERSIAN guards, it would have been impoſſible for us to paſs along. At laſt, we reached the end of our journey; a noble palace, in the middle of the city, with a garden, three courts, and apartments ſufficient for the ambaſſador and all his retinue.

THE ORDER OF THE ENTRY.

An officer.
Three dragoons.
A kettle-drum.
Four trumpets.
Thirty dragoons, three abreaſt, with drawn ſwords.
Six ſpare horſes with ſumptuous trappings.
The ſteward.
Twelve footmen.
Two pages.

Three

TO ISPAHAN.

Three footmen.
Two interpreters.
Two hey-dukes in HUNGARIAN habits.
The ambaſſador, with the maymander, baſha and interpreter.
The prieſt and one gentleman.
Myſelf and one gentleman.
Two clerks.
Faulconers, huntſmen, &c.

CHAPTER VI.

Occurrences during our ſtay at ISPAHAN.

THE 15th, the agents of the ENGLISH and DUTCH factories, *viz.* Mr. COPPIN the ENGLISH agent, ſent Meſſieurs BATSON and REYNARDSON, the DUTCH agent likewiſe ſent two gentlemen of their company, to ſalute the ambaſſador.

The 16th, the maymander baſha invited the ambaſſador to an audience of the Etmadowlett, or prime miniſter, which he would not comply with till he had an audience of the Shach, and delivered his cre-

den-

dentials, though it is ufual firft to take an audience of that minifter. This day I vifited the ENGLISH factory, where I met with a friendly reception.

On the 27th was a great fall of rain, fuch as had not been at ISPAHAN for feven years. It was the caufe of great joy in this fultry dry climate, though to me it feemed nothing extraordinary.

April 1ft, I went to JULFFA to fee a friend, accompanied by Mr. BATSON. It is a large place in the fuburbs, inhabited by ARMENIANS, who have the free exercife of the CHRISTIAN religion. On the 10th, I dined at the DUTCH houfe, the weather very hot.

May 4th, the ceremonial part of the ambaffador's introduction to the Shach being previoufly agreed on, he was this day to have his firft audience. In the morning horfes were fent from the King's ftables, all of them magnificently equipped, with grooms to attend them; many of the faddles and bridles were garnifhed with gold and filver.

We marched in the fame order as at our entry above mentioned, only the dragoons had not their fwords drawn. After paffing through feveral ftreets we we came into the great market place called BAZAR, and then to a gate called ALLA-CAPY, *i. e.* GOD'S-GATE, where we difmounted. Acrofs this gate is hung a chain, and none are permitted to enter on horfe-back, except the Shach himfelf. We walked through the guards, drawn up on each fide, to an inner court, and thence to an arched gate, furrounded with benches, and fpread with carpets. Here the ambaffador was defired to fit down till the Shach was ready to receive him. We waited at leaft two hours, during which time all the minifters of ftate, and officers of the houfhold, paffed us in great ftate. After them came a large elephant, mounted by his keeper, and adorned with gold and filver ftuff; then two large lions, led by their keepers with chains of maffy gold.

CHAP. VI. 1717.

When this parade was over, an officer informed the ambaffador that the Shach waited for him. Whereupon, proceeding immediately through the gate, we entered a fpacious garden. The firft thing that prefented was a noble view of twenty horfes ftanding in a row, richly caparifoned, having all their faddles and bridles ornamented with gold and silver,

silver, and some of them set with saphires, emeralds, and other precious stones of great value. The horses were all tied to a rope fixed to the ground, at the extremities, by a stake of gold, near which lay a mallet of the same metal for driving it, according to the custom of PERSIA; the hind-feet were also fastened to a rope, to prevent kicking: this is an excellent precaution; for, though they were all stoned horses, they could neither hurt one another, nor any thing else: the chains that bound their hind-feet, with the stakes, and mallets were also of gold. The PERSIAN horses are well managed; neither do I think them so vicious as those in EUROPE: whether they are naturally more gentle I shall not determine, perhaps it is intirely owing to the milder treatment of their grooms. At each end of the row stood a large vessel of gold full of water, for the horses to drink.

Approaching nearer to the hall of audience, we passed the two lions, chained to the ground, one on each side of the passage, near them were placed two basons of gold, filled with water for drink. Next to the lions stood the elephant, with his keeper on his back. As the ambassador passed, both the lions couch-

couched, and the elephant bent his fore-knee, at a word pronounced by the keepers.

We now turned to the left, and had a full view of the hall of audience, about an hundred yards diſtant. It ſeemed to ſtand by itſelf in the middle of the garden; it is indeed contiguous to the ſeraglio, on the ſouth, but is quite open to the north. Before the entry is a large fountain of pure water, which ſprings upward in three pipes, and falls into a baſon filled with roſes, jeſſamine, and many other fine flowers.

When we came to the ſtair we were deſired to put off our ſlippers, and our ſervants were no farther admitted. The ambaſſador only and ſix of his retinue (among whom I was) entered the hall. We aſcended by eight ſteps of marble, the whole breadth of the hall. From the roof hung a canvaſs which was ſtretched out over the ſtair, and ſhaded the whole inſide of the edifice. The hall is a ſpacious ſquare building, with a terrace roof. The cieling is very magnificent, being all arched, and ſet with mirrours of different magnitudes till within three feet of the floor; which is quite covered with ſilk-
car-

carpets, interwoven with branches, and foliage, of gold and silver. In the middle were two basons, into which several pipes, each about eight feet high, spouted water, which, falling upon roses and other flowers, has a fine effect on a hot day. The farther end of the hall is a semicircle. Here sat the Shach upon a sofa, raised about a foot from the floor, which was elevated four steps above the rest of the hall. He was attended by twenty eunuchs; one carried his sabre, another his bow, a third the quiver with arrows, a fourth the calianne, or tobacco pipe, so that each had his office of state.

The ambassador was received in the hall by the master of the ceremonies, called Ish-aggan Basha, to be by him introduced to the Shach. He continued sitting upon his sofa, with his legs acrofs, while all his ministers of state stood in their places, clothed magnificently in their robes; which they never wear, except on solemn days; and when these are over they leave them in a wardrobe at court, appointed for keeping them. I must confess the appearance was very splendid, and put me in mind of of the accounts left us by the ancients, of the magnificence of the Kings of PERSIA.

At our entry into the hall we were stopped about three minutes at the first fountain, in order to raise the greater respect; the pipes were contrived to play so high that the water fell into the bason like a thick rain. Nothing could be distinguished for some time, and the Shach himself appeared as in a fog. While we moved forward, every thing was as still as death. The master of the ceremonies took the ambassador by the arm and conducted him within six yards of the throne, who, offering to advance, in order to deliver his credentials, was prevented by the etmadowlett, or prime minister. This minister received the credentials, and laid them before the Shach, who touched them with his hand, as a mark of respect. This part of the ceremony had been very difficult to adjust. For the ambassador insisted on delivering his letters into the Shach's own hands. The PERSIAN ministers, on the other hand, affirmed, that their Kings never received letters directly, from the ambassadors of the greatest emperors on earth.

CHAP. VI.
1717.

The ambassador now made a short speech, which the Sophy answered, through the Etmadowlett, in very obliging terms. He then enquired after his Czarish Majesty's health, and asked several questions about the SWEDISH war; and whether the ambassador had suffered any hardships on the road during so long a journey? To all which he returned answers suitable to the occasion. At last, he was desired to take his seat, to which he was led by the master of the ceremonies. It was about a foot high, and placed at the distance of ten yards from the King. A little behind the ambassador were placed his attendants, on seats nearly of the same height. During all this ceremony, musick played; consisting of a variety of instruments, which are not unharmonious, and the mufty, or high-priest, read, without intermission, chapters of the Koran.

Before the ambassador was seated, the presents from his Czarish Majesty to the Sophy, carried by fifty men, were brought to the entry, and received by the proper officers. They consisted of sables, and other valuable furrs, falcons, a variety of fine tea, musical clocks, gold-watches set in diamonds, &c.

As

As soon as the ambassador had taken his seat, all the ministers of state sate down on their hams, on both sides of the hall, in rows; for none are allowed to sit crofs legged in prefence of the Sophy.

There was now placed before the company little tables, on which were set all kinds of sweet-meats, and confections; and before the ambassador was laid a golden calianne, or tobacco-pipe; which the PERSIANS reckon an high instance of respect.

The musick continued playing, and the mufty still continued reading; but every thing elfe was very silent. Several messages passed between the King and the ambassador, by means of the master of the ceremonies, and our interpreter. The King spoke the PERSIAN language, and the ambassador the RUSSIAN, while the other two used the TURKISH.

In the mean time some pure water, with a bit of ice in it, was brought in golden bafons to drink. About an hour after, victuals were brought by a number of fervants, who carried them on their heads, in large fquare baskets. First the Shach was ferved, and next the ambaffador with his retinue, then all the officers of state that sat in the hall.

The grand steward of the houshold waited on the King, and his assistants on the rest of the company, according to their different ranks. At the same time our servants were entertained in the garden.

The entertainment consisted mostly of different kinds of rice boiled with butter, fowls, mutton, boiled and roasted lamb. The whole was served in large gold or china dishes, and placed in the baskets, which stood on a long cloth spread above the carpet. The dishes were intersperfed with saucers filled with aromatic herbs, sugar and vinegar. But, according to the custom of the country, we had neither napkins, spoons, knives nor forks; for the Shach himself eat with his fingers, and every one followed his example. There were indeed, besides the common bread, some very large thin cakes, which we used instead of napkins, to wipe our fingers. They are made of wheat-flower, the PERSIANS sometimes eat them, they are not disagreeable. Our drink was sherbet, and water cooled with ice. Formerly it was usual, on such occasions, to drink wine, and have women to dance and sing. But the present Sophy, being a sober and devout prince,

thought

thought it proper to abolish a custom productive of so many indecencies, and directly contrary to the rules of the Koran. We had therefore only men to sing, and no dancing.

The ambassador, and all the gentlemen who were admitted into the hall, continued with their heads covered during all the time of the audience. They only, on entering the royal presence, uncovered once and bowed to his majesty.

When the entertainment was over, the ambassador took his leave and returned to his lodgings, conducted by the maymander basha, in the same manner as in the morning. The streets were lined with the Sophy's guards to prevent any inconvenience from the vast crouds of people.

The same evening the Shach sent a present to the ambassador of the golden calianne he had used at court; it was neatly wrought in filigree, and valued at forty or fifty pounds Sterling: also twenty large dishes of solid gold, filled with variety of sweetmeats. Those who brought them returned immediately, leaving the plate; which remained at the ambassador's lodgings above six weeks. All this time

time it was uncertain whether such a valuable treasure was forgot, or intended as a present. The dishes however were at last demanded, and delivered. They weighed about thirty pounds a-piece; but were of mean workmanship, being all beat out with a hammer. From this, and many similar instances, some conception may be formed of the immense riches whereof the Sophy is possessed.

The Shach's name is HUSSEIN; he is about thirty years of age, of a middle stature, open countenance, and has a short black beard. It is said his legs are remarkably short, in proportion to his body. He is very good natured, and of a beneficent disposition. He has several children by different ladies. TACHMAZ the oldest, at present in his minority, seldom appears out of the HARAM. HUSSEIN himself, though a prince adorned with many virtues, yet being educated in the HARAM among the women, is little acquainted with the world, and leaves the management of the empire wholly to his ministers: in them he places an intire confidence; and they, in their turn, persuade him, that it is below his dignity to attend to any publick affairs whatever. As this

this very time there was a formidable rebellion be- CHAP. VI.
gun at CHANDAHAR, a strong town on the borders 1717.
of INDIA, by MERY-MAHMUT, an enterprising and
powerful chief, who took advantage of the weak-
ness of the present administration.

The PERSIAN ministry neglected and despised
these rebels, threatning, in their stile, to send some
troops to cut them all to pieces. Time hath shown
the vanity of these high words. I must observe that
they wanted neither men nor money; but their soldiers were undisciplined, and, above all, they had
no officers of sufficient abilities to command them.

The 9th of May, the ambassador had his first
audience of the Etmadowlett. We were conducted
in the same manner as when we went to court. The
entertainment was likewise of the same kind, but
much more magnificent. The palace was grand,
and had a fine garden adjoining. The Etmadowlett, whose name is PHATALY-CHAN, was by birth a
GEORGIAN, of CHRISTIAN parents, but educated in
the seraglio. He is a tall well shaped man, of a
friendly aspect, and a great favourite of the Sophy.
After we returned home, the Etmadowlett sent the
ambas-

ambassador a present of a fine horse, with a saddle and bridle, richly mounted, after the PERSIAN fashion, and a gold calianne, little inferior to that given by the Shach. It was reported that no foreign ambassador had ever been treated with so much respect.

The 11th, the ambassador had a second audience of the Sophy, at the same palace as formerly, called TAVALEA TELEAR, *i. e.* the palace near the stables; it was very short, and no entertainment was given. Next day he received from the Shach a present of some excellent SHERASS wine, and a gold bottle, that contained about two quarts, with a small cup of the same metal.

On the 15th the ambassador had a second audience of the Etmadowlett, relating to the subject of the embassy.

Three days after, the Hackim Basha, or chief physician, sent me an invitation to visit him. He received me in a very courteous obliging manner; and detained me above two hours, talking on different subjects. He told me that the physicians in PERSIA made vegetables, and their virtues, their chief study; they

they dealt but little in minerals and chymical preparations. Then he asked me whether the EUROPEAN physicians admitted opium in their prescriptions? I told him they did with great success. To which he replied, that the qualities of that drug were known to very few. He inquired whence tea came? how it should be made? and what were its virtues? All which I answered to his satisfaction. Hence it is evident that the PERSIANS have no correspondence nor commerce with the CHINESE. The physician is an elderly man, of a grave deportment, and might pass for a doctor any where. On taking my leave, he told me he was sorry he could not converse with me but by means of an interpreter, which was tedious and disagreeable.

The same day the DUTCH commissary Myn-heer VONKETTLER, made his publick entry at ISPAHAN, as envoy from the governor of BATAVIA to the Shach of PERSIA. He was preceded by six elephants, sent as a present to the King by the governor. He had a numerous retinue; and was attended by several gentlemen, and made as grand an appearance as if he had been a minister from any court of EUROPE.

He

He took up his lodgings at the DUTCH factory. Mr. KETTLER told me, that he was born in COURLAND; that, in his youth, he inlisted as a soldier in the service of the DUTCH EAST-INDIA company; by his uncommon abilities he had raised himself, from that low situation, to the honourable place he now held.

The following day Mr. KETTLER sent two of his retinue to compliment our ambassador. And, both our gentlemen being indisposed, I was sent next day to return the compliment.

The 28th, I dined at the DUTCH house, where we had a grand entertainment.

June 2d, the ambassador intended to go a hunting, and to take a view of the country about ISPAHAN. But an officer came from court, desiring him to delay it till another opportunity; for the Shach had pitched on that day to visit a country-house, in company with his ladies; on which occasions it is death for any one to be seen near the place where the court passes. To prevent accidental transgressions in this respect, a cryer is previously dispatched to warn the inhabitants, who proclaims through the streets,

streets, and along the road, that nobody under pain of death shall appear either in the way, or from any house near it, by which his majesty and the ladies are to march. The Shach rides on horse-back, attended only by eunuchs. The ladies are mounted astride, some on horses, others on mules and asses. They are all vailed with white muslin; so that nothing can be seen of them but the eyes and nose.

The PERSIANS tell a pleasant story of SHACH ABBASS's behaviour on an occasion of this nature. The Shach at a certain time was riding along, attended by his concubines, when he happened to meet a poor country fellow upon the road. He was immediately brought before the King, and, expecting instant death, fell on his knees, most submissively begging pardon for so heinous an offence, and pleaded ignorance in his excuse; having neither seen nor heard of any cryer. The prince was pleased with the simplicity and innocence of the peasant, ordered him to take courage, and all the ladies to unveil; then desired him to pick out any of his concubines he liked best, and he should have her for a wife. This treatment dispelled his fear; he pitched on one that pleased him most. The Shach approved so much of his taste, that he carried him to court; where he soon became a great favourite.

The 9th, I dined at the ENGLISH factory, where Mr. COPPIN, and the other gentlemen belonging to the company, received me in the most friendly manner. The day was very hot, and in the evening we supped near a fountain in the garden. On a sudden we felt a gust of wind, as hot as if it had come from the mouth of an oven. It was soon over without any bad effect. But I was informed that these hot winds are very dangerous, in travelling over the deserts, and often kill people immediately. The only resource, on perceiving them coming, is to fall down flat, with the face to the ground, and continue in that posture till they are gone.

On the 12th, the ambassador had a third audience of the Shach at FARRABBATT, a country-house near the city. It is an extremely pleasant place, adorned with gardens, fountains and cascades, surrounded with parks for all kinds of game. While we were at supper on the terrace, we had a squal of wind which almost carried away every thing, and actual-

actually swept off the thin broad cakes, which the Persians use instead of napkins.

The 16th, Monsieur RICARD, whom I mentioned at TAURIS, and twelve missionaries of different orders, were invited to dine with the ambassador. Several of these gentlemen had been long in INDIA, and ETHIOPIA; which rendered their conversation very entertaining.

The 21st, the ambassador was invited to dinner by the Devettar, or keeper of the great seal and standish. Here, as in all other countries, this is an office of great trust. We were entertained with more magnificence than by the prime minister, or even at court. Soon after we entered, there were served up a great variety of sweet-meats, and all kinds of fruit that the climate afforded. Coffee and sherbett were carried about by turns. We were placed crofs-legged on the carpets, except the ambassador, who had a seat. During this part of the feast we were entertained with vocal and instrumental musick, dancing-boys, tumblers, puppets and juglers: all the performers executed their parts with great dexterity. Two of them counterfeiting a quarrel, one beat off the other's turban with his foot, out of which dropped about fifteen or twenty large serpents, which run or crawled about the room. One of them came towards me, with great speed, which soon obliged me to quit my place. On seeing us alarmed they told us the creatures were altogether inoffensive, as their teeth had been all drawn out. The fellow went about the room and gathered them again into his turban, like so many eels. The victuals were now served in a neat and elegant manner. Every thing was well dressed in the PERSIAN fashion. Our host was very chearful, and contributed every thing in his power to please his guests. He excused himself handsomely enough for not having wine, as it was not then used at court.

On the 23d, the Maymander Basha brought a message from the Shach to the ambassador, intimating, that the business of his embassy being now finished, he might chuse his own time to depart. This was not very agreeable news to the ambassador; who alledged, that, before he could procure shipping, to transport him to ASTRACHAN, the season

son would be far advanced, and oblige him to winter in some part of PERSIA.

July 1st, the Shach sent the ambassador, and the principal persons of his retinue, what the PERSIANS call the kalatt. It consists of a tunic, a long robe of gold and silver stuff, a sash and turban, and some pieces of PERSIAN silk; whereof about ten or a dozen fell to my share. The whole value was not considerable; but the Shach bestows this mark of favour to all foreign ministers, who come on friendly errands. On this occasion he sent the ambassador, in particular, a present of two fine horses from his own stables.

The 3d, the ambassador had his last audience of the Shach, at a palace in the city; when he received an answer to the Czar's letter, and immediately took leave standing, without further ceremony.

The 8th, the Shach sent the ambassador another present; consisting of an elephant, two lions, two leopards, six monkeys of different kinds, three parrots, two white and one green, three fine horses, and an INDIAN bird, called myana; it is in colour, shape,

and

and size like a black-bird, and whistled a very fine note.

August the 3d, we began to prepare for our journey homeward, which took up much time. The 18th, we removed from our lodgings in the city to a house belonging to the Shach, in the northern suburbs, called TAUCHTZY.

The 26th, I took leave of my friend Mr. COPPIN, who set out this day on his journey to ENGLAND, by way of ALEPPO. The ENGLISH factory at ISPAHAN are very well situated in the middle of the city, have a spacious garden adjoining, and are separated from the rest of the town by a wall. Most of the great houses in the city are surrounded in the same manner, which renders it very extensive.

ISPAHAN is situated nearly in thirty two degrees north latitude, on a fruitful plain, in the province of HIERACK, anciently the kingdom of the PARTHIANS. About three or four ENGLISH miles distant from the city, to the south, runs an high ridge of mountains from east to west. SHACH ABBASS the Great transferred the seat of the PERSIAN government from CASBIN to this place.

ISPA-

ISPAHAN is plentifully supplied with water from the river SCHENDEROO, which runs between the city and the suburbs, keeping its course to the north. It rises near the city, and is fordable almost every where, unless during great rains, which seldom happen. After passing this place, its course is but short, for it soon loses itself in dry parched plains. Over the SCHENDEROO there are three stately stone bridges in sight of one another; but the one in the middle, betwixt the city and that part of the suburbs called JULPHA, which terminates the spacious street TZAR-BACH, far exceeds any structure of that kind I ever saw. It is broad enough for two carriages and a horseman to pass abreast, and has galleries on each side, which are covered, for the convenience of people on foot; and watch-men are stationed at each end to prevent disorders. There are few houses in the town which have not their chaufes, *i. e.* cisterns of water, conveyed in pipes from the river: a most salutary and refreshing circumstance in such a dry and sultry climate.

The city is populous, and, as I already observed, very extensive. As most of the inhabitants have their houses apart, surrounded with gardens, planted with fruit and other trees, at a distance it appears like a city in a forest, and affords a very agreeable prospect.

The streets are generally very narrow and irregular, except that leading to the great bridge, already mentioned. This noble street is very broad and straight, and near an ENGLISH mile in length. On each side are the King's palaces, courts of justice, and the academies for the education of youth, with two rows of tall chinar trees, which afford a fine shade. These trees have a smooth whitish bark, and a broad leaf like the plane-tree. At certain distances there are fountains of water that play continually, round which are spread carpets; and thither the PERSIANS resort to drink coffee, smoak tobacco, and hear news: which, I must confess, is very agreeable in hot weather.

About half a mile below the city is a fine plain upon the bank of the river, where the PERSIANS, every evening, exercise their horses in riding, and accustom them to the discharge of fire-arms. They also shoot at butts with bows and arrows, and throw blunt-

blunted darts at one another; at which they appear very dextrous.

The city is almoſt quite defenceleſs, having only a ſlight wall round it, built of mud dried by the ſun, which is broken down in many places: ſo that, if the army is defeated in the field, ISPAHAN cannot defend itſelf one day; for even all the artillery I ſaw, conſiſted of about twenty braſs cannon, which ſtood in the grand court before the palace gate, and were more for parade than real uſe.

The houſes here, as in other places of PERSIA, are generally built with bricks hardened by the ſun. The roofs are flat, and covered with a terrace; they make but a mean appearance from the ſtreet, though within they are neat and clean; and very convenient for the PERSIAN manner of life. The Shach's palaces, the publick edifices, and the houſes of all perſons of diſtinction, are built with ſtone.

As the ſtreets are not paved, when it is windy, the city is ſometimes involved in ſuch a cloud of duſt, that the ſun is ſcarcely viſible. This obliges the inhabitants to water the ſtreets, at leaſt every evening. Theſe guſts of wind are very diſagreeable;

but

CHAP. VI. but they happen seldom, and are of short duration.

1717. At ISPAHAN are many manufactories of silk and cotton, and a great many silk-worms in the neighbourhood. As the consumption of silk is very considerable at this place, little of it is exported. The making carpets, however, employs the greatest number of hands; for which the demand is great, as they are preferable in quality, design, and colour to any made elsewhere.

The fields about the city are very fertile, and produce plentiful crops of excellent wheat and barley; but then they must all be watered on account of the dryness of the soil, which is a work of labour and expence: besides these I saw no other grain.

The PERSIANS tread out their corn with oxen or asses: for this purpose they make a circle, about twenty or thirty feet in diameter, on the circumference whereof the shaves are laid; there is a light sledge or hurdle drawn by the cattle, in which the driver sits and directs them round and round, as often as is necessary; and new shaves are always added when the former ones are trodden sufficiently: This operation also softens the straw, and renders

it

it very good provender; there is no hay in Persia, and the best horses are kept in a condition for any service by this food, and a small quantity of dryed barley twice a day.

They have flocks of large sheep, whereof the mutton is very good, but the wool coarse. In the province of KARAMENIA indeed they have exceeding fine wool, some of which I have seen little inferior to silk. Their horned cattle are buffalos; which afford them milk, and are used in plowing the ground and drawing carriages. They have also the common kind of cattle of different sizes. The better sort of people eat chiefly mutton and fowls, but very little beef.

Besides the cattle I have mentioned, there is another kind, having a high rising upon the shoulder, with clean limbs, which are very handsome.

As I have formerly observed, that the PERSIANS make use of ice to cool their water in summer, it may be asked, where are got such quantities, in so hot a climate, as are daily sold in the streets, for that purpose? I was informed, that there were people who made it their business to watch the frosty nights,

nights, in the winter season; on which occasions they went to the mountains near the city, and threw water on certain places, which being frozen, they continued to repeat the operation till the ice was of convenient thickness; then they cut it in pieces, and carry it into caves, hewn in the rocks, where it is preserved during the summer; what they cannot carry off before the sun rises is covered, to defend it from his heat.

While I remained at ISPAHAN, I visited the Shach's aviary. It contains a great variety of all kinds of birds, many of which had come from INDIA, and other foreign parts. Among the rest were a couple of turkeys, which it seems are rare birds in PERSIA. The place is very neat and elegant; the aviary is about fifteen feet high, and covered with a net-work of brass-wire, to prevent the birds flying away.

Provisions of all kinds are very dear at ISPAHAN, which is sufficiently apparent from the number of poor that go about the streets. Nothing however is so extravagantly high as fire-wood.

The ROMAN CATHOLICS have three convents in the city; *viz.* those of the CARMELITES, CAPUCHINS, and

and AUGUSTINS. The JESUITS and DOMINICANS have their separate convents in the suburbs of JULPHA, which is inhabited by ARMENIANS, who are allowed the free exercise of their religion.

There is a confiderable number of JEWS in the city, who are either merchants or mechanics.

In the neighbourhood of the city is a tribe of people, called by the PERSIANS GIAUR, who worfhip fire, being the pofterity of the ancient inhabitants of this country, who paid divine honours to that element. They are a poor indolent race, and live in nafty huts, or in tents. They fpeak a different language from the PERSIAN; have black hair, and are of a fwarthy complexion. They have fome fheep and cattle; but many of them go about the ftreets begging.

About three or four miles to the fouthward of the city, are to be feen the ruins of a tower on the top of a mountain, where, it is said, DARIUS fat when ALEXANDER the Great fought the fecond battle with the PERSIANS. I was alfo told, that about two days journey from ISPAHAN, are diftinguifhable the remains of the tomb of Queen ESTHER, a lady celebrated

brated in holy writ for many virtues. These, and many other places, I intended to have examined on the spot, but was unluckily prevented for want of time.

While we lay at TAUCHTZY, waiting for horses and camels, two of our servants were stung with scorpions; but were soon cured, by timely application of the oil of scorpions, prepared after the PERSIAN manner, without any other remedy. The jackals made a dismal howling under our windows every night.

I have now finished my observations on whatever seemed most remarkable in, and about the city of ISPAHAN. I shall only add, that, among the many lofty and pompous titles which this mighty monarch assumes, there are some very extraordinary; of which I shall mention one, ' That the greatest kings of the ' earth may think it an honour to drink out of his ' horses footsteps.' Several more instances might be given, in the Oriental stile, fully as extravagant.

TO ISPAHAN.

THE SHACH'S PALACES.

1. TZEL SOOTUN, or that of forty pillars.
2. TEVELA TELEAR, near the stables.
3. HASTA-BEHASI, chambers of paradise.
4. OTHIAT TALLARD, near the HARAM.
5. GULDESTA, house of eunuchs.
6. TAUCHTZY, at the north entry.
7. FARRABBATT, south east from the city.

PERSIA is at present divided into sixteen provinces, many of them of great extent. I shall mention their present names, and, opposite to them, those they seem to have born among the ancients.

MODERN NAMES.	ANCIENT.
1. TURKOMANIA,	GREAT ARMENIA.
2. DIARBECK,	MESOPOTAMIA.
3. KURDISTAN,	part of ASSYRIA.
4. HIERACK ARABEE,	CHALDEA, or BABYLON.
5. HIERACK AGGEMY,	region of the PARTHIANS.
6. SHIRVAN,	towards the north-west coast of the CASPIAN sea.
7. GUILAN and MESANDERAN,	HYRCANIA.
8. ASTRABATT,	MARGIANA.

MODERN NAMES.	ANCIENT.
9. USBECK,	BACTRIA.
10. KORASSAN,	ARIA.
11. SABLESTAN,	PARAPOMISIA.
12. SIGISTAN,	DRANGIANA.
13. ARACHOSIA.	
14. MACHRAN.	
15. KARAMENIA,	reaching to the gulph of ORMUS.
16. PHARSISTAN,	OLD PERSIA, whereof PERSEPOLIS was the capital city.

I have added the ancient names according to the best information I could procure; for, under the various revolutions of this country, the records have been almost wholly either lost or destroyed: so that the PERSIANS themselves know very little of the ancient history of their country.

CHAP.

CHAPTER VII.

From ISPAHAN *to* SHAMACHY: *Occurrences during our stay there.*

SEPTEMBER 1ft, having procured horfes and camels, and every thing neceffary, and having alfo got a conductor from the Shach, we this day left ISPAHAN in order to return to RUSSIA. We travelled fhort ftages along the fame road by which we came to ISPAHAN. Little material happened for a confiderable time, and I fhall not repeat what I formerly obferved; I fhall only take notice, that many of the places, through which we paffed, were much infefted by ftrong gangs of high-way men. We were therefore obliged to travel very cautioufly, and to keep our people together, near the baggage; but particularly to procure a fafe caravanfery for our lodgings. The weather continuing very hot, was the reafon of our making eafy marches; and thefe chiefly in the mornings and evenings, and fometimes in the night, when it could be done with fafety.

CHAP. VII.
1717.

We travelled in this manner till the 26th of September, when we arrived at a village called ARRAZANT, where we lodged. Next day, instead of pursuing the same route by TAURIS, we turned to the right and took the road leading to CASBIN and GUILAN.

The 27th, we proceeded five agatz to MEMBERECK; and the 28th four, to the city of CASBIN. This place is situated in a spacious plain, having a ridge of high mountains to the north. I mentioned formerly, that CASBIN was once the seat of government, and the residence of the PERSIAN monarchs. There are still to be seen the ruins of many stately mosques, palaces, and other publick edifices. The city appears to have been, in former times, very large and flourishing, but is now much contracted and decayed.

The plague raged here all the preceeding summer, which had almost depopulated the place. And although the fury of that contagious distemper was much abated, people continued to die daily; which made us resolve to remain no longer than was absolutely necessary, in order to prepare things for our journey to GUILAN. This could not be soon accomplished at a time of such publick calamity.

In the mean time, many of our people were seized with pestilential fevers, who all recovered but one. He died suddenly, with the usual symptoms of the plague. I and several of our people were likewise taken with fevers, occasioned by our being lodged in houses where the PERSIANS had lately died. These circumstances made the ambassador resolve to leave the place at all events. During the time therefore which we were obliged to wait for horses and camels, we removed out of town about a mile, to a garden belonging to the Shach, provided for us by the commandant of the city and province. Here we set up our tents; and in this situation, by the help of free air and good water, our people recovered surprisingly: so that, in a short time, most of them were able to ride, another gentleman only and myself were carried in litters between two mules.

The 12th of October, we set out again, pursuing our journey northward. After travelling about two leagues through a plain, we ascended an high and steep

steep mountain, and, proceeding onward about a league, came to a small village where we lodged. All the inhabitants had forsaken their houses. Whatever else was wanting, we had here the comfort of pure air; which had such an effect on me, that, next day, I was able to mount on horse-back, though at setting out, I was scarcely in condition to bear the easy motion of the litter.

We continued our journey, ascending and descending many steep rocks and mountains for four days, when we arrived at MENZYLY, a little town situated in a charming valley; where grow abundance of citrons, oranges, olives, beside grapes and other fruits. These I own were tempting objects; but sad experience taught many of us to value them no more than sloes or bramble berries. MENZYLY is governed by a kalentar, or judge; it is a pretty romantick place, encompassed by high mountains on all sides, which decline to the north, and are covered with grafs. This is a rare fight in PERSIA, and is caused by the great autumnal rains; for along the south coast of the CASPIAN sea, it rains at this season, almost without intermission, for the space

space of six weeks or two months. In this and the neighbouring villages are bred a great number of silk-worms, which produce the best and greatest quantities of raw-silk made in the province of GUILAN; from whence it is exported by the ARMENIAN merchants, partly through RUSSIA to HOLLAND, and partly by land to ALEPPO, for the LEVANT trade.

Having staid two days at MENZYLY, we set out again in heavy rains, through deep roads, which greatly incommoded our camels; for they often slipped, and sometimes fell down under their burdens; however, in five days we reached RESHD, the capital of the province of GUILAN.

RESHD stands in a plain, surrounded with great woods on every side, about a day's journey from the nearest shore of the CASPIAN sea, where is a very good harbour for ships of small burden

The houses are thinly scattered, resembling rather a large village than a town. As the ground at this place is very flat, the inhabitants are obliged to chuse the dryest places to build on. In the market place, I saw about eight pieces of cannon, mounted on sorry carriages; among which was a neat

neat brass field-piece, with the name of that noted prince the Duke of HOLSTEIN GOTTORP upon it: it seems to have been left here accidentally by the ambassadors of that Duke to the then Shach of PERSIA.

The houses are mean, in comparison with those in other parts of PERSIA; the roofs are raised and tiled, to carry off the great falls of rain.

The marshes and pools, with which RESHD is surrounded, renders it very unhealthy, especially in the heat of summer, when it is often visited with the pestilence; and, although it is a place of the greatest plenty, the inhabitants look as half starved. I was told they were obliged to confine themselves to a scanty diet; that, if they allowed themselves the least indulgence, even so far as to eat their rice with butter, they were liable to agues, the reigning distemper in this climate. Many of our people were actually seized with these agues, though none of them proved mortal. Here, as at the capitals of the other provinces, we were obliged to remain a considerable time, much longer than we inclined. For every province bears the expence of ambassadors,

dors, from the time they arrive at its capital, till they reach the capital of the next province, where fresh supplies of money and cattle are to be procured. The obtaining these things and the rainy weather detained us in this disagreeable place. The pools are full of frogs that chatter like magpies, and make such a loud croaking, besides their chattering, that a person cannot sleep till he is accustomed to that noise.

The country about RESHD is very fruitful; particularly in rice, which grows plentifully on the marshy grounds; and is sufficient to supply most of the other provinces of PERSIA: there is also plenty of fruit natural to the climate. The ARMENIANS, who inhabit RESHD, make good wine both red and white; and even in the woods you may see the vines, loaden with clusters of grapes, twisting about the trees, which are left to the birds, as they are not worth gathering, amid such plenty.

Great flocks of fieldfares, thrushes, black-birds, with vast quantities of storks, cranes, swans, wild-geese, and all other kinds of water-fowl, come hither,

ther from the north, during the winter, and return to the northern regions in the spring.

The staple of GUILAN is raw-silk, of which they make great quantities, both for their own consumption and for exportation.

While we remained at RESHD, two ambassadors arrived from the AIJUKA chan, prince of the KOLMUCK-TARTARS, in their way to ISPAHAN.

November 9th, we left RESHD and travelled through thick woods to the shore, along which we kept to the left, in all about five agatz, and then lodged in a small empty village.

The 13th, we proceeded six agatz to a small town called KESHKER. This day the road lay through pleasant woods. At some distance from the sea we met with some groves of orange trees, where we found blossoms, ripe and green fruit on the same tree. The great rains detained us some days at KESHKER: during which a new maymander arrived from ISPAHAN, who arrested the former one for some fault he had committed on the road.

The 20th, we travelled from KESHKER to the shore, three agatz, and halted a little; then along the

the shore four agatz farther, and at midnight reached an empty village: a disagreeable circumstance, after marching in constant rain the whole day, which had rendered the rivers almost impassable to camels.

From the 21st to the 27th, we advanced along the shore. The roads were very good. At last, we came to a town called ASTARA, where we halted for refreshment. There is nothing remarkable about this place, except its pleasant situation.

December 1st, we reached SIARAKENT, a large village. And next day LANGGARA, situated on the shore at the mouth of a river, an agatz distant from the former. And the 3d, to KYZILLAGATCH, five agatz from LANGGARA. This day we passed along several large bridges, over very deep rivers. In great rains, and strong northerly winds, these rivers swell above their banks, and, spreading to a great extent round the bridges, render them impassable.

The 5th, we travelled five agatz to TZAMACHAVA. I was surprized at the great flocks of water-fowl near this place: so numerous were they that one of our people killed eight geese at one discharge.

The 7th, we entered the plains of MUGAN. I described

scribed what seemed most remarkable in this desert, when going southward, and shall not recapitulate any thing I formerly observed. The road was very good. We lodged at the river BULGARA, six agatz from TZAMACHAVA; the water of the river is muddy and brackish. Next day we advanced seven agatz, and lodged again in tents; for there are no houses in this plain, and only pit water, very brackish.

On the 9th, we travelled seven agatz to some small huts, beyond the river KURE, which we passed on a bridge of boats. We passed this river about a day's journey above this place, in going to ISPAHAN, when I made my remarks upon it. Seven agatz from these huts, stands a place called KARAKURODY, the last stage in the desert, where we lodged on the 11th.

The 12th, we arrived at SHAMACHY, five agatz from the last stage. Since the time we left this place, it had suffered grievously by the plague, which raged here all the preceeding summer. It was now much abated, though not quite extinguished. This was a disagreeable circumstance, many of our people were sickly, and two of them died of of the diftemper: for the empty houfes, where the PERSIANS had died, notwithftanding every precaution, particularly fmoaking the walls, ftill proved infectious.

I was informed, that about feventy thoufand perfons had been carried off by the peftilence, within the laft eight months, in SHAMACHY and the province of SHIRVAN.

The 15th, my old acquaintance, Monfieur YEIISKY the DANTZICKER, whom I formerly mentioned, came to vifit me. He was fo altered by ficknefs that I fcarce knew him. He told me what difmal havock the plague had made, particularly in his own family. I asked, why he did not retire to the country for better air? His anfwer was, whither could he fly from GOD ALMIGHTY! This I find to be the general opinion of the MAHOMETANS, both PERSIANS and TURKS. The fame day I had a vifit from father BACKOND, the only miffionary at prefent in thefe parts, his companion, father RICARD, being dead of the plague.

The feafon being now far advanced, it became proper to pitch on fome place for winter quarters.

CHAP. VII.
1718.

The terrible pestilence which had prevailed so long, and with such destruction, greatly deterred us from chusing this place. The superior convenience, however, of it; the present abatement of the plague; and chiefly because a province is not obliged to support the expences of an ambassador till he arrives at the capital; and several other reasons, determined us to winter at SHAMACHY.

January 15th, 1718, the Chan came to town from the country, where he had been all the last summer.

The 21st, the ambassador paid the Chan a visit; which was returned the 25th.

Nothing material happened during the winter; only we often heard of the bad success of the Shach's forces, which were sent to CHANDAHAR, against the rebel MERY MAHMUT; and of many incursions into the PERSIAN provinces, made by the mountaineers who inhabit between the BLACK and CASPIAN seas.

March 10th, one of our gentlemen, Monsieur LO-PUCHIN, was sent away by land to ASTRACHAN, with an elephant and all the horses. He was escorted by thirty RUSSIAN soldiers, and some ASTRACHAN TAR-
TARS.

TARS. In his march, between DERBENT and TERKY, he was attacked by some hundreds of the mountaineers, called SHAFFKALLS, who killed one man and two horses, and wounded several men and the elephant. Meeting, however, with a warm reception they thought proper to retire, but carried off three of the horses. The gentleman arrived safe, without any further misfortune, at ASTRACHAN.

April 14th, ships, commanded by captain RENTLE, arrived at NIEZABATT, in order to transport the ambassador to ASTRACHAN. He could not, however, proceed immediately to embark; for we were obliged to wait for an answer to an express, which the Chan had dispatched to ISPAHAN on affairs of importance, which did not return till the end of May. All of us impatiently desired to leave SHAMACHY before the great heat came on. In the mean time, we diverted ourselves with hunting. I went often to see the silk-worms feeding on mulberry leaves. The inhabitants were apprehensive that the plague would break out again in the summer; and we had already buried twenty two of our people, since our arrival on the frontiers of PERSIA.

O 2

On the night of the eight of May there was such flashes of lightning, as had not happened in the memory of man; though the night was dark, I could plainly see the cattle in the adjacent fields, by means of the coruscations. The lightning was accompanied with dreadful claps of thunder, which lasted above two hours.

CHAPTER VIII.

From SHAMACHY *to* ST. PETERSBURG.

JUNE 16th, we left SHAMACHY, and in four days arrived safe at NIEZABATT, where we found ships waiting to receive us.

On the 21st we began to load the vessels with all possible dispatch, which was soon accomplished by the assistance of some RUSS soldiers, who had wintered at this place. Since I have mentioned these soldiers, I shall briefly relate how they happened to be on this coast.

The people of CHIVA, a territory (see p. 42.) eastward from the CASPIAN sea, having several times rob-

robbed and plundered some caravans of RUSSIAN merchants going to BUCHARIA, his Czarish Majesty determined to send a small body of regular troops and some cossacks, to demand satisfaction for such outrages committed in time of peace. For this purpose Mr. BECKVITZ, a captain of the guards, who was appointed to command this expedition, repaired to ASTRACHAN, in summer 1716, in order to make all the necessary preparations against next spring. Having accordingly embarked his men, provisions, and ammunition, at the proper season, he steered his course along the CASPIAN sea, and landed at a place called KRASNA-VOODA, *i. e.* red water, as near to CHIVA as he conveniently could. This place was barren, and uninhabited. Having therefore moored his transports, he erected a small fort to secure his retreat, in case of accidents.

In the mean time, he sent a friendly message to the Chan of CHIVA, to notify his arrival, and to desire he would furnish him with provisions and quarters for his men; for which he offered to pay ready money. The crafty TARTAR returned for answer, that he might come to CHIVA with the greatest safety,

where

where all his demands should be granted. At the same time, sent him a present of fruits and fresh provisions, and guides to conduct him on the road, accompanied with the highest expressions of respect to his Czarish Majesty. Mr. BECKVITZ, having left about three hundred men in the fort, to guard the camp and provisions, proceeded with the rest, and a few field-pieces, towards CHIVA.

In three or four days he arrived in the neighbourhood of the town, where he was met by several of the chiefs, who came with compliments from the Chan, and to settle matters relative to the cantonment of the soldiers. This particular was difficult to adjust.

Mr. BECKVITZ insisted, that all his men should be quartered in the town, and nothing but infatuation could have influenced him to alter so prudent a resolution. But the TARTARS started many objections against putting it in execution, and pretended that the Chan and themselves were willing to agree to it; but the people were averse, and jealous of having so many armed men lodged within their walls. And therefore they proposed, as a means of quieting the minds of the people, that he should separate his men, in order to be quartered more conveniently in the adjacent villages; that himself should have lodgings in the town, with a sufficient guard to attend him. This motion was strongly opposed by all the old officers, who looked on it as a stratagem laid for their destruction. And such in reality it proved in the end.

Mr. BECKVITZ, deluded by false promises, at last consented to canton his men. No sooner were they divided into small parties than they were inclosed, and attacked by great numbers of TARTARS; and most of them either killed or taken prisoners, who were afterwards sold for slaves. A few of them taking the alarm stood to their arms, and made a brave defence for some time, endeavouring chiefly to regain their camp and ships; but having a barren desert to pass, and the TARTAR horse harrassing them day and night, they were at last obliged to submit to fatal necessity. The imprudence of the general was the sole cause of all these misfortunes; for, being in no want of provisions or ammunition, had he only kept his men together, the whole combined power

CHAP. VIII. power of these TARTARS could not have prevented
1718. his regaining the camp and shipping.

The camp was next attacked by the TARTARS. But they were repulsed by the garrison, which, having now intelligence of what had passed at CHIVA, demolished the fort, reimbarked the men and stores, and set sail for ASTRACHAN. The season was now too far advanced to gain that port: this circumstance, together with hard gales of contrary winds, obliged them to put into NIEZABATT in order to pass the winter. Here they were hospitably received by the PERSIANS; and the presence of the ambassador at SHAMACHY, contributed greatly to the relief of these poor unfortunate people.

Unhappy BECKVITZ himself, happened to be taken prisoner. He was sent for to the Chan's tent, on some pretence of business, where they first struck off his head; then after venting their barbarous rage on his dead body, they flayed it, and, having stuffed the skin with straw, placed it, a miserable spectacle, on one of the city gates.

This unfortunate gentleman was the son of a petty prince, or chief of a tribe in TZERKESSIA, and had been

been sent to RUSSIA in his infancy, as a hostage for his father's fidelity.

Being now on the point of departing from PERSIA, called by the PERSIANS IRAN, and also PHARSISTAN, I shall close what I have to offer regarding that country, by giving a list of the principal officers of state who attend that mighty monarch at the megiliss, *i. e.* publick audience of ambassadors; they sit in the hall of audience according to their respective ranks, and have all of them, on those occasions, magnificent caps, and robes of state, kept in the king's wardrobe for that purpose.

1. The Etmadowlett, prime minister.
2. Spasselaar, general in chief.
3. Kurtsy Basha, general of 12,000 men.
4. Kular-agassy, director of the prisons.
5. Tfengy Basha, general of musketeers.
6. Ishek-agassy Basha, master of ceremonies.
7. Divan Begg, chief justice.
8. Toptshy Basha, master of the ordinance.
9. Vaggian Aviz, secretary of state.
10. Merish-kaz Basha, grand falconer.
11. Dgevedar Basha, general of the artillery.

12. The Milachurd Basha Giloff, master of horse.
13. Milachurd Yaffy Basha, master of the field-horses.
14. Kolopha.
15. Mamalek, comptroller of the houshold.
16. Kchaffa, cabinet secretary.
17. Nazyr Daftar, steward of the houshold.
18. Visir ISPAHAN, chief magistrate of ISPAHAN.
19. Visir Kurtsy, general of horse.
20. Visir Kule.
21. Chasnadar Basha, chief treasurer.
22. Kaliphar Kashkar, chief judge in civil affairs.
23. Doroga Taftar, judge of the city.
24. Sachapt Tauchtzy.
25. Sachapt Narvifs, chief astrologer.
26. Hakim Basha, chief physician.

The following officers attend the Shach wherever he goes.

1. The Ibrahim Aga, chief of the eunuchs.
2. Yeush Basha, chief of the white eunuchs.
3. Achmet Aga, chief of the black eunuchs.
4. Klitch Kurtshy, sword-bearer.
5. The

5. The Tzatyn Bafha, quiver-bearer.
6.   Saddach Kurtfhy, bow-bearer.
7.   Tfang Kurtfhy, musket-bearer.
8.   Dgid Kurtfhy, dart-bearer.
9.   Kalchan Kurtfhy, target-bearer.

The following are the chief doctors of the Law of MAHOMET.

1. Sadyr Chaffa, the fame office in PERSIA as that of the Mufty in TURKEY.
2. Sadyr Mammalck.
3. Fazyl.
4. Shach Iflam.
5. Chazy.
6. Mullah Bafha.
7. Mudarafs.
8. Pifhnamafh.
9. Mutafhett Bafha.
10. Moafham Bafha.

Thefe are the principal; befides whom, there are many other officers too numerous to recite. With the foregoing lift I clofe what I have to fay regarding PERSIA.

The 26th, we fet fail from NIEZABATT with a fair wind

wind at south-east, which lasted only a few hours; after which we were becalmed for three days.

July 2d, the wind became again fair, and carried us, with a gentle breeze, out of the deep water into foundings; but turning contrary, we came to anchor in thirty fathom water, where we lay till the 10th, when it blew a very hard gale, which drove us from our anchors out to sea; and, continuing for two days, brought us again in sight of the PERSIAN shore, which was at this time no very agreeable object.

The 13th, the wind chopped about favourable, and so continued, with little variation, till the 18th, when we arrived safe at ASTRACHAN, to the great joy of all our company.

September 7th, leaving ASTRACHAN, we sailed up the VOLGA. Our progress, contrary to the course of the river, was very slow and tedious. In calms the boats were drawn up by men, who went upon the banks; but in hard gales we were obliged to haul them near the side and ly still.

October 12th, after a voyage of five weeks, we arrived at the town of SARATOFF, about eight hundred verst distant from ASTRACHAN. The winter draw-

drawing on prevented our farther progress by water. We therefore unloaded, and discharged the boats, being resolved to remain here till the snow fell, when we might proceed by land in sledges.

November 1st, there had now been a little fall of snow, sufficient to smooth the roads, and this day we set out from SARATOFF in sledges.

The 3d, we came to a little town called PETROSKY, about ninety verst from SARATOFF.

The 8th, we came to a large town called PENZE, ninety verst from the former. As we advanced to the north the frost and snow dayly increased, which made the roads very smooth and easy. Before we left this place a sudden rain obliged us to halt a few days. Here we met with Brigadier KROPOTOFF, who, with some regiments of dragoons, had winter quarters at this place.

The 14th, the frost and snow returning, we set out from PENZE.

The 15th, we reached SARANSKY, eighty verst from the former. Here we found many SWEDISH officers taken at POLTAVA, who were well quartered in a plentiful country.

The

CHAP. VIII.
1718.

The 17th, we left SARANSKY, and the 21ſt, arrived at ARZAMASS, an hundred verſt from SARANSKY.

The 24th, we came to MURUM, three hundred and ſixty verſt from SARATOFF, which I mentioned in going ſouthward by water. From SARATOFF to PETROSKY the country is ſomewhat dry and barren; but the reſt of the country through which we paſſed is very fruitful, producing all kinds of corn, fine woods, particularly of oaks, interſperſed with many villages; and the face of the country, conſtantly varied by plain and gently riſing grounds, affords a moſt beautiful proſpect. From MURUM we came to the town of WOLODIMIR, an hundred and thirty verſt from MURUM: this place is large and well peopled, and famous for being formerly the reſidence of a great prince of the ſame name.

The 30th, we arrived ſafe at the city of MOSCO, an hundred and forty verſt from the former, and ſeven hundred and ſeventy from SARATOFF.

December 19th, we proceeded towards ST. PETERSBURG, where we arrived on the 30th. Nothing material happened during our return through RUSSIA, and what was moſt remarkable in the country

I

I described in going southward. I cannot help taking notice of an extraordinary case of one of our people in an exceſſive cold night. The fellow, expecting to baniſh all feeling of cold from himſelf, drunk a large quantity of ſpirits; which produced a drowſineſs that ended in ſleep in an open ſledge. On arriving at a village, the perſon was found ſtiff, ſpeechleſs, and apparently quite dead; but being carried to a brook hard by, and plunged ſeveral times in the water, and then rubbed with ſnow and brought into a warm room, with proper regimen he ſoon recovered, and was able to proceed next day.

CHAP. VIII.
1718.

I have often obſerved in other inſtances, that the uſe of ſpirituous liquors in cold weather, is the worſt of remedies: for, though they warm at firſt, they leave a chilneſs behind them, not to be got clear of for a conſiderable time. I have found by experience nothing preferable to weak warm liquors mixed with a little ſpirits. The RUSSIAN travellers carefully avoid the exceſſive uſe of brandy in ſtrong froſts.

Thus have I finiſhed my account of a long, tedious, and dangerous journey, which laſted for three years, attended with many difficulties not eaſily conceived

ceived by those who have not travelled the same road. At our return to ST. PETERSBURG, we found his majesty at that place, who, I was informed, was well satisfied with the conduct of his ambassador, whose principal errand was to cultivate and cement amity, and a good correspondence, between the two crowns of RUSSIA and PERSIA.

Notwithstanding the war with SWEDEN had continued near twenty years, this active monarch had not neglected, nor even suspended, the building and adorning his new capital. During my absence the appearance of things were so changed that I could scarce imagine myself in the same place: so surprising was the alteration in so short a time. Besides, this prince had fitted out a navy of thirty ships of war, and three hundred gallies: enterprises which might have been the work of ages, but not superior to the single industry and activity of PETER the first.

A

A JOURNEY FROM Sᵗ· PETERSBURG IN RUSSIA, TO PEKIN IN CHINA,

WITH AN EMBASSY FROM HIS IMPERIAL MAJESTY, PETER THE FISRT, TO KAMHI EMPEROR OF CHINA, IN THE YEAR MDCCXIX.

NAMES OF THE PRINCIPAL PERSONS WHO COMPOSED THE TRAIN OF THE AMBASSADOR.

LEOFF VASSILOVICH ISMAYLOFF.

LAURENCE DE LANGE,	Secretary of the Embassy.
IVAN GLAZUNOFF,	the Ambassador's Secretary.
KNEAZ ALEXANDER SASECKIN,	
NICOLAUS DE PAULI KRESTITZ,	
LUKIAN NESTEROFF,	Gentlemen of the Embassy.
ALEXIE DIVOFF,	
DAVID GRAVE,	
The AUTHOR of this JOURNAL,	
GREGORY,	a Priest.

Interpreters, clerks, a band of music, valets, footmen, &c. in all to the number of about sixty persons; besides a troop of twenty five dragoons, for our escort from TOBOLSKY to PEKIN, and back.

A JOURNEY FROM St PETERSBURG TO PEKIN.

CHAPTER I.

From ST. PETERSBURG *to* TOBOLSKY *the capital of* SIBERIA.

WHEN I arrived at ST. PETERSBURG from ISPAHAN, I met with a very sensible mortification, on finding that my very worthy friend, DR. ARESKINE, was no more; he died about six weeks before my arrival. Not long after which, upon being informed that an embassy was preparing for CHINA, and that his majesty had nominated LEOFF VASSILOVICH ISMAYLOFF, a gentleman of a family very well known and much respected in RUSSIA, and a captain of the guards, for that employment, I became very desirous of making that journey in his train.

Upon my acquainting my very good friend, ARTEMY PETROVICH VALENSKY, with my desire, he, without

out loss of time, recommended me to LEOFF VASSILO-VICH ISMAYLOFF, the appointed ambassador, in such a manner as produced, on all occasions, marks of friendship and regard for me, as well during the journey, as also after our return, untill he died in 1736.

The time, between my return from ISPAHAN and my setting out for PEKIN, I spent with much satisfaction with my friends and acquaintance at ST. PETERSBURG. Among whom I esteemed as such, not only several worthy persons of my own countrymen, as well in trade as in the service of his majesty; but also not a few of the RUSSIAN gentry, to whom I became known on occasion of my journey to PERSIA, and of whom I found many to be persons of much worth and honour.

At length the presents for the Emperor of CHINA being got ready, as well as the ambassador's dispatches, I set out from ST. PETERSBURG the 14th of July, 1719, in company with Messieurs LANGE and GRAVE, attended by a few servants; the first was a native of SWEDEN, and the other of COURLAND. We travelled to the city of MOSCO in small parties, the more easily to procure post horses. The weather being very hot obliged us to make short stages, confining us mostly to the mornings and evenings. Having in my PERSI-
AN

AN journal deſcribed what is moſt remarkable on this road, I have nothing to add to what I have there obſerved.

Nothing material happened during our journey to MOSCO, where we arrived on the 30th of July, and joined the ambaſſador, who had arrived there two days before, having paſſed us on the road. We took up our lodgings at the houſe of Mr. BELAYOF, near the triumphal arch. Here we ſpent five weeks in preparing barques to go by water to CAZAN, and neceſſaries for ſo long and unfrequented a road. This interval we paſſed very agreeably, being invited to all the entertainments the place afforded.

September 9th, having ſhipped our baggage, and prepared every thing for our departure, we went ourſelves on board; and, after firing nine guns, rowed down the river MOSCO. There is a ſhorter way from MOSCO to SIBERIA through YAROSLAVE; but, as we were incumbered with heavy baggage, conſiſting chiefly of preſents from his majeſty to the emperor of CHINA, it was thought beſt to proceed as far as poſſible by water.

Accordingly we continued our courſe down the MOSCO river to KOLUMNA, then into the river OCKA; and

and passing PERESLAVE-RESANSKY, MURUM, and other towns of less note, we arrived at NISHNA-NOVOGOROD, situated to the right hand, on a high bank of the OCKA, at its confluence with the VOLGA. Leaving NISHNA, we entered the river VOLGA and proceeded towards CAZAN.

After a voyage of six weeks we arrived at CAZAN on the 20th of October. We intended to have continued our route farther down the VOLGA to the river KAMA, which falls into the VOLGA about sixty verst below CAZAN, and then up the KAMA to SOLIKAMSKY; but the advancement of the season, and the frost coming on apace, made us resolve to remain at CAZAN till the winter set in; least we should run the hazard of being frozen up near some uninhabited place on the KAMA.

In consequence of this resolution the barques were discharged, and we took up our lodgings in the city. Here I found many of my old friends and acquaintance, particularly the SWEDISH officers; among others, general HAMILTON, general ROSEN, and baron WACHMAITER, who still remained prisoners of war, regretting the hard fate of their long captivity. We staid here about five weeks, waiting for the snow falling to smooth the

the roads, and in the mean time were employed in preparing fledges, and other neceffaries for our journey. Having formerly made my remarks on this route, and particularly on CAZAN and its neighbourhood, I fhall now purfue our journey towards SIBERIA.

November 24th, we fent off the heavy baggage: but Monfieur ISMAYLOFF, with a few of the gentlemen, remained fome days longer; becaufe it was difagreeable travelling on rough roads with loaded fledges. At laft on the 28th, late in the night, the ambaffador quitted CAZAN, keeping to the north-eaftward. There being many villages on the road we changed horfes as often as occafion required.

The 29th, we travelled through woods, confifting chiefly of tall oaks, fir, and birch. This part of the country is very fruitful, producing plenty of cattle, corn, and honey. The hives are not made like thofe in ENGLAND: the inhabitants take the trunk of a lime-tree, afpin, or any foft wood, of about five or fix feet long; having fcooped it hollow, they make a large aperture in one fide, about a foot in length and four inches broad; they then fix crofs rods within the trunk, for the bees to build upon, and, having done this, clofe up the place carefully with a board, leaving fmall notches for the bees to go in and out. These hives are planted in proper places, at the side of a wood, and tied to a tree with strong wythes, to prevent their being destroyed by the bears who are great devourers of honey. The wax and honey exported yearly from CAZAN make a very considerable article of trade. I have seen above an hundred hives near one village; and was informed, that they have a method of extracting the honey and wax without killing the bees, which would certainly be worth knowing; but I was told it so indistinctly, that I could not understand it, and had no opportunity of seeing it practised.

The villages, through which we passed, were mostly inhabited by the TZEREMISH and TZOOWASH TARTARS, whom I have formerly mentioned. The three following days the roads were rough and narrow, lying through dark woods, interspersed with some villages and cornfields. We passed the ICK and several smaller rivers, and then the VIATKA, a pretty large one, all which discharge themselves into the KAMA.

After a tedious journey of six days, we came to a small town called KLINOF, or more commonly VIATKA, from the river of that name running near it. The situation of this place is very pleasant, having round it it corn-fields, and fine pasture, and the rivers in the neighbourhood abounding with great variety of fish.

The country about KLINOF is reckoned so proper pasturage for sheep, that his majesty ordered some thousands of GERMAN sheep, most esteemed for their wool, to be bought and sent thither, with a view to establish a manufactory at this place for clothing his army. He also caused a GERMAN shepherd to be engaged in his service, who is settled here, and enjoys a considerable salary. The flocks are already so numerous, that I am persuaded they will in time answer the end proposed. A thousand other instances might be produced of the unbounded genius of this great and active Prince, who spares no expence, and overlooks nothing that can contribute either to the honour or advantage of his empire. I cannot omit another seemingly inconsiderable article, I mean pump leather: this commodity was formerly brought from ENGLAND and HOLLAND at no small charge; to save which, his majesty gave orders to engage an ENGLISH tanner for a certain number of years, whom he sent to CAZAN, where the best hides are, to teach the natives the art of dressing them. This scheme has fully answered the end in view, and produced abundance, not only of pump leather, but of every other kind of leather whereof that country hath any need.

There being no verst posts on this, though on most other roads in RUSSIA, I compute the distance between CAZAN and KLINOF to be about five hundred verst; each verst measures one thousand one hundred and sixty six yards and two feet ENGLISH. Here I met with several SWEDISH officers, who passed a solitary life in a pleasant and plentiful country. We halted one day to refresh ourselves, and the next, being the 5th of December, we left the baggage to follow leisurely, and set out again toward SOLIKAMSKY. On the 7th, we reached KAY-GOROD, a small town. We perceived the cold becoming daily more intense as we proceeded northward along the banks of the KAMA.

The 8th, we quitted KAY-GOROD in a vehement cold. Though there was little wind and a thick fog, the frost continued so penetrating that several of our people, who were most exposed, had their fingers and toes frozen. Most of them recovered by the common method of rubbing the numbed parts with snow: but had we not halted from time to time, at villages to let them warm themselves, they must have perished by cold. On the 9th, we arrived at the town of SOLIKAM-SKY,

sky, derived from SOLE salt and KAMA the river, on the banks of which it is situated. Our arrival was a most agreeable circumstance, as the piercing frost still prevailed.

SOLIKAMSKY is a large and populous town, and the capital of a province of that name; which is at present annexed to the government of SIBERIA. Its situation is very pleasant, upon the eastern bank of the KAMA. This river is of great fame in these parts of the world. It rises far to the north, and, in its course, receives the PARMA, PILVA, KOYVA, and many other rivers, which together form a mighty stream, very nearly equal to the VOLGA; into which it discharges itself, about sixty verst below the city of CAZAN, and loses its name. Its long course to the south-west is now turned short, by the current of the VOLGA, and carried toward the south-east. The KAMA is well stored with variety of excellent fish. On the banks are fine corn-fields and pasture-grounds; but often interrupted by thick woods, especially to the north. These woods are stocked with different kinds of game, and wild beasts, natural to the climate.

SOLIKAMSKY is famous for having many salt-pits in its neighbourhood, the property of my worthy friend

Baron

Baron STROGANOF, by virtue of a grant from his majesty. The Baron has brought thefe works to fuch perfection, that he is able to ferve all RUSSIA with falt; and could befides furnifh a confiderable quantity for exportation, were there any demand. The falt is of a brownifh colour, and very good of the kind.

The common method of procuring this falt is as follows: They dig pits in the earth till they come to the falt-rock, which feems to ly in thefe parts at a certain diftance from the furface, as coals do in other places of the world. When the pit is finifhed, it is naturally, and of courfe, filled with water; which ftanding for a convenient time, till it is fufficiently impregnated with the falt, is then drawn out with pumps and other engines, and put into large iron caldrons, where it is boiled to a proper confiftence; when, the water being evaporated, the falt is left upon the bottom.

I was informed of another curious and extraordinary procefs, by which they draw falt-water from a frefh-water river, which I cannot omit taking notice of. In the rivers near this place there is a mixture of falt-water arifing from the fprings, which either have their fource in the falt-rocks, or run through them: it is the bufinefs of the inhabitants to difcover

ver the places where these springs empty themselves into the rivers, which they do by diving, or some other manner; having done this, they make a large frame of strong thick balks or beams joined very close, about fifteen or twenty feet square, and of depth enough to reach the bottom of the river, while part of it remains above the surface; when the ice is very strong they sink this machine into the river, over the place where the salt spring issues, and drive strong piles of wood all around, to hinder its being forced from this position by the current, or by floating ice in the end of winter. During the winter they draw out all the water, mud and sand, contained within the machine, and sink it still deeper until it hath penetrated the bottom of the channel of the river, and prevented all further communication between it and the salt spring: the frame is now filled only with the salt-water, issuing from the spring, from whence it is drawn, and the salt extracted as formerly described.

However tedious and expensive this process may seem, these people perform it with great readiness and ease; and, what is still more extraordinary, without regular instruction in any art subservient to that purpose, but by the mere force of natural genius. The Baron

Baron has a great number of hands constantly employed in this service. And the woods for fewel are inexhaustible.

When the salt is made, it is laid up in granaries, till the season of transporting it to MOSCO, ST. PETERSBURG and other places: the barques, for this purpose, called by the RUSSIANS Lodia, are of a construction somewhat uncommon. I have seen some of them longer and broader than any first rate man of war in ENGLAND, and not one iron-nail in the whole fabrick. All of them are flat-bottomed, having one tall tree for a mast, and a sail of light canvass in proportion. To manage this mighty machine, six or eight hundred men are necessary; the rudder is nearly as long as the barque; and so unwieldy, that sometimes it requires forty or fifty men to steer it. They load these ships very deep, and let them float down the KAMA into the VOLGA; where, if the wind is not favourable, they are obliged to draw them, against the stream, to the place of their destination.

I cannot leave SOLIKAMSKY without mentioning the rich iron-mines in the country adjacent, at KATHENABURG, and other places of that district, which produce iron, equal perhaps in quality to the best in the world.

These

These works have of late been brought to great perfection, by the skill and indefatigable industry of Mr. DEMIDOF, a native of RUSSIA, enabled and encouraged to carry them on by a beneficial grant from his majesty; who is always ready to assist and protect those, who, by their ingenuity, form projects to the advantage of his country.

These works, I am informed, are still capable of great improvement. The ore is very good, and rises in many places to the very surface of the earth, and may be dug at a small expence. As for wood to smelt it, no place in the world can have greater advantage. Besides, all the machines may be driven by water; and there is an easy communication by the rivers, to ST. PETERSBURG for exportation, and to many other parts of RUSSIA, for inland consumption.

In these mines are often found magnets of various sizes. I have seen some of them very large, and of high virtue.

There are several other iron-works in RUSSIA; for instance, at TULA, OLONITZ, and other places; but the metal is of an inferior quality to that of SIBERIA. Besides these of iron, there are also rich mines of excellent copper at this place, which, being lately discovered ed, are capable of great improvement. The copper-ore also rises to the very surface.

In the neighbourhood of SOLIKAMSKY is found the fossil called asbestos; of which is made a kind of cloth like linen, that may be put into the fire and taken out again unconsumed. This cloth was known among the ancients, and used by them on several occasions. At present, it goes by the name of the incombustible linen.

The asbestos, like many both curious and useful discoveries, was found out by mere accident in these parts. I shall briefly relate in what manner: A certain huntsman being about to load his fowling-piece, and wanting wadding, observed a great stone in the woods, which seemed to have some flakes upon it like loose threeds; he soon found that by rubbing it turned into a soft downy substance fit for his use: he therefore filled his pocket with it; but having fired his piece, was surprised to see that the gun-powder had no effect upon the wadding: this raised his curiosity so far, that he kindled a fire on purpose, into which he put the asbestos; but still took it out intire, and of the same use as formerly: this experiment so frightened the poor sportsman, that he imagined the devil had

had taken poffeffion of the foffil. On returning home, he narrated what had happened to the prieft of the parifh; who, amazed at the relation, repeated it fo frequently, that, at laft, he told it to a perfon who was acquainted with that quality peculiar to the asbeftos; and, on examination, found the flakes to be that foffil.

The weather is much colder at SOLIKAMSKY than at other places fituated feveral degrees nearer to the north pole; perhaps its great diftance from any part of the ocean may be partly the caufe of the exceffive cold which fometimes prevails.

December 10th, the ambaffador took poft horfes, and fet out for TOBOLSKY, leaving the baggage to follow as fhould be moft convenient. About midnight we came to a village called MARTINSKY; here having changed horfes, we foon reached the mountains named VERCHATURSKY-GORY, where we found the fnow very deep, and a ftrong froft ftill continued. We kept on our journey, afcending and defcending thefe high and fteep mountains for the fpace of fifteen hours. In fuch of the valleys as are fit for culture, are found RUSSIAN villages well peopled. And, where the woods are cut down, there appeared a beautiful landfkip, even at this bleak feafon.

CHAP. I.
1719.

These mountains divide RUSSIA from SIBERIA. They run in a ridge from north to south, inclining a little to the east and west of these points. They are quite covered with wood, consisting of tall firs of different kinds, larinxes, birch, and other trees natural to the climate; and abound with game and various kinds of wild beasts. Their length, from north to south, I cannot ascertain; but compute their breadth, where we passed, to be about forty ENGLISH miles. But they are not near so high as the mountains I have seen in PERSIA, and other parts of the world.

Having passed these mountains, we descended, on the 11th, into a country finely varied with plains and rising grounds, interspersed with woods, villages, corn-fields, and pasturage; and, in the evening, reached the town called VERCHATURIA, from verch which signifies high, and TURA the name of the river on which the town stands. This river is navigable, and runs to the east till it discharges itself into the TOBOL. VERCHA-TURIA is pleasantly situated upon a rising ground, and fortified with a ditch and palisades. It is governed by a commandant, who has under him a garrison, consisting of some regular troops and cossacks. What makes VERCHATURIA considerable, is its being a frontier town,

and

and commanding the only entry from RUSSIA into SIBERIA. Here is a custom-house, where all merchants are obliged to make entry of what sums of money or merchandise they carry into SIBERIA, or from SIBERIA into RUSSIA; on all which is charged a duty of ten per cent to his majesty. Though this impost may appear high, it is really very moderate, considering the profits which the trade yields, and it extends only to the money to be employed in traffick; for every merchant is allowed a certain sum for his expences, free of all duty.

The country, adjacent to VERCHATURIA, is inhabited by a race of people called VOGULLITZ, who differ in language, dress, and manners, from any nation I ever saw. Their features and persons have a resemblance of the TZOOWASHIANS near CAZAN. They have some obscure notions of the Deity; and are very fond of a kind of wizards called SHAMANS, whom they hold in great esteem. I shall have occasion to speak more fully of these SHAMANS afterwards. The VOGULLITZ know nothing of agriculture; but live in huts in the woods, and subsist by hunting and fishing. They are an honest inoffensive people, but not very numerous; arising perhaps from their unsocial and uncomfortable manner of life. The archbishop of TOBOLSKY hath
of

CHAP I.
1719.
of late, by his pious labours, converted many of them to CHRISTIANITY; who now begin to build houses, and cultivate some appearance of society; and, probably, in time, the rest will follow so laudable an example: this however will depend much on the encouragement they meet with, from the clergy and subgovernors of provinces. I visited them as often as any opportunity offered, both in their huts and houses, and endeavoured to procure some information about their original, or from whence they came to settle in these northern parts; but could obtain nothing satisfactory on either of these heads.

Before we enter SIBERIA, it will not be perhaps improper to give a short account of the singular manner in which this most extensive country was discovered by the RUSSIANS.

About the beginning of the last century, a certain DON-COSSACK, named YARMAK TIMOTHEOVITZ, being obliged, by some accident, to leave his native country, and having no means of subsistence, he, with a few accomplices, betook themselves to robbing on the highways. He soon became famous and powerful; for he robbed only the rich; and, by a generosity uncommon in such a character, liberally bestowed to such as

were

were in want. He never killed, nor even hurt any person, unless compelled to such outrages in his own defence. This behaviour so raised his reputation, that all the idle fellows in the country enlisted themselves in his gang, proud to follow so brave and enterprising a leader. He became at last so troublesome that the governors of the southern provinces sent out troops to apprehend him; but, being previously informed of the design, he withdrew from the land, and procuring boats upon the VOLGA, commenced pirate on that river. Being attacked here also, he was forced to cross the CASPIAN sea, and shelter himself on the PERSIAN shore, where he passed some time under the disguise of a merchant. Being again discovered, he was obliged by the PERSIANS to quit their coast: and now his only refuge was to return to the VOLGA, where he behaved with great circumspection, often lurking in woods and villages; and, being in no want of money, paid the inhabitants liberally for every thing he needed. Foreseeing however that such a numerous gang could not be long concealed, he took the resolution of leaving the VOLGA, and steered his course up the river KAMA, at that time little frequented by the RUSSIANS, or any other nation; here he hoped to find, at least, leaft, a fafe retreat during the winter. YARMAK, therefore, with his followers, amounting to the number of two hundred, continued their voyage up the KAMA, till they were ftopped by the ice, at no great diftance from a large village, now belonging to Baron STROGANOF. The inhabitants were alarmed at the fight of fo many armed men, whom they were not able to oppofe, and therefore gave them an hofpitable reception. YARMAK demanded only provifions, and winter quarters, for his money, promifing to leave them unmolefted next fpring. In confequence of this declaration, he and his followers paffed the winter very quietly in this remote place; afraid, however, at the approach of fummer, of being difcovered by the government, and uncertain what courfe to fteer; it was at laft determined to crofs the mountains of VERCHATURIA, and go to the eaftward, in hopes of finding fome inhabited country; or, at leaft, a fafe retreat.

Having paffed the mountains, they arrived at the river TUR; and, finding it navigable, foon made a fufficient number of canoes for the whole gang. After rowing for fome days down the TUR, they difcovered feveral villages of MAHOMETAN TARTARS, who were furprifed at the fight of fuch a number of ftrangers; of whom

whom they had before never so much as heard. YAR-MAK having got what intelligence he could procure of the situation and government of the country, pursued his voyage to the river TOBOL; where he found the towns populous, and the land well cultivated. His approach alarmed the king of the TARTARS, who assembled a numerous body of horse and foot, armed with bows and arrows, lances, and other such weapons, with whom our adventurer had many skirmishes, and defeated great multitudes by means of his fire-arms; which had never before been known in these parts. The poor TARTARS were as much amazed, and terrified, at the sight of the RUSSIANS and their arms, as the inhabitants of MEXICO on the arrival of the SPANIARDS in AMERICA; to which SIBERIA may, in many respects, be compared.

YARMAK, finding his enemies daily more numerous, the nearer he approached the residence of the TARTAR king; having also lost many of his men, in continual encounters, and spent the greatest part of his ammunition; knowing, besides, of no place of safety, where he might pass the winter, which is both long and severe in this quarter; at last determined to retreat. He therefore steered his course to the west, up the TOBOL and TUR rivers. The furious TARTARS gave him no rest, but haraſſed him perpetually from the banks. He himſelf and few more eſcaped, with a conſiderable booty, and returned to the village where they wintered the preceeding year. The inhabitants, on ſeeing the rich furs and other ſpoils, gave them a welcome reception. And YARMAK did not forget to diſpenſe his favours liberally, among thoſe who had entertained him in his diſtreſs, when he fled from juſtice.

Our adventurer had now time to reflect on his miſerable circumſtances. He conſidered, that his lurking in theſe parts, though remote from any town, could not be long a ſecret; to make another attempt againſt the TARTARS with a handful of men, ill provided with arms and ammunition, might perhaps be ruinous, and certainly unſucceſsful. He therefore reſolved to ſubmit himſelf to his majeſty's clemency, in hopes of obtaining a gracious pardon for himſelf and his accomplices, on condition of pointing out the way to a rich and eaſy conqueſt of a country which he had lately diſcovered. The propoſal was made at court by a friend, and was of too great importance to be neglected. In ſhort, YARMAK was brought to MOSCO, under a ſafe conduct, where he communicated the whole

whole affair. He begged his majesty's pardon, and asked a certain number of troops, which he promised to lead to a glorious conquest. His majesty granted him a pardon, approved of the expedition, and gave immediate orders for the troops to attend him. They marched to SOLIKAMSKY, where they passed the winter in making preparations for the enterprize, which was to be undertaken in the spring.

During this interval, YARMAK behaved with surprising prudence and activity, and discovered himself to be a person of uncommon genius. He collected such of his former followers as remained, and formed them into a company, in whom he could confide on all occasions.

At the proper season, the troops set out towards SIBERIA. On coming into the inhabited part of the country, they found many straggling parties of TARTARS in arms, ready to oppose them, and a number of boats upon the rivers, full of armed men: the king of the TARTARS himself was on board one of these vessels. This expedition was of short duration; and, in the issue, fully answered the expectations of the RUSSIANS. I cannot omit a few particulars of the last action. The TARTARS in the boats, being pursued by the RUSSIANS, a battle enfued on the river IRTISH. YARMAK, obferving the king's barge, ordered his crew to board her; which he endeavouring to do at the head of his men, jumped fhort, fell into the river, and was drowned; to the great grief of all his followers. Thus fell poor YARMAK! Notwithftanding this misfortune, the RUSSIANS gained a complete victory. The brave king of the TARTARS loft his life in the action. His fon and the reft of the royal family were taken prifoners, and fent to MOSCO; where they were honourably received by the Czar, and treated according to their quality. The prince had an extenfive property granted him in RUSSIA; which the family enjoys to this day, together with the title of Sibirsky Czarevitz, or Prince of SIBERIA; which, I believe, is a more generous treatment of the conquered than any of the mighty monarchs of PERU or MEXICO, or any of their lineage, have experienced.

December 11th, we left VERCHATURIA, in deep fnow. The cold was exceffive, and the sky clear.

Next day, we came to a large village, having a few of the VOGULLITZ TARTARS in the neighbourhood; and, the 13th, arrived at the town of EPANTSHIN. From VERCHATURIA to this place the country is moftly ly covered with woods. About the villages there are large plains, for corn or pasturage. The cattle are in good condition. The horses, particularly, being of the TARTAR breed, are larger, and better shaped than ordinary, and fit for any use.

EPANTSHIN is but a small place, fortified with a ditch and palisades, and defended by a few soldiers in garrison. This place is sometimes alarmed with incursions of the TARTARS, called KOSSATSHY-ORDA, and KARA-KALPACKS; but the RUSSIANS have of late so fortified their frontiers, that these rovers appear seldomer than formerly. Both these tribes are MAHOMETANS, live always in tents, and spread themselves, with their flocks, in the great desert; both are very numerous, and own subjection to different chiefs, whom they call Batteer, which signifies a hero. These are chosen by themselves, and are the most famous among them for their abilities in military exploits. They are at continual war with the KALMUCKS, who inhabit along the VOLGA, and with all their other neighbours. They are not able to stand against regular troops; and, when attacked by them, retire into the wide desert, with their families and cattle; whither none, but people accustomed to their manner of life, can follow them.

The

CHAP. I.
1719.

The country of the KARA-KALPACKS, or BLACK-CAPS, so called from a kind of caps they commonly wear turned up with black lamb-skins, lies to the south-west, towards the VOLGA. That of the KOSSATSHY-ORDA extends to the south-east, as far as the river IRTISH. The course of this river I shall have occasion to mention afterwards.

The 14th, we came to a pretty large town, called TUMEN, situated upon the north bank of the river TUMA, from whence the place takes its name. The banks of the TUMA are high and steep. There is a very convenient wooden-bridge at this place. The TUMA has its source far to the west; and, in its course, is augmented by the TURA, and several other rivers. It continues to run to the east, till, meeting with the TOBOL, it loses itself and name.

The country between EPANTSHIN and TUMEN begins to be more open, and better peopled, than that westward of these places. For, besides the RUSSIANS, who make the greatest part of the inhabitants, we met with several villages inhabited by the descendents of the ancient MAHOMETANS, who were natives of these places. These TARTARS subsist by agriculture; and pass their lives without care or disturbance, in the free

free exercife of their religion and other privileges.
Tumen is a pretty neat place, and well fortified. The ftreets are fpacious, and the houfes built in a ftraight line. The adjacent country is covered with fine woods, interfperfed with villages, corn-fields, and pafturage; and provifions of all kinds are very plentiful. The merchants of this place have a confiderable trade in furs, particularly the skins of foxes and fquirrels; which, indeed, are not fo valuable here as they are to the eaftward.

Early on the 15th, we left this place, keeping on our courfe along the banks of the TUMA, till we arrived at the river TOBOL, which we croffed, and proceeded along the eaftern bank, through a fine country, and well peopled. Though the froft ftill continued ftrong, it was not near fo violent and piercing as about SOLIKAMSKY; which may proceed from the woods being cut down and the country cultivated. On the other fide of the river, indeed, the face of the country appeared flat and morafly, abounding with tall and dark woods.

The 16th, about noon, we were in fight of the city of TOBOLSKY, though diftant from us about twenty ENGLISH miles. It ftands upon a very high bank of
the

the TOBOL. The walls are white; and the crosses and cupolas of the churches guilded, and make a very fine appearance. About two o'clock, we arrived safe at the city of TOBOLSKY, the capital of this mighty province, and the residence of the governor. We lodged in the broad-street, leading to the governor's palace and the courts of justice.

We travelled between TUMEN and TOBOLSKY, about two hundred and fifty verst, in the space of thirty hours. Sledges are the most simple and convenient machines for travelling on snow that can be imagined. And the person in the sledge may either sit, or ly along upon the couch, according to his inclination.

CHAPTER II.

Occurrences at TOBOLSKY; *Observations on the* KALMUCKS, &c. *and journey continued to* TOMSKY.

TOBOLSKY is situated in latitude fifty eight degrees forty minutes north, at the conflux of the IRTISH and TOBOL. From this last the city has its name. Both these rivers are navigable for several hundred miles above this place. The IRTISH, after receiving the TOBOL, becomes a noble stream, and discharges es itself into the OBY. This situation was chosen by the RUSSIANS, both for its strength and beauty. Formerly the TARTAR princes had their abode at a place about thirty verst south from TOBOLSKY, which is now neglected and ruinous.

TOBOLSKY is fortified with a strong brick-wall, having square towers and bastions at proper distances; and is well furnished with military stores. Within the town stand the governor's palace, courts of justice, several churches built of brick, particularly a large cathedral, and the palace of the archbishop. From the walls you have a very extensive prospect of a fine country, especially to the south. To the west the land is also flat, and overgrown with tall woods. The inhabitants are chiefly RUSSIANS, of different professions; many of them are merchants, and very rich, by the profitable trade they carry on to the borders of CHINA, and many places of their own country.

These live mostly upon the hill. Under the hill in the suburbs, along the banks of the river, are several large streets, called the TARTAR-streets, occupied by the remains of the ancient inhabitants of these parts. Here, as at other places, these people enjoy the free exercise of their religion, and the priviledges of trade.

They resemble, in their persons, religion, language, and manners, the TARTARS of CAZAN and ASTRACHAN. Their houses are very cleanly. They are very courteous to strangers, and esteemed honest; on which account they get great credit in their commercial affairs. Besides the fortification, formerly mentioned, about the town, the whole suburbs are surrounded with a ditch and palisades.

When we were at TOBOLSKY, SIBERIA was superintended by Mr. PETROF SOLOVOY, vice governor, a person well acquainted with the business of the government, and a captain of the guards. The former governor, KNEAZ GAGARIN, had incurred his majesty's displeasure and was recalled; and his successor, KNEAZ ALEXIE MICHAYLOVITZ CHERKASKY, a nobleman worthy of such an important trust, was not yet arrived.

As in most other towns, through which we passed, we found here many SWEDISH officers of distinction; among others, Monsieur DITTMAR, formerly secretary to CHARLES XII. king of SWEDEN. He was a native of LIVONIA, and equally esteemed for his probity and capacity. He was much respected by the late governor; who, indeed, was a friend to all these unfortunate gentlemen. They were allowed to walk about at large, a hunting or fishing, and even permitted to travel to other places to visit their countrymen. For my part, I think the greatest favour his majesty shewed these prisoners, was the cantoning them in these parts; where they may live well at small expence, and enjoy all the liberty that persons in their circumstances can expect.

I cannot but observe, that the SWEDISH prisoners, dispersed in most of the towns in this country, contributed not a little to the civilizing the inhabitants of these distant regions; as they were the means of introducing several useful arts, which were almost unknown before their arrival.

Many of the officers, being gentlemen of liberal education, the better to support their tedious captivity, devoted their time to the study of the more agreeable and entertaining parts of science, particularly musick and painting; wherein some of them attained to great perfection. I was present at several of their concerts, and was not a little surprised to find such harmony, and variety of musical instruments, in this part of the world.

They sometimes amused themselves with teaching young gentlemen and ladies the FRENCH and GERMAN languages, musick, dancing, and other similar accomplifhments; whereby they gained many friends among the people of diftinction; a circumftance, to men in their fituation, both honourable and ufeful.

In TOBOLSKY there are always about five or fix thoufand regular troops, horfe and foot, befides a number of irregulars. Thefe troops, added to the natural ftrength of the place, effectually fecure it from any attacks of the neighbouring TARTARS.

The woods and fields about TOBOLSKY are ftored with all kinds of game natural to the climate; fuch as the coq-limoge, coq-bruiere, and gilinots; the laft are about the fize of a partridge, their flefh is white and very agreeable. There is another kind of thefe gilinots, fomewhat larger, with rough feet; which, in the winter, turn white as a dove. Alfo the common partridge, which, on the approach of winter, flies off to more temperate climates; wood-cocks, a great variety of fnipes, which fly off in autumn, after having hatched their young. As for water-fowl, no country in the world can produce fuch numbers, and variety; they are alfo birds of paffage. In my PERSIAN journal I gave an account of the vaft flocks of thefe fowls on the fhores of the CASPIAN fea.

Here alfo you meet with feveral kinds of fmall birds, about

about the size of a lark, particularly those called snow-birds. They come to SIBERIA in vast flocks in autumn, and remain till the spring, when they disappear. Many of them are white as snow, some speckled, and others all over brown. They are reckoned a very fine and delicious dish.

I observed another very pretty bird, about the size of a thrush, having beautiful red and yellow feathers in the wings and tail, with a tuft of brown feathers on its head, which it raises at pleasure. These are also birds of passage; and, as they breed no where in EUROPE or ASIA that I know of, perhaps both these and the snow-birds may come to SIBERIA from the northern parts of AMERICA. This conjecture will appear not improbable, when it is considered, that these birds are of a hardy nature, and the flight not so far as is generally imagined.

In the woods are various kinds of wild beasts; such as bears, wolves, lynxes, several sorts of foxes, squirrels, ermins, sables, martins and rosio-macks, called feel-frefs by the GERMANS. The furs are better of their kinds than those of any other country. The ermins commonly burrow in the open fields, and are caught in traps baited with a bit of flesh; this is done only

only in the winter, when they are altogether white, and the fur moft valuable. In fummer moft of thefe animals turn brown; when they are not killed, becaufe, at this feafon, the fur is of little ufe. There are alfo ottars in the rivers and lakes, whofe skins yield a confiderable profit. Indeed, furs of all forts, in this country, are very profitable. At prefent, few fables are caught in this neighbourhood; it is faid they fly from fmoke, which, perhaps, is partly true; yet I am apt to believe, that thefe poor animals are chafed away towards the north, to the wild woods, on account of the high value of their skins.

The woods of SIBERIA abound alfo with venifon of feveral forts; as elk, rain-deer, roe-buck, together with an incredible number of hares, which change their colour, from brown in the fummer to white in winter. The hares are generally caught by the country people in toils, more on account of their skins than their flefh, of which they make but little ufe. The skins are bought by the merchants, and fent, in great quantities, to ST. PETERSBURG, and other ports, in order to be exported to ENGLAND, HOLLAND, and other countries; where they are chiefly manufactured into hats.

Having defcribed the land-animals, I fhall now give fome

some account of the fish. In my opinion, there are few countries in the world so well watered, with fine navigable rivers and lakes, as SIBERIA; and few rivers and lakes produce greater quantities, or more variety, of excellent fresh-water fish, than those in this country. For, besides sturgeon, white fish, sterlet, and others, to be found in the VOLGA, and the rivers in RUSSIA, there are several kinds peculiar to this part of the world; particularly the muchsoon, about the size of a large carp, and much esteemed by persons of delicate taste.

Southward from TOBOLSKY the soil is fruitful, producing abundance of wheat, rye, barley, oats, and other grain. The cattle also are very numerous, and in winter are fed with hay. In a word, provisions of all kinds are extremely reasonable. From what I have said, it will appear, that TOBOLSKY is by no means such a disagreeable place as is generally imagined. Whatever the opinions of mankind may be, it is the business of a traveller to describe places and things without prejudice or partiality; and exhibit them fairly, as they really appear. This principle it shall be my study to keep always in view.

Captain TABAR, a SWEDISH officer, was at this time writ-

writing a history of SIBERIA. He was a gentleman very capable for such a performance; and, if it shall ever be published, it cannot fail of giving great satisfaction to the curious.

Before I leave TOBOLSKY, it will not be improper to give a short account of the famous river IRTISH, that passes this place. It continues its course a little to the eastward of the north, in a strong but smooth current, visiting several small towns and villages, and receiving many lesser streams, and a large river called KONDA, running eastward, till it discharges itself into the OBY, at a town called SAMARIOFSKY-YAMM, about six hundred verst below TOBOLSKY.

The IRTISH takes its rise from a great lake, named KORZAN, in a mountainous country, about fifteen hundred verst to the southward of TOBOLSKY. The country about this lake is inhabited by the BLACK KALMUCKS, a mighty and numerous people, governed by a prince called Kontaysha. From these the KALMUCKS on the VOLGA are descended. After the IRTISH hath run for many miles, through a hilly country covered with wood, it passes through a fine fruitful plain, inhabited by the KALMUCKS, till it comes to a house called SEDMY-PALATY, or the SEVEN ROOMS, situated

to

to the right in coming down the river. It is very surprising to find such a regular edifice in the middle of a desert. Some of the TARTARS say it was built by TAMERLANE, called by the TARTARS TEMYR-ACK-SACK or LAME-TEMYR; others by GINGEEZ-CHAN. The building, according to the best information I could obtain, is of brick or stone, well finished, and continues still entire. It consists of seven apartments under one roof, from whence it has the name of the SEVEN PALACES. Several of these rooms are filled with scrolls of glazed paper, fairly wrote, and many of them in gilt characters. Some of the scrolls are black, but the greatest part white. The language in which they are written is that of the TONGUSTS, or KALMUCKS. While I was at TOBOLSKY, I met with a soldier in the street with a bundle of these papers in his hand. He asked me to buy them; which I did for a small sum. I kept them till my arrival in ENGLAND, when I distributed them among my friends; particularly to that learned antiquarian Sir HANS SLOANE, who valued them at a high rate, and gave them a place in his celebrated museum.

Two of these scrolls were sent, by order of the Emperor PETER the First, to the Royal Academy at PARIS. The Academy returned a translation, which I saw in the rarity-chamber at ST. PETERSBURG. One of them contained a commission to a lama or priest; and the other a form of prayer to the Deity. Whether this interpretation may be depended on I shall not determine. The TARTARS esteem them all sacred writings, as appears from the care they take to preserve them. Perhaps they may contain some curious pieces of antiquity, particularly of ancient history. Above the SEDMY PALATY, towards the source of the IRTISH, upon the hills and valleys, grows the best rhubarb in the world, without the least culture.

Several days journey from the PALACES, down the IRTISH, on the western bank, stands an old tower named KALBAZINSHA-BASHNA, or the the tower of KALBAZIN. Below this is the lake YAMISHOFF, to the right, where the RUSSIANS have built a small fort, for the conveniency of making and gathering salt from that lake, great quantities whereof are made by the sun; it is brought in barques down the river to TOBOLSKY, and other places. This fort created some jealousy to the Kontaysha; he sent an ambassador to the governor of SIBERIA, requesting to have it demolished; but this demand not being granted, the difference came to an open rupture, the event of which time must discover.

Descend-

Descending farther, you meet with another settlement of the RUSSIANS, called SHELEZINSKY, from a rivulet of that name in its neighbourhood. A little below SHELEZINSKY stands OMUSKA, a considerable town, which also derives its name from a river. Both these places are situated on the eastern bank of the IRTISH. You now pass some inconsiderable places before you arrive at TARA, a little town situated on the western bank, on the road leading from TOBOLSKY to TOMSKY, through a country called BARABA, of which I shall give some account as we proceed to the east.

Between TARA and TOBOLSKY are a few small towns, and many villages, inhabited by MAHOMETAN TARTARS. And the country abounds with corn, cattle, and fine pasturage.

I have now pointed out the course of the IRTISH till it reaches TOBOLSKY, and from thence till it empties itself into the river OBY. I have nothing further to remark concerning TOBOLSKY and the country around it, and should therefore now pursue our journey to the eastward; but, before I leave this place, I imagine it will not be improper to subjoin a few more particulars relative to the Kontaysha, prince of the KALMUCKS, whom I formerly mentioned. I am the more inclined

CHAP. II.
1719.

to do this, as I can entirely depend on my intelligence; having procured it from persons who have been in that country, and seen this prince; but particularly from an ingenious and penetrating gentleman, who fills a public office in this place, and was employed in several messages to him from the late governor of SIBERIA.

The territories of this prince are bounded by three of the most potent empires in the world; on the north by RUSSIA, by CHINA on the east, and by the country of the Great Mogul to the south. From the two first he is separated by desert plains, and from the third by almost impassable mountains. To the south-west his frontiers reach near to BUCHARIA. The Kontaysha is a very powerful prince, and able to bring into the field, at a short warning, an hundred thousand horsemen, who are all of them able-bodied men, well mounted, and armed with bows and arrows, lances and sabres. This is a greater number of horse than any prince that I know can muster, except his RUSSIAN Majesty, and the Emperor of CHINA. These TARTARS live in tents, all the year, removing from place to place, as called by necessity or inclination. This is the most ancient and pleasant manner of life. It is entertaining to hear them commiserate those who are confined to one place of abode,

abode, and obliged to support themselves by labour, which they reckon the greatest slavery.

The Kontaysha has always some thousands of his subjects encamped near himself, who treat him with great veneration and respect. And, in justice to him, it must be confessed, that he is as attentive to the interests of his people; and as assiduous in the administration of justice, in particular, as if they were his own children.

The KALMUCKS are not such savage people as they are generally represented; for I am informed a person may travel among them with greater safety, both to his person and effects, than in many other countries.

The Kontaysha received the deputies from the governor of SIBERIA, like ambassadors from foreign princes, and treated them accordingly. This shows what high respect these eastern princes entertain for his Czarish Majesty, when the governor of SIBERIA is regarded as a sovereign. The ceremony on these occasions was as follows.

The deputy with his servants were admitted into the tent, where the Kontaysha sat, with his queen and several children about him. He desired all of them to sit down on carpets or mats; for the KALMUCKS, like most

most ASIATICS, use no chairs. They were entertained with tea before dinner; and, after it, the Kontaysha dismissed the deputy in a friendly manner, telling him, he would send for him next day to receive an answer to the governor's letter, which he punctually performed. This answer was expressed in very plain and concise terms. These TARTARS in general write with brevity and perspicuity. I have seen several of their letters translated, which pleased me extremely, as they contained no tedious preambles, nor disgusting repetitions, which serve only to perplex the reader.

The Emperor of CHINA was some time ago engaged in a war with the Kontaysha, about some frontier towns, of which the latter took possession, and maintained his claim with a strong army. The Emperor sent against him an army of three hundred thousand men, under the command of his fourteenth son, who is reckoned the best general of all his children. Notwithstanding their superiority in numbers, the Kontaysha defeated the CHINESE in several actions. The Emperor at last thought it best to accommodate the difference, and a peace was concluded to the satisfaction of both parties.

It must be observed, that the CHINESE, being obliged

to

to undertake a long and difficult march, through a desert and barren country, lying westward of the long wall; being also incumbered with artillery, and heavy carriages containing provisions for the whole army during their march; had their force greatly diminished before they reached the enemy. The Kontaysha, on the other hand, having intelligence of the great army coming against him, waited patiently on his own frontiers, till the enemy was within a few days march of his camp, when he sent out detachments of light horse to set fire to the grass, and lay waste the country. He also distracted them, day and night, with repeated alarms, which, together with want of provisions, obliged them to retire with considerable loss.

This method of carrying on war, by wasting the country, is very ancient among the TARTARS, and practised by all of them from the DANUBE eastward. This circumstance renders them a dreadful enemy to regular troops, who must thereby be deprived of all subsistence, while the TARTARS, having always many spare horses to kill and eat, are at no loss for provisions.

I have only to add, that the Kontaysha must be the same prince, who, in our EUROPEAN maps, is generally called the Great Cham of TARTARY. As no EURO-
PEANS

PEANS travel through that country, these maps must be very erroneous. It is however to be expected, that the RUSSIANS will, in time, make a more complete discovery of the eastern parts of ASIA.

Our baggage did not arrive at TOBOLSKY till the 23d of December. The people refreshed themselves till the 27th, when they again set out, taking the road along the IRTISH to TARA. The ambassador and his retinue remained to pass the rest of the holidays.

January 9th, 1720, we proceeded towards TARA. We passed though many TARTAR villages, and at night lodged in one of their little huts, and warmed ourselves at a good fire on the hearth. These houses consist generally of one or two rooms, according to the ability of the landlord. Near to the hearth is fixed an iron-kettle to dress the victuals. In one end of the apartment is placed a bench, about eighteen inches high, and six feet broad, covered with mats, or skins of wild beasts, upon which all the family sit by day, and sleep in the night. The walls are built of wood and moss, consisting of large beams, laid one above another, with a layer of moss between every two beams. All the roofs are raised. A square-hole is cut out for a window, and to supply the want of glass, a piece of ice

ice is formed to fit the place exactly, which lets in a good light. Two or three pieces will last the whole winter. These TARTARS are very neat and cleanly, both in their persons and houses. They use no stoves, as the RUSSIANS do. Near the house there is commonly a shade for the cattle.

We continued our journey along the banks of the IRTISH, having the river to the right or left, as the road lay from one TARTAR village to another.

The 15th, we reached TARA, a small town, reckoned about five hundred verst from TOBOLSKY; in all this road we did not meet with a RUSSIAN village, except a small one near TARA. The country abounds with woods, corn-fields, and fine pasturage, which appeared sufficiently from the quantities of hay, and the good condition of the cattle, though the face of the country was covered with deep snow. We found the air at TARA much milder than at any place since we left KAZAN.

TARA is situated on the IRTISH, and fortified with a deep ditch, strong palisades, and wooden towers, sufficient to defend it against the sudden attacks of the TARTARS, called KOSSATSHY-ORDA, who inhabit west-ward

ward of the IRTISH, and are very troublesome neighbours.

Here we laid in provisions for our journey over the BARABA; which signifies, in the TARTAR language, a marshy plain. Its inhabitants are a mixture of different TARTAR tribes, called BARABINTZY, from the name of the country in which they live. They are a poor miserable people, being treated as subjects both by the Emperor and the Kontaysha; and obliged to pay a tribute, in furs and skins of wild beasts, to each. They have no grain nor cattle of any kind, except a few raindeer; and subsist by hunting and fishing. What fish they consume not in the summer, are dried and smoked for their winter provisions. They are partly of the MAHOMETAN and partly of the KALMUCK religion; but this difference causes no disputes.

It is generally reckoned, that more robberies are committed in BARABA, than in any country on the road to CHINA; not by the natives, for they are very honest and hospitable; but by the KALMUCKS, who come to collect tribute for the Kontaysha; who sometimes pick up travellers, and carry them off with all their effects. It was said, that a strong party of them, having intelligence that the ambassador was to pass that way, waited ed to intercept him; on which account he took thirty dragoons and some cossacks, from the garrison of TO-BOLSKY, to escort him to TOMSKY; which was a sufficient guard against any robbers who might attack us: and he knew the Kontaysha was too polite a prince to authorise his subjects to molest any foreign minister who had done him no injury, notwithstanding the differences that subsisted between him and his Czarish Majesty.

Our baggage having waited at TARA till our arrival, we left that place on the 18th; and, next day, came to a large RUSSIAN village, sixty verst from TARA, and the last inhabited by RUSSIANS, till you pass the BARABA and come to the river OBY.

In the places through which we passed, the ambassador sent for all the hunters and sportsmen, that he might inquire what kinds of game and wild beasts were in their neighbourhood. Hunting is the employment of most of the young fellows in this country; and is very profitable, as they sell the furs to great advantage. We found that this place produced great plenty both of game and wild beasts, but few sables. In the spring, a number of elks and stags come hither, from the south; many of which are killed by the in-

CHAP. II.
1720.

habitants, both on account of their flesh and their hides. What of the flesh is not consumed fresh they salt. The hides are very large, and are dressed into excellent buff. The huntsman, having found the track of a stag upon the snow, pursues it upon his snow-shoes, with his bow and arrows, and little dog; till the animal is quite fatigued: for, the snow on the surface, being melted by the heat of the sun, and congealed, at night, by the frost, but not strong enough to bear the weight of such an animal; he sinks deep at every step, and the sharp ice cuts his ancles, and lames him; so that he becomes an easy prey to the hunter.

One of these hunters told me the following story, which was confirmed by several of his neighbours. That, in the year 1713, in the month of March, being out a hunting, he discovered the tract of a stag, which he pursued; at overtaking the animal, he was somewhat startled, on observing it had only one horn, stuck in the middle of its forehead. Being near this village he drove it home, and showed it, to the great admiration of the spectators. He afterwards killed it, and eat the flesh; and sold the horn to a comb-maker, in the town of TARA, for ten alteens, about fifteen pence

pence Sterling. I inquired carefully about the shape and size of this unicorn, as I shall call it, and was told it exactly resembled a stag. The horn was of a brownish colour, about one archeen, or twenty eight inches long; and twisted, from the root, till within a finger's length of the top, where it was divided, like a fork, into two points very sharp.

The 19th, we entered the BARABA, and continued travelling through it, for ten days, when we came to a large RUSSIAN village called TZAUSKY OSTROGUE, from a rivulet of that name; which discharges itself into the OBY, a little distance eastward from this place. Here is a small fort, surrounded with a ditch and palisades; mounted with a few cannon, and garrisoned by some militia of the country, in order to prevent the incursions of the KALMUCKS. We staid a day at this place; to refresh ourselves; and, having changed horses, proceeded towards TOMSKY.

BARABA is really what its name signifies, an extensive marshy plain. It is generally full of lakes, and marshy grounds, overgrown with tall woods of aspin, alder, willows, and other aquatics; particularly many large birch-trees, having their bark as white and smooth as paper. The lakes abound with various kinds of fishes; such as

pikes

pikes, perches, breams, eels; and, particularly, a fish called karrafs, of an uncommon bigness, and very fat. These the inhabitants dry, in summer, for winter provisions; which are all the food to be found among them. I have eat of it often, and thought it not disagreeable. In winter, they use melted snow for water. They are very hospitable; and desire nothing, in return of their civilities, but a little tobacco to smoke, and a dram of brandy, of which they are very fond. The dress, both of men and women, consists of long coats of sheep-skins, which they get from the RUSSIANS and KALMUCKS, in exchange for more valuable furs. As they wear no other apparel, not even shirts, they are very nasty. Their huts are most miserable habitations, and sunk about one half under ground. We were glad, however, to find them, as a baiting-place in such a cold season.

The BARABINTZY, like most of the ancient natives of SIBERIA, have many conjurers among them; whom they call shamans, and sometimes priests. Many of the female sex also assume this character. The shamans are held in great esteem by the people; they pretend to correspondence with the shaytan, or devil; by whom, they say, they are informed of all past and future

ture events, at any distance of time or place. Our ambassador resolved to inquire strictly into the truth of many strange stories, generally believed, concerning the shamans; and sent for all of fame, in that way, in the places through which we passed.

In BARABA, we went to visit a famous woman of this character. When we entered her house, she continued busy about her domestic affairs, without almost taking any notice of her guests. However, after she had smoked a pipe of tobacco, and drunk a dram of brandy, she began to be more chearful. Our people asked her some trifling questions about their friends; but she pretended to be quite ignorant, till she got more tobacco, and some inconsiderable presents; when she began to collect her conjuring tools. First, she brought the shaytan; which is nothing but a piece of wood, wherein is cut something resembling a human head, adorned with many silk and woolen rags, of various colours; then, a small drum, about a foot diameter, to which were fixed many brass and iron rings, and hung round also with rags. She now began a dismal tune, keeping time with the drum, which she beat with a stick for that purpose; several of her neighbours, whom she had previously called to her assistance, joined in the chorus

chorus. During this scene, which lasted about a quarter of an hour, she kept the shaytan, or image, close by herself, stuck up in a corner. The charm being now finished, she desired us to put our questions. Her answers were delivered very artfully, and with as much obscurity and ambiguity, as they could have been given by any oracle. She was a young woman, and very handsome.

On the 29th of January, we reached the OBY, which we crossed on the ice, and entered a country pretty well inhabited by RUSSIANS; where we found provisions, and fresh horses as often as we wanted them. The country is generally covered with woods, except about the villages; where are fine corn-fields, and good pasture grounds. Our course lay a little to the northward of the east from TZAUSKY OSTROGUE.

February 4th, we arrived safe at the town of TOMSKY, so called from the noble river TOMM, upon the eastern bank of which it stands.

CHAP.

CHAPTER III.

Occurrences at TOMSKY; *Observations on the* TZULIMM TAR-TARS, &c. *and journey continued to* ELIMSKY.

THE citadel of TOMSKY is situated on an eminence, and contains the commandant's house, publick offices, and barracks for the garrison. The fortifications, like most others in this country, are of wood. The town stands under the hill, along the banks of the river TOMM. The country about this place is pleasant and fruitful. From the top of the hill you have a very extensive view every way, except to the south, where it is interrupted by hills. Beyond these hills there is a large, dry, and open plain, which stretches a great way southward.

About eight or ten days journey from TOMSKY, in this plain, are found many tombs, and burying places of ancient heroes; who, in all probability, fell in battle. These tombs are easily distinguished by the mounds of earth and stones raised upon them. When, or by whom, these battles were fought, so far to the northward, is uncertain. I was informed by the TARTARS in the BARABA, that TAMERLANE, or TIMYR-ACK-SACK, as they call him, had many engagements in that country with the KALMUCKS; whom he in vain endeavoured to conquer. Many persons go from TOMSKY, and other parts, every summer, to these graves; which they dig up, and find, among the ashes of the dead, considerable quantities of gold, silver, brass, and some precious stones; but particularly hilts of swords and armour. They find also ornaments of saddles and bridles, and other trappings for horses; and even the bones of horses, and sometimes those of elephants. Whence it appears, that when any general or person of distinction was interred, all his arms, his favourite horse and servant, were buried with him in the same grave; this custom prevails to this day among the KALMUCKS and other TARTARS, and seems to be of great antiquity. It appears from the number of graves, that many thousands must have fallen on these plains; for the people have continued to dig for such treasure many years, and still find it unexhausted. They are, sometimes indeed, interrupted, and robbed of all their booty, by parties of the KALMUCKS, who abhor the disturbing the ashes of the dead.

I have seen several pieces of armour, and other curiosities, that were dug out of these tombs; particularly

larly an armed man on horse-back, cast in brass, of no mean design nor workmanship; also figures of deer, cast in pure gold, which were split through the middle, and had some small holes in them, as intended for ornaments to a quiver, or the furniture of a horse.

While we were at TOMSKY, one of these grave-diggers told me, that once they lighted on an arched vault; where they found the remains of a man, with his bow, arrows, lance, and other arms, lying together on a silver table. On touching the body it fell to dust. The value of the table and arms was very considerable.

The country about the source of the river TOMM, near which these tombs are, is very fruitful and pleasant. At the source of the TOMM the RUSSIANS have a small town called KUZNETSKY. This river is formed by the KONDOMA, and many lesser rivers; all which run to the north.

In the hills above KUZNETSKY, there had lately been discovered rich mines of copper, and some of silver; which, since I was in this country, have been greatly improved.

On the hills, and in the woods near this place, are many sorts of wild beasts; particularly the urus, or uhr-ox, one of the fierceft animals the world produces, and exceeding, in fize and ftrength, all the horned fpecies. Their force and agility is fuch, that no wolf, bear, nor tiger, dare to engage with them. Thefe animals are found in the woods of POLAND, and fome other parts of EUROPE. As they are well known I need not defcribe them.

In the fame woods is found another fpecies of oxen, called bubul by the TARTARS; it is not fo big as the urus; its body and limbs are very handfome; it has a high fhoulder and a flowing tail, with long hair growing from the rump to the extremity, like that of a horfe. Thofe I faw were tame, and as tractable as other cattle. Here are alfo wild affes. I have feen many of their skins. They have, in all refpects, the head, tail, and hoofs, of an ordinary afs; but their hair is waved, white and brown, like that of a tiger.

There is, befides, a number of wild horfes, of a chefnut colour; which cannot be tamed, though they are catched when foals. Thefe horfes differ nothing from the common kind in fhape, but are the moft watchful creatures alive. One of them waits always on the heights, to give warning to the reft; and, upon the leaft approach of danger, runs to the herd, making all the noife noise it can; upon which all of them fly away, like so many deer. The stallion drives up the rear, neighing, biting and kicking those who do not run fast enough. Notwithstanding this wonderful sagacity, these animals are often surprized by the KALMUCKS; who ride in among them, well mounted on swift horses, and kill them with broad lances. Their flesh they esteem excellent food; and use their skins to sleep upon, instead of couches. These are the animals peculiar to this part of the country; and, besides these, there are many more, common to this place with the rest of SIBERIA.

The river TOMM, having passed KUZNETSKY, TOMSKY, and several other towns of less note, empties itself into the OBY, at a place called NIKOLSKY, about an hundred verst below TOMSKY, in a country overgrown with thick woods. Here the TOMM loses its name, and makes a great addition to the OBY, which now commences a mighty stream.

The TOMM abounds with variety of fine fish; such as sturgeon, sterlet, muchsoon, and the largest and best quabs, called in FRENCH guion, that I have any where seen. The method of catching these fish is by planting pales across the river, in which there is left one narrow opening for the fishes to pass through; above this opening

ing, a hole is cut in the ice; and near it is placed a fire, upon some stones laid for that purpose. The fish, on seeing the light of the fire, stops a moment in its passage; and, at this instant, the fisherman strikes it with a spear, through the hole in the ice. This exercise requires great quickness; for the fish is gone in a trice. I killed several of them myself.

Thus, having made a short excursion up and down the TOMM, and given a brief description of the country adjacent, I return again to TOMSKY.

TOMSKY is a good market for furs of all sorts; but particularly of sables, black and red foxes, ermins, and squirrels. The squirrels called TELEUTSKY, from the name of the district where they are caught, are reckoned the best of that species. They have a blackish stripe down their back.

Besides the common squirrel, there is another species found here called the flying squirrel. There is little peculiar in its shape or size; only, it has, at the upper joint of the thigh of the fore-leg, a small membrane, stretching to the shoulder, somewhat like the wing of a bat, which it extends at pleasure; and is thereby enabled to spring much farther, from tree to tree, than it could do without the help of these wings.

Both

Both the ermins and fquirrels are caught only in winter; becaufe in fummer their fur is quite brown, fhort, and of little ufe.

We waited fome days at TOMSKY for the arrival of our baggage. Here we found feveral SWEDISH officers; who had good quarters in a plentiful, though diftant, place. After our people had refrefhed themfelves for two days, they fet out again on the road to YENISEYSKY.

During our abode in TOMSKY, we diverted ourfelves with fifhing and hunting. We were prefent alfo at feveral concerts of mufick, performed by the SWEDISH officers, at Mr. KOSLOFF's, commandant of the place. Thefe gentlemen were not lefs expert in touching their inftruments, than their companions at TOBOLSKY. Mr. KOSLOFF is a good-natured and chearful gentleman, and treats thefe officers with great humanity. They had along with them a SWEDISH parfon, Mr. VESTADIUS, a man of genius and learning.

The 9th, we were entertained at the commandant's; where were affembled fome hundreds of his COSSACKS, or light horfe, armed with bows and arrows. After going through their ufual exercife, they fhowed their dexterity in fhooting on horfe-back at full fpeed. They
erected

erected a pole, for a mark, in an open field; and, passing it, at full gallop, let fly their arrows; and soon split it all to shivers.

The 12th, about midnight, we went into our sledges, and set out on our journey towards YENISEYSKY. For the two following days, we had tolerably good roads, lying through a pretty fine country, inhabited by RUSSIANS. The villages are but thinly scattered, yet sufficiently near one another to afford provisions and fresh horses.

On the 14th, we reached a large navigable river, called TZULIMM. We went up this river upon the ice. We met with neither house, nor inhabitant, for the space of six days. We could get no fresh horses, and were obliged to carry both provisions and forage along with us; which made this part of the road very tedious. During all this time, we had no where to warm ourselves, or dress our victuals, but in the thick overgrown woods, which occupy both sides of the river. There is great plenty of fallen trees in these woods, of which we made large fires. The trees are chiefly pitch-fir, rising like a pyramid, with long spreading branches hanging to the ground; which render these woods almost impassable to man or beast. We frequently

quently set fire to the moss and dried fibres of these firs. In the space of a minute the fire mounts to the top of the tree, and has a very pretty effect. The kindling so many fires warmed all the air around.

In summer, the banks of this river are inhabited by a tribe of TARTARS, called by the RUSSIANS TZULIMM-ZY, from the name of the river, who live by fishing and hunting. We found several of their empty huts, as we went along. In autumn, these people retire from this inhospitable place, towards the south, near to towns and villages, where they can find subsistence.

The 20th, we arrived at a RUSSIAN village, called MELETZKY-OSTROGUE, where we staid a day to refresh ourselves and horses. In the neighbourhood of this place we found many huts of these TZULIMM-TARTARS, who seem to be a different race from all of that name I have yet mentioned. Their complexion indeed is swarthy, like that of most of the other descendents of the ancient natives of SIBERIA; but I have seen many of them having white spots on their skins, from head to foot, of various figures and sizes. Many imagine these spots natural to the people; but I am rather inclined to believe they proceed from their constant diet of fish and other animal food, without bread. This, of course, creates a scorbutick habit of body, which often breaks out in infants; and the scars falling off, leave that part of the skin as if it had been scalded, which never recovers its natural colour. I have however seen several children with these spots, who seemed healthy.

The TZULIMMS, like other TARTARS, live in huts half-sunk under ground. They have a fire in the middle, with a hole at the top to let out the smoke, and benches round the fire, to sit or ly upon. This seems to be the common method of living among all the northern nations, from LAPLAND, eastward, to the JAPANESE ocean.

The TZULIMMS speak a barbarous language, composed of words from many other languages. Some of our people, who spoke TURKISH, told me, they had many ARABICK words, which they understood. They are poor, miserable, and ignorant heathens. The archbishop of TOBOLSKY, in person, came lately hither, and baptised some hundreds of them, who were inclined to embrace the CHRISTIAN faith. As they are a well-disposed and harmless people, probably in a short time they may be all converted.

The river TZULIMM has its source about three hundred

dred verst above MELETSKY OSTROGUE; from this place it continues its course to the northward, till it meets with the river OBY, at a place called SHABANNSKY OSTROGUE. OSTROGUE, in the RUSSIAN language, signifies a strong palisade, inclosing a certain piece of ground. On the first settlements made by the RUSSIANS in these parts, such inclosures were necessary to prevent any surprise from the inhabitants.

The 21st, early in the morning, we left MELETSKY, and travelled through thick woods, along narrow roads. Next day, we came to a small RUSSIAN village, called MELAY-KEAT; where we found our baggage, for the first time, since we quitted TOMSKY. Near this place the river KEAT has its source; and runs towards the west, till it meets with the OBY. Having changed horses at MELAY-KEAT, we left our baggage, and proceeded on our journey.

On the evening of the 22d, we came to a zimovey, where we halted a little, to refresh ourselves and bait our horses. A zimovy is a house or two, built in a place at a great distance from any town or village, for the convenience of travellers; and is a sort of inn, where you generally find a warm room, fresh bread, and a wholesome and agreeable liquor, called quafs, made of malt, or rye-meal, steeped and fermented; with hay and oats, at easy rates.

From this place we travelled to BELOY, a large village, where we changed horses, and proceeded. From hence to YENISEYSKY the country is well cultivated. Upon the road are many RUSS villages, where we got fresh horses, as often as we pleased, without halting ten minutes. Thus we continued travelling, day and night, till we arrived, on the 23d, at the town of YENISEYSKY; where we had a friendly reception, and good entertainment, from the commandant, Mr. BECKLIMISHOF, who had come some miles from town to meet his old friend the ambassador.

Here I found Mr. KANBAR NIKITITZ AIKINFIOF, with whom I got acquainted at CAZAN, while we wintered there, in the journey to PERSIA. Some cross accident had been the occasion of his coming to this place. He enjoyed full liberty to walk about at pleasure. He understood several languages, was well acquainted with history, and a chearful good-natured companion.

Here we passed the holidays called Masslapitza, or the Carnaval, which is held on the week before Lent. In the mean time our carriages arrived, which were dispatched again as soon as possible.

The

The town of YENISEYSKY is pleasantly situated in a plain, on the western bank of the river YENISEY, from which the town takes its name. It is a large and populous place, fenced with a ditch, palisades, and wooden towers. Here is a good market for furs of all sorts; particularly of the animals called piessy, which are of two colours, white and dove-colour. These creatures are caught far to the northward of this place. They are nearly of the shape and size of a fox; having a short bushy tail, and a thick soft downy fur, very light and warm, which is much esteemed by the great men in the northern parts of CHINA; and, by them, made chiefly into cushions, on which they sit in winter.

Besides the above, there is here another creature called rossomack in RUSS, and feel fress by the GERMANS; because they imagine it eats a great deal more in proportion than other animals. I have seen several of them alive. They are very fierce, and about the shape and size of a badger. The neck, back, and tail are black; but about the belly the hair is of a brownish colour. The blacker they are, the more valuable. The skin, being thick, is only used in caps and muffs. Also elks, rain-deer, and stags. The latter retire to the south on the approach of winter, and return in the spring.

spring. Here are likewife an incredible number of white-hares, which perhaps I may mention afterwards.

I muft not omit the black foxes, which are in great abundance about YENISEYSKY. Their fur is reckoned the moſt beautiful of any kind; it is even preferred to the fable with refpect to lightnefs and warmnefs. I faw here one of their skins valued at five hundred crowns, and fome of them far exceed this fum.

Before I leave this place I fhall give a fhort defcription of the courfe of the famous river YENISEY, according to the beſt information I could procure. It rifes in a hilly country, at a great diftance fouthward from this place. Being joined by many rivers in its courfe, it grows into a mighty ſtream; and is, at YENISEYSKY, full as large as the VOLGA. It runs the longeſt courfe of any river on this vaſt continent. The firſt town, of any note, in coming down this river, is KRASSNO-YARR, which ſtands on the weſtern bank. It is a place of confiderable trade, particularly in furs. From this place, along the banks, are many villages, till the YENISEY meets the lower TONGUSTA, a large river, coming from the eaſt, a few verſt above YENISEYSKY. Below this place there are many inconfiderable ſettlements, till you come to MANGASEYSKY, a town

town famous for furs, and the shrine of an illustrious saint, called VASSILE MANGASEYSKY, much frequented by the devout people in these parts.

Above this place the YENISEY receives the PODKA-MENA-TONGUSTA, a large river, running from the south east; and, at MANGASEYSKY, it meets another river, called TUROCHANSKY, coming from the west. The YENISEY now continues its course, almost due north, till it discharges itself into the ocean. This river abounds with variety of excellent fish; such as I have already mentioned, but in lesser quantities.

The 27th, we left YENISEYSKY, and travelled about eight or ten verst along the south bank of the river, when we came to thick and tall woods, which obliged us to leave the land and march along the river, on the ice, which was very uneven. This roughness is caused by the frost setting in about autumn, with a strong westerly wind, which drives up great cakes of ice upon one another, in some places four or five feet high. If the frost happens to begin in calm weather, the ice is very smooth, and easy for sledges.

The 28th, we proceeded along the YENISEY, meeting sometimes with villages. The rigour of the cold was much abated; but the face of winter appeared e-
very

very where, without the least sign of spring. At evening, we entered the river TONGUSTA, which we found as rough as the former; but, as both the banks were overgrown with thick woods, we were obliged to keep along the ice.

Next day, we still proceeded along the river, in blowing weather and driving snow.

The 1st of March, we overtook our baggage, which we passed; it being thought more convenient, both in order to procure lodging and fresh horses, that the heavy carriages should travel behind.

We continued our journey, for several days, along the TONGUSTA. We found, now and then, little villages, or single houses, on the banks. One day we chanced to meet a prodigious flock of hares, all as white as the snow on which they walked. I speak within compass when I say there were above five or six hundred of them. They were coming down the river, very deliberately, on a small path, of their own making, close to the beaten road. As soon as they saw us, all of them run into the woods, without seeming much frightened. I am informed that these hares travel to the south, in much greater flocks than this, every spring, and return in autumn, when the rivers

vers are frozen and the snow falls. In most of the villages, we found plenty of this sort of venison; the inhabitants, however, value it but little; for they catch these hares more on account of their skins, of which they make considerable profits, than their flesh.

The TONGUSY, so called from the name of the river, who live along its banks, are the posterity of the ancient inhabitants of SIBERIA, and differ in language, manners, and dress, and even in their persons and stature, from all the other tribes of these people I have had occasion to see. They have no houses, where they remain for any time, but range through the woods, and along rivers, at pleasure; and, wherever they come, they erect a few spars, inclining to one another at the top; these they cover with pieces of birchen bark, sewed together, leaving a hole at the top to let out the smoke. The fire is placed in the middle. They are very civil and tractable, and like to smoke tobacco, and drink brandy. About their huts they have generally a good stock of rain-deer, in which all their wealth consists.

The men are tall and able-bodied, brave, and very honest. The women are of a middle size, and virtuous. I have seen many of the men with oval figures, like wreaths, on their fore-heads and chins; and sometimes

times a figure, resembling the branch of a tree, reaching from the corner of the eye to the mouth. These are made, in their infancy, by pricking the parts with a needle, and rubbing them with charcoal, the marks whereof remain as long as the person lives. Their complexion is swarthy. Their faces are not so flat as those of the KALMUKS, but their countenances more open. They are altogether unacquainted with any kind of literature, and worship the sun and moon. They have many shamans among them, who differ little from those I formerly described. I was told of others, whose abilities in fortune-telling far exceeded these of the shamans at this place, but they lived far northward. They cannot bear to sleep in a warm room, but retire to their huts, and lie about the fire on skins of wild beasts. It is surprizing how these creatures can suffer the very piercing cold in these parts.

The women are dressed in a fur-gown, reaching below the knee, and tied about the waist with a girdle. This girdle is about three inches broad, made of deer's skin, having the hair curiously stitched down and ornamented; to which is fastened, at each side, an iron-ring, that serves to carry a tobacco-pipe, and other trinkets of small value. Their gowns are also stitched down the

the breast, and about the neck. Their long black hair is plaited, and tied about their heads, above which they wear a small fur-cap, which is becoming enough. Some of them have small ear-rings. Their feet are dressed in buskins, made of deer-skins, which reach to the knee, and are tied about the ancles with a thong of leather.

The dress of the men is very simple, and fit for action. It consists of a short jacket, with narrow sleeves, made of deer's skin, having the fur outward; trousers and hose of the same kind of skin, both of one piece, and tight to the limbs. They have besides a piece of fur, that covers the breast and stomach, which is hung about the neck with a thong of leather. This, for the most part, is neatly stitched and ornamented by their wives. Round their heads they have a ruff, made of the tails of squirrels, to preserve the tips of the ears from the cold. There is nothing on the crown, but the hair smoothed, which hangs in a long plaited lock behind their backs.

Their arms are a bow and several sorts of arrows, according to the different kinds of game they intend to hunt. The arrows are carried, in a quiver, on their backs, and the bow always in their left hand. Besides these, they have

have a short lance, and a little hatchet. Thus accoutred, they are not afraid to attack the fiercest creature in the woods, even the strongest bear; for they are stout men, and dexterous archers. In winter, which is the season for hunting wild beasts, they travel on what are called snow shoes, without which it would be impossible to make their way through the deep snow. These are made of a very thin piece of light wood, about five feet long, and five or six inches broad, inclining to a point before, and square behind. In the middle is fixed a thong, through which the feet are put. On these shoes a person may walk safely over the deepest snow; for a man's weight will not sink them above an inch; these however can only be used on plains. They have a different kind for ascending hills, with the skins of seals glued to the boards, having the hair inclined backwards, which prevents the sliding of the shoes; so that they can ascend a hill very easily; and, in descending, they slide downwards at a great rate.

The nation of the TONGUSY was very numerous; but is, of late, much diminished by the small pox. It is remarkable, that they knew nothing of this distemper, till the RUSSIANS arrived among them. They are so much afraid of this disease, that, if any one of a family

mily is seized with it, the rest immediately make the patient a little hut, and set by him some water and victuals; then, packing up every thing, they march off to the windward, each carrying an earthen pot, with burning coals in it, and making a dreadful lamentation as they go along. They never revisit the sick, till they think the danger past. If the person dies, they place him on a branch of a tree, to which he is tied, with strong wythes, to prevent his falling.

When they go a hunting into the woods, they carry with them no provisions; but depend entirely on what they are to catch. They eat every animal that comes in their way, even a bear, fox, or wolf. The squirrels are reckoned delicate food; but the ermins have such a strong rank taste and smell, that nothing but starving can oblige them to eat their flesh. When a TONGUSE kills an elk or deer, he never moves from the place, till he has eat it up, unless he happens to be near his family; in which case, he carries part of it home. He is never at a loss for fire, having always a tinder-box about him; if this should happen to be wanting, he kindles a fire by rubbing two pieces of wood against each other. They eat nothing raw, but in great extremity.

The

The sables are not caught in the same manner as other animals. The fur is so tender, that the least mark of an arrow, or ruffling of the hair, spoils the sale of the skin. In hunting them they only use a little dog, and a net. When a hunter finds the track of a sable upon the snow, he follows it, perhaps, for two or three days, till the poor animal, quite tired, takes refuge in some tall tree; for it can climb like a cat; the hunter then spreads his net around the tree, and makes a fire; the sable, unable to endure the smoke, immediately descends, and is caught in the net. I have been told, by some of these hunters, that, when hard pinched with hunger, on such long chaces, they take two thin boards, one of which they apply to the pit of the stomach, and the other to the back opposite to it; the extremities of these boards are tied with cords, which are drawn tighter by degrees, and prevent their feeling the cravings of hunger.

Although I have observed, that the TONGUSY, in general, worship the sun and moon, there are many exceptions to this observation. I have found intelligent people among them, who believed there was a being superior to both sun and moon; and who created them and all the world.

I shall

I shall only remark farther, that from all the accounts I have heard and read of the natives of CANADA, there is no nation, in the world, which they so much resemble as the TONGUSIANS. The distance between them is not so great as is commonly imagined.

The 4th of March, we came to a little monastery, called TROYTZA, dedicated to the Holy Trinity; where we found about half a dozen monks, who gave us an hospitable reception in their cells, and furnished us with provisions and fresh horses. The monastery stands upon the north-side of the river, on a very pleasant though solitary bank, encompassed with woods, cornfields, and good pasturage. Most of the villages are on the north side of the river, as it is higher than the south side.

The same day, we proceeded on our journey along the river. We met with, daily, great flocks of hares in their progress to the westward, and many TONGUSIANS in their huts. It is to be observed, that, from this river northward to the frozen ocean, there are no inhabitants, except a few TONGUSIANS on the banks of the great rivers; the whole of this most extensive country being overgrown with dark impenetrable woods. The soil, along the banks of this river, is good; and produces

duces wheat, barley, rye, and oats. The method taken by the inhabitants to destroy the large fir-trees, is, to cut off a ring of bark from the trunk, about a foot broad, which prevents the ascending of the sap, and the tree withers in a few years. This prepares it for being burnt in a dry season; by which means, the ground is both cleared of the wood, and manured by the ashes, without much labour.

The RUSSIANS observe, that, where the sort of fir, commonly called the SCOTCH fir, grows, the ground never fails of producing corn; but it is not so where the pitch, or any other kind of fir, prevails.

The 7th, we came to the head of the TONGUSKY, which is formed by the conflux of two other rivers, the ANGARA and the ELIMM. The first issues from the great BAYKALL lake; and runs towards the west, till it meets the TONGUSKY, when it loses its name. We left the ANGARA and TONGUSKY on our right hand, and proceeded along the ELIMM, which we found much smoother than the TONGUSKY. The ELIMM is a considerably large and navigable river. The banks on the south side are very high, and covered with rugged rocks, overgrown with woods; but, to the north, you meet with several villages, corn-fields, and pasturage.

We

We kept on our courſe up the ELIMM, a little to the northward of the eaſt, till the 9th, when we arrived at the town of ELIMSKY, ſo called from the name of the river, which ſtands in a narrow valley, on the ſouth ſide of the river, encompaſſed with high hills and rocks covered with woods. This place is but ſmall, and is only conſiderable as it ſtands on the road to the eaſtern parts of SIBERIA; for travellers to CHINA generally take to the ſouth-eaſt, towards IRKUTSKY; and thoſe who travel to YAKUTSKY and KAMTZATSKY, to the north-eaſt.

CHAPTER IV.

Obſervations on YAKUTSKY *and* KAMTZATSKY, *&c. Journey continued to* IRKUTSKY, *and occurrences there, &c.*

AT ELIMSKY I met with general KANIFER. He was adjutant general to CHARLES XII. of SWEDEN, and much eſteemed by that great warrior, for his military exploits. KANIFER was a native of COURLAND. He was taken priſoner by the RUSSIANS in POLAND, and ſent hither; where he lived in eaſe and ſolitude, and was regularly viſited by all travellers.

This gentleman had a creature called kaberda, which

was brought to him when a fawn, by some of the TON-GUSY. It is the animal from which the sweet-smelling drug called musk is taken. The musk grows about the navel, in form of an excrescence, which is cut off, and preserved, when the creature is killed. There are many of them in this country; but the musk is not so strong scented as that which comes from CHINA, and more southern climates. The general had bred this creature to be very familiar. He fed it at his table with bread and roots. When dinner was over, it jumped on the table, and picked up the crumbs. It followed him about the streets like a dog. I must confess it was pleasing to see it cut caprioles, and play with children like a kid.

The kaberda is a size less than the fallow-deer, and its colour darker. It is of a pretty shape, having erect horns, without branches; is very swift, and haunts rocks and mountains, of difficult access to men or dogs; and, when hunted, jumps from cliff to cliff with incredible celerity, and firmness of foot. The flesh is esteemed better venison than any of the deer kind, of larger size; whereof there is great variety in these parts.

Before I leave ELIMSKY, I shall, as usual, give a short account

account of some of the places adjacent; particularly those to the north-east, towards the river LENA, and YAKUTSKY, according as I have been informed by travellers, on whose veracity I could entirely depend.

The people who travel in winter, from hence to these places, generally do it in January, or February. It is a very long and difficult journey; and which none but TONGUSIANS, or such hardy people, have abilities to perform. The RUSSIANS frequently finish it in six weeks. The common method is as follows: After travelling a few days in sledges, when the road becomes impassable by horses, they set themselves on snow-shoes, and drag after them what is called a nart, containing provisions and other necessaries; which are as few and light as possible. This nart is a kind of sledge, about five feet long, and ten inches broad, which a man may easily draw upon the deepest snow. At night, they make a large fire, and lay themselves down to sleep in these narrow sledges. As soon as they have refreshed themselves, they again proceed on their snow-shoes, as before. This manner of travelling continues about the space of ten days, when they come to a place where they procure dogs to draw both themselves and their narts. The dogs are yoked by pairs; and are more or fewer in number, according to the weight they have to draw. Being trained to the work, they go on with great spirit, barking all the way; and the person, who lies in the sledge, holds a small cord to guide the dog that leads the rest. They are fastened to the sledge by a soft rope, which is tied about their middle, and passes through between their hind legs. I have been surprised to see the weight that these creatures are able to draw; for travellers must carry along with them provisions, both for themselves and the dogs. These watchful animals know the time of setting out in the morning; and make a dismal howling, till they are fed and pursue their journey. This way of travelling would not, I believe, suit every constitution; the very sight of it satisfied my curiosity. Thus, however, these people proceed for near three weeks, till they arrive at some villages on the LENA; where, leaving the dogs, they procure horses, with which they travel to the town of YAKUTSKY. This place has its name from a rivulet, called YAKUT, which empties itself into the LENA.

I have been, perhaps, too particular in describing the method of travelling with snow-shoes and dogs; but, as these things are known to few EUROPEANS, I concluded an account of them would not be disagreeable. I have seen several SWEDISH officers who have travelled to YAKUTSKY in this manner. I tried the snow-shoes myself, and found them very fatiguing; but time and practice make them easy and familiar.

There is a more agreeable road, from ELIMSKY to YAKUTSKY, than that I have mentioned, which is by water, down the river LENA; but this rout will not agree with the time and circumstances of every traveller. Those who travel from IRKUTSKY, by this course, go, by land, to a place called VERCHOLENSKY OSTROGUE, situated near the source of the LENA, where they embark and fall down the stream. Those who go from ELIMSKY, cross the country directly, about two days journey, to the first convenient place upon the LENA, where they procure vessels, and sail down the river to YAKUTSKY, or any other place; but in this passage, by water, they are pestered with numbers of large gnats and muskitoes, which lessen the pleasure of the voyage.

Before I proceed to the northward, it will not be improper to give a short description of the famous river LENA; which, for the length of its course, and quantity of water, may be compared to any of the largest rivers in the world.

The

CHAP. IV.
1720.

The LENA rifes at a fmall diftance northward from the BAYKALL lake, and runs to the north, with little variation, till it difcharges itfelf into the NORTHERN ocean. I compute the length of it, from the fource to the ocean, to be about two thoufand five hundred ENGLISH miles, though it is much more by common report. It is navigable during this whole courfe, having no cataracts fo great as to prevent the paffage of veffels of confiderable burden. It receives many great rivers, moft of which come from the eaft. It may eafily be imagined, that the LENA cannot fail of being ftored with various kinds of excellent fifh, when the other rivers in SIBERIA afford fuch plenty and variety. The banks are generally overgrown with tall thick woods; wherein are abundance of game, and wild beafts. The country, between its fource and the BAYKALL lake, is well peopled, abounding with many RUSS villages, and corn-fields, along the banks of the river.

Having formerly mentioned YAKUTSKY and KAMTZATSKY, I fhall add a few obfervations on thefe two provinces.

The town of YAKUTSKY, capital of the province of that name, is fituated on the weft bank of the river LENA, and governed by a commandant; whofe office is reckoned very lucrative, as many fables, and other valuable furs, are found in that province.

The winter here is very long, and the frost so violent, that it is never out of the earth, in the month of June, beyond two feet and an half below the surface. When the inhabitants bury their dead above three feet deep, they are laid in frozen earth; for the heat of the sun never penetrates above two feet, or two feet and an half: so that, I am informed, all the dead bodies remain in the earth, unconsumed; and will do so till the day of judgment.

The town, and many villages in its neighbourhood, are inhabited by RUSSIANS; who have horses and cows, but no sheep nor corn. They are plentifully supplied with corn from the southern parts of the country, by water-carriage along the LENA. And, in summer, they make hay enough to feed their cattle in winter.

The province of YAKUTSKY is inhabited by a numerous tribe of TARTARS; by which name the RUSSIANS call the whole of the natives of this country, however they differ from one another in religion, language, and manners. Those of this province are named YAKUTY. They occupy a great space of territory round this place,

place, especially to the east, where they border with the extensive province of KAMTZATSKY.

The YAKUTY differ little from the TONGUSIANS, either in their persons or way of life. Their occupation, like that of the other natives, is fishing and hunting. They have flattish faces, little black eyes, and long black hair, plaited, and hanging down their backs. Many of the men are marked in the face with charcoal, after the manner of the TONGUSIANS. I have, however, seen many of these people, both men and women, of good complexions. They often sell their children to the RUSSIANS, who are very fond of them; as they generally make trusty servants.

These people, though otherwise humane and tractable, have, among them, one very barbarous custom: When any of their people are infirm through age, or seized with distempers reckoned incurable, they make a small hut for the patient, near some river, in which they leave him, with some provisions; and seldom, or never, return to visit him. On such occasions, they have no regard to father or mother; but say, they do them a good office in sending them to a better world. Whereby it appears, that, even these rude ignorant people have a notion of a future state.

Under

Under KAMTZATSKY I include all that vast tract of land, reaching from the river AMOOR, along the shore of the EASTERN, or JAPANESE ocean, called by the RUSSIANS TIKOE MORE, or the CALM SEA, to the north-east point of the continent. The country, along the shore, is very pleasant and healthy, especially to the south, where the climate is temperate. This part of the country produces grain, and, as I have been informed, even grapes, and other fruits. The inhabitants are very humane and hospitable.

When the RUSSIANS first entered this province, the KAMTZEDANS endeavoured to oppose them. For this purpose they assembled great numbers of men, armed, after the fashion of their country, with bows, arrows, and short lances, headed with bone, sharpened at the point. Whence it appears, that these people knew no more the use of iron, than the MEXICANS on the arrival of the SPANIARDS in AMERICA. Their multitudes were soon dispersed by a few RUSSIANS with fire-arms, which, in those days, had rifled barrels, and a small bore, which killed at a great distance. The poor KAMTZEDANS, seeing their people fall without any visible wound, and astonished with the fire and noise of the gun-powder, left the field in the utmost consterna-

CHAP. IV.
1720.
tion. Their dispositions now were wholly inclined to peace; and a few of their chief men were sent to the RUSSIANS, in order to obtain it. They prostrated themselves, in the most submissive manner, before the leader of the party, and begged of him to grant them peace; which he did, on condition of their paying to his Majesty an annual tribute of sables, or other furs. This condition they have punctually performed ever since.

Many parts of KAMTZATSKY are hilly and mountainous, particularly to the north, and covered with tall woods. At OCHOTSKY is a good harbour, and timber enough to build a royal navy. There are many great and small rivers, that run through the country, and empty themselves into the Eastern Ocean, among which is a great river, called ANADEER. To the north of this river, towards the ocean, lies an extensive tract of land, little known, and inhabited by a fierce and savage people, called, by the RUSSIANS, ANADEERTZY, who continue very untractable.

I have nothing further to add concerning these remote provinces; only, I am persuaded that the islands of JAPAN can be at no great distance from the southern parts of KAMTZATSKY. What confirmed me in this

this opinion is, that I saw at ST. PETERSBURG a young man, a native of JAPAN, who, I believe, is yet alive in the Academy of Sciences at that place. I asked him, by what accident he was brought so far from his own country; and he gave me the following account. That his father and himself, with a few persons more, being at a noted town called NAGGISAKY, on the west coast of the island, employed about some affairs of trade, and having finished their business, intended to return to their own habitations, on the north shore, by sailing round the coast. Therefore went they on board a small boat, and begun their voyage homeward; but, meeting with a strong gale off the land, they were unfortunately driven out to sea; and, in a few days, were cast upon the coast of KAMTZATSKY, half-starved, and in the greatest distress. In this condition they met with a RUSSIAN officer, who afforded them all that assistance which common humanity dictates on such occasions. Notwithstanding all his care, several of the old people died; being quite spent with fatigue, and want of victuals. That he and another youth, who was since dead, were sent to ST. PETERSBURG, where his Majesty was pleased to order that they should be provided for in the Academy. This young man could read

CHAP. IV. read and write both the JAPANESE and RUSSIAN lan-
1720. guages.

We set out from ELIMSKY on the 12th; and next day, in the evening, came to a small village, upon the north bank of the river ANGARA, about eighty verst distant from ELIMSKY. During these two days we saw no house, nor any inhabitants; the whole of the country, through which we passed, being covered with tall and thick woods. There is a narrow road cut for sledges; and the trees on each side, meeting at the top, shade it by day; and in the night make it very dark, and almost dismal.

We passed the night in this village, where we got fresh horses; and, next morning, repeated our journey almost due east, up the river ANGARA, upon the ice. Along the banks we found many villages well-peopled. The face of the country had now a different aspect, from what I had seen for several months; sometimes we saw a fine champaign country, exhibiting a beautiful and extensive prospect; at other times, the view was agreeably varied with woods, and rising grounds. The north-side of the river is mostly over-grown with woods. There are some openings along the banks;
where

where we found villages, and abundance of cattle and provisions.

The 15th, we arrived at a large village, called BAL-LAGANSKY; situated on the south-side of the ANGARA, near a rivulet, running from the south, called UNGA. The situation of this place is very pleasant, as it stands in a fruitful plain, and has many corn-fields and woods in the neighbourhood.

Here we found another tribe of the natives of SIBE-RIA, who differ, in some particulars, from all those I have formerly described. They are called by the RUS-SIANS BRATSKY, but by themselves BURATY. They live in tents all the year; and, having large flocks of sheep, and many cows and horses, they remove from place to place, as the convenience of grazing requires. Their language has a great affinity to that of the KAL-MUCKS; and they have priests among them who can read and write that language. As to their dress, and manner of life, I could observe little difference between them and the KALMUCKS on the VOLGA; and therefore conclude they have both descended from the same original. Their faces, however, are not quite so flat as those of the KALMUCKS; their noses being somewhat higher, and their countenances more open.

The

CHAP. IV.
1720.

The BURATY are stout active men, but hate all kind of labour. For, though they have the example of the RUSSIANS plowing and sowing their ground, and living plentifully on the produce of this rich and fertile soil, they chuse still to live in their tents, and tend their flocks, on which their subsistence intirely depends.

The chief exercise of the men is hunting and riding. They have a good breed of saddle-horses; and their horned cattle are very large. Their sheep have broad tails, and their mutton is excellent. They have also great abundance of goats. For all these animals they make no provision of fodder; but leave them to feed in the open fields. When the snow falls to a great depth, which seldom happens in these parts, they drive them southward to rising grounds, where little snow lies.

Their arms are bows and arrows, lances and sabres; all of which are used on horse-back; for, like the KALMUCKS, they have no infantry. They are dexterous archers, and skilful horsemen.

These people were formerly subject to a prince of the MONGALS; but now live very quietly under the RUSSIAN government. They are at present a very numerous people, reaching towards the east and south
of

of the BAYKALL lake; and are generally reckoned very honest and sincere.

As to their dress, the men wear a coat, or rather gown, of sheep-skins, girt about the middle, in all seasons; a small round cap, faced with fur, having a tassel of red silk at the top; which, together with a pair of drawers and boots, makes up the whole of their apparel. The women's dress is nearly the same; only their gowns are plaited about the waist, and hang down like a petticoat. The married women have their hair hanging in two locks, one on each side of the head, drawn through two iron rings to prevent its floating on the breast; and looking very like a tye-wig. Round their fore-head they wear a hoop of polished iron, made fast behind; and on their head a small round cap, faced with fur, and embroidered, in their fashion, to distinguish it from those of the men. The maids are dressed in the same manner; only, their hair is all plaited, hanging in separate locks round their head, and is as black as a raven; some of them have good complexions. Both the men and women are courteous in their behaviour. I should like them much better if they were a little more cleanly. Both their persons and tents are extremely nasty, from their using only

skins

skins to preserve them from the cold; on these they sit, or lie, round a little fire, in their tents.

The religion of the BURATY seems to be the same with that of the KALMUCKS, which is downright Paganism of the grossest kind. They talk indeed of an almighty and good being, who created all things, whom they call BURCHUN; but seem bewildered, in obscure and fabulous notions, concerning his nature and government. They have two high priests, to whom they pay great respect; one is called Delay-Lama, the other Kutuchtu. Of these priests I shall have an opportunity to give some account afterwards.

In passing the tents of the BURATY, I often observed a long pole; whereon was hung, by the horns, the head and skin of a sheep. On inquiring the reason of this appearance, I was told that the animal, whose head and skin these were, had been slain, and offered in sacrifice, to the God who protected their flocks and herds. I could observe no images among them, except some relicks given them by their priests, which they had from the Delay-Lama; these are commonly hung up in a corner of their tents, and sometimes about their necks, by way of an amulet, to preserve them from misfortunes.

The 16th, we came to another large village, called KAMENKA, situated on the north bank of the river, where we found many of the BURATY in their tents. This day we had some rain, which melted much snow, and made it dangerous to travel upon the ice; so that we were obliged to leave the river, and make the best of our way along the banks; for several of our horses broke through the ice, and were got up again with no small difficulty.

The 17th, our route lay to the south-east. The alteration of the weather was now very perceptible; the heat of the sun was very intense, and the snow suddenly disappeared, leaving no marks of winter, except the ice upon the river, which was vanishing very fast. Thus, in the space of a few days, we passed from a cold winter to a warm spring; and one would almost have imagined we had been imperceptibly dropped into another climate. Our sledges, in which we had travelled and lodged, for most part, during the winter, could now be of no use; and we left them to be put on wheel carriages, in order to follow us as should be convenient.

Having procured such horses and furniture as the place afforded, we proceeded along the north bank of

CHAP. IV.　the ANGARA, towards IRKUTSKY. We were escorted
1720.　by some COSSACKS, and a party of the BURATY, armed
with bows and arrows. We hunted all the way as we travelled; and were not a little surprised to see the BURATY kill many hares with their arrows. This exercise was very seasonable, as we had been confined to sledges for more than three months, during our journey from CAZAN to this place.

On the 18th of March, we arrived at the town of IRKUTSKY, so called from the rivulet IRKUT, which falls into the ANGARA near it. It stands on the north bank of the ANGARA, in a large plain, to the north of which the grounds are very high, and covered with woods. On the south side of the river, towards the BAYKALL lake, are high hills, rising to the south, and covered with tall trees; among which are many larinxes and SIBERIAN cedars. The larinx, called in RUSS lisvinitza, is a well known tree in these parts; near the root of it grows a famous drug, called agarick, in form of a mushroom. It sheds its leaf in autumn, and in summer it looks like a pine; it grows very straight and tall, and is reckoned good timber for ship-building; it bears a cone like the fir-tree, containing the seed, but not half so large.

What

What is called the cedar is a large tall tree, which never shades the leaf; it is white and smooth, but has not the least smell of cedar. They use it chiefly in building houses; and it makes the finest white floors, and freest from knots, of any wood I know. The leaves are like those of a pine; but grow in tassels, very beautiful. The cones are large; and, instead of seed like the fir, contain a small nut with a kernel; of which the people in this country are very fond, and eat it by way of a desert, in place of better fruit. It has a pleasant taste, like that of raisins; and is esteemed good for the stomach.

The town of IRKUTSKY is fortified with a ditch, and strong palisades, having towers at certain distances. The garrison consists of some regular troops, besides a number of cossacks, or the militia of the country. The town contains about two thousand houses; and the inhabitants are plentifully supplied with provisions of all kinds, from the neighbouring villages. The adjacent woods abound with variety of game. The river affords sturgeon, and many other kinds of fish, but no sterlet; because, as I apprehend, they delight in muddy streams; and the water at this place

place is so clear, that, in two fathoms depth, one may see the pebbles at the bottom.

At IRKUTSKY is a good market for furs of all sorts, and likewise for many kinds of CHINESE goods. All merchandise must be entered at the custom-house, in this place, and pays a duty of ten per cent; which produces a considerable revenue to his majesty.

The 25th of March, our baggage arrived, after surmounting many difficulties on the road. They had been obliged to leave many of the sledges, after taking the baggage off them, and putting it on wheel-carriages.

Our design was to have crossed the BAYKALL sea upon the ice, and then proceeded, by land, to the town of SELINGINSKY; but we came too late for that purpose. The season was so far advanced, that, before our carriages arrived, the river was almost free of ice. We were informed, indeed, that the ice, upon the lake, was sufficiently strong to bear horses; but, upon considering the matter, it was thought most advisable to remain here, till the ice in the sea was also melted, that we might go by water to SELINGINSKY; and orders were immediately given that vessels should be prepared for this purpose.

April

April 1ſt, we croſſed the river, accompanied by Mr. RAKITIN the commandant, in order to take a view of the country towards the ſouth. We rode through fine woods, of ſtately oaks and other trees, formerly mentioned. We hunted all the way, and found abundance of game. At laſt, we came to a ſmall RUSSIAN village, in a fruitful valley, encompaſſed with hills covered with woods, where we lodged. Next day we went ten or a dozen miles farther, in ſearch of wild beaſts; but, finding none, we returned to the ſame village, and the day following to IRKUTSKY.

The 10th, we were entertained with a famous BURATSKY ſhaman, who was alſo a lama, or prieſt, and was brought from a great diſtance. As theſe ſhamans make a great noiſe in this part of the world, and are believed, by the ignorant vulgar, to be inſpired, I ſhall give ſome account of the behaviour of this one, in particular, by which it will appear that the whole is an impoſition.

He was introduced to the ambaſſador by the commandant, accompanied by ſeveral chiefs of his own tribe, who treat him with great reſpect. He was a man of about thirty years of age, of a grave aſpect and deportment. At his introduction he had a cup of
brandy

brandy presented to him, which he drank, but refused any more.

After some conversation, he was desired to exhibit some specimen of his art; but he replied, he could do nothing in a RUSSIAN house; because there were some images of saints, which prevented his success. The performance was therefore adjourned to a BURATSKY tent in the suburbs. Accordingly, in the evening, we went to the place appointed, where we found the shaman, with several of his companions, round a little fire, smoking tobacco; but no women among them. We placed ourselves on one side of the tent, leaving the other for him and his countrymen. After sitting about half an hour, the shaman placed himself crosslegged upon the floor, close by a few burning coals upon the hearth, with his face towards his companions; then he took two sticks, about four feet long each, one in each hand, and began to sing a dismal tune, beating time with the sticks; all his followers joined in the chorus. During this part of the performance, he turned and distorted his body into many different postures, till, at last, he wrought himself up to such a degree of fury that he foamed at the mouth, and his eyes looked red and staring. He now started up up on his legs, and fell a dancing, like one diftracted, till he trode out the fire with his bare feet. Thefe unnatural motions were, by the vulgar, attributed to the operations of a divinity; and, in truth, one would almoft have imagined him poffeffed by fome demon. After being quite fpent with dancing, he retired to the door of the tent, and gave three dreadful fhrieks, by which, his companions faid, he called the demon to direct him in anfwering fuch queftions as fhould be propofed. He then returned, and fat down in great compofure, telling he was ready to refolve any queftion that might be asked. Several of our people put queftions in abundance; all which he anfwered readily, but in fuch ambiguous terms that nothing could be made of them. He now performed feveral legerdemain tricks; fuch as ftabbing himfelf with a knife, and bringing it up at his mouth, running himfelf through with a fword, and many others too trifling to mention. In fhort, nothing is more evident than that thefe fhamans are a parcel of jugglers, who impofe on the ignorant and credulous vulgar.

The 6th of April, we went to a monaftery, about five miles to the weftward of this place, where we dined with the archbifhop of TOBOLSKY. This prelate had

had lately come hither to visit some monasteries; and, in his way, had baptized a number of OSTEAKS and other heathens. From this time till the 8th of May, little material happened. We waited patiently for the dissolving of the ice on the BAYKALL lake, of which we expected to receive the most certain knowledge by means of the floating-ice on the ANGARA; for, when this happens, that river is filled with floating-cakes, which are driven along with great fury by the wind and current.

The 11th, the river was now clear of ice. Our baggage was shipped on board large flat-bottomed boats, and drawn up the stream; the wind being southerly made the progress of the boats very slow. The ambassador therefore resolved to remain at this place, till he heard they had nearly reached the lake, which is about forty verst from IRKUTSKY.

Before we left this place, Mr. KREMENSKY, our interpreter for the LATIN tongue, died of a hectick disorder. He was a POLISH gentleman, and had laboured under this distemper for some years.

CHAP.

CHAPTER V.

From IRKUTSKY, *cross the lake* BAYKALL, *to* SELINGINSKY; *some account of the* KUTUCHTU, *&c.*

THE 15th of May, the weather being very hot, we did not set out till after dinner, when we left IRKUTSKY, accompanied by the commandant and some other officers of the place. We rode along the north bank of the river, through pleasant woods, and some open fields, till we came, about midnight, to a few fishermen's huts, where we halted for a few hours, and repeated our journey early next morning.

At noon, we arrived at a small chapel, dedicated to ST. NICOLAS, where travellers usually pay their devotions, and pray for a prosperous passage over the lake. About this religious house there are a few fishermen's huts. Two monks constantly attend, to put people in mind of their duty, and receive a small gratuity from the passengers.

Here we found our boats, waiting for us, below the falls of the ANGARA. From hence you can see the lake, bursting out betwixt two high rocks, and tumbling down over huge stones, that ly quite cross the river, which I reckon to be about an ENGLISH mile broad. The whole channel of the river is covered with these rocks, from the mouth of the lake down to the chapel of ST. NICOLAS, about the distance of an ENGLISH mile. There is no passage for the smallest boats, except along the east shore, through a narrow strait, between the rocks and the land. In the most shallow places there is about five or six feet water, and breadth, all the way, sufficient for any single vessel. But if, by stress of weather, or any other accident, a boat should have the misfortune to miss this opening, and be thrown upon the rocks, she must immediately be dashed to pieces, and the whole crew inevitably perish. The waters, dashing upon the stones, make a noise like the roaring of the sea; so that people near them can scarce hear one another speak. I cannot express the awfulness with which one is struck, at the sight of such astonishing scenes of nature as appear round this place, and which, I believe, are not to be equalled in the known world. The pilots and sailors, who navigate the lake, speak of it with much reverence; calling it the Holy Sea, and the mountains about it, the Holy Mountains; and are highly displeased with any person, who speaks of it with disrespect, or calls it a lake. They tell

tell a ſtory of a certain pilot, who always gave it that appellation, but was ſeverely puniſhed for his contempt. Being on a voyage in autumn, he and his crew were toſſed from ſide to ſide of the lake, till they were half-ſtarved, and in great danger of periſhing. Neceſſity, at laſt, forced this hardy mariner to comply with the prevailing cuſtom, and pray to the Holy Sea and Mountains to have compaſſion on him in ſuch diſtreſs. His prayers were effectual, and he arrived ſafe to land; but was obſerved, ever after, to ſpeak of the ſea with the greateſt reſpect.

The afternoon was ſpent in adjuſting the tackle, and preparing the barques for being drawn up the ſtrong narrow current.

The 17th, the wind being contrary, and blowing pretty freſh, the pilots would not venture out. I, and three more of our company, took this opportunity of walking up to the top of the mountains, where we had a full view of the ſea, and the land to the ſouth, on the other ſide of it, and alſo to the weſt as far as it extends. The land on the ſouth ſide of the lake riſes gradually, till it terminates in hills moſtly covered with wood; but, on the weſtern ſhore, there are very high mountains, ſeveral whereof are overſpread with deep ſnow,

snow, which we could easily discern, though at a great distance.

The BAYKALL sea, opposite to the mouth of the SE-LINGA, is reckoned about fifty ENGLISH miles broad, though it is much broader in some other places; and about three hundred miles in length. It is wholly fresh water, and is supplied by the SELINGA and many other rivers, from the south, and by the higher ANGARA from the east. The course of the sea is from south-west to north-east, and has very few shelves or rocks. There is only one large island, near the middle of it, called OLCHON. It is bounded on the north by a ridge of high rocks, which run from one end of it to the other. The only opening, by which it discharges itself, is that into the ANGARA; which, though it is a natural passage, appears as if cut through the rocks by art. In my opinion, one cannot imagine a more beautiful prospect of nature, than is seen from the top of these mountains; which may easily be perceived from the short and imperfect sketch I have drawn of it. The woods, on the summit of the rocks, are short, and thinly scattered; but, on their declivity towards the north, and in the valleys, the trees become gradually both taller and larger. There is abundance of game and

and wild beasts in these woods, particularly the wild boar, which was the first of that species we found in this country; a certain sign of a temperate climate; for these animals cannot endure the excessive cold in more northerly parts. The hunting of these animals being a dangerous kind of sport, we carefully avoided their haunts. In the evening we returned to our barques at the chapel of ST. NICOLAS.

The BAYKALL is abundantly furnished with various kinds of excellent fish; particularly sturgeon, and a fish called omully, in shape and taste resembling a herring, but broader and larger. The sea produces also great numbers of seals, whose skins are prefered, in quality, to those of seals caught in salt-water. I am of opinion, that both the seals and fish in the BAYKALL came originally from the NORTHERN ocean, as the communication between them is open, though the distance be very great.

The seals are generally caught in winter, by strong nets hung under the ice. The method they use, is, to cut many holes in the ice, at certain distances from one another, so that the fishermen can, with long poles, stretch their nets from one hole to another, and thus continue them to any distance. The seals, not being able

able to bear long confinement under the ice for want of air, seek these holes for relief; and thus entangle themselves in the nets. These creatures indeed commonly make many holes for themselves, at the setting in of the frost. In this manner they catch not only seals, but fish of all kinds, in winter.

The 18th, the wind being favourable, we put off from ST. NICOLAS's. As we had workmen enough, we left part of them on board to assist the pilot, by setting poles; while the rest were employed on shore, in towing the barques against a strong current. In about the space of three hours we got clear of the current, and all hands came on board. We were now quite becalmed, and obliged to take to our oars. We rowed along shore to the eastward, till about noon; when we had an easy breeze, which soon carried us two-thirds over the sea, under our main-sail. The wind now chopped about to the east, and blew so fresh, that we could not make the river SELINGA; which was the port where we intended to land. As these barques cannot turn to windward, we were drove about ten miles to the westward of the POSSOLLSKY monastery; which stands about six miles to the westward of the SELINGA, in a pleasant and fruitful plain, furnishing an extensive view

view in all directions; where, endeavouring to get to land at any rate, we steered into a bay, in which, we fancied, we saw the shore covered with cockle-shells or white sand. On a nearer approach our mistake appeared. For what seemed shells or sand, at a distance, was only great and small cakes of ice, beating with the waves against the main body of the ice; which lay firm, and covered the whole bay. Our people, on distinguishing the ice, immediately struck sail, and were in no small confusion. But Mr. ISMAELOFF ordered the sail to be again set, and to steer directly for the ice. In the mean time, all hands were employed in hanging boards about the bow of the vessel, to prevent the cutting of the planks; and in setting poles to push off the large cakes. At last we came among the ice, which made a terrible rattling at first; but the farther we advanced, the easier our barque lay, till we came to the main body of the ice, where she remained as unmoved, as if she had been in a mill-pond, though it still continued to blow hard. We now quitted the ship, and walked about upon the ice, which was yet strong enough to carry horses. By this time the sun was set, which prevented our design of going ashore; for the distance was, at least, five ENGLISH miles; and there was a great gap in the ice near the place where we lay.

About midnight the wind turned westerly; and at break of day we left our station, and sailed to the eastward; and, about noon, entered the river SELINGA; where we found our other three barques. They, having been two or three miles before us the preceeding night, had time enough to reach anchoring-ground; and, by this means, escaped the ice, so little expected at this season of the year. We ourselves, before entering the bay, had sounded, in order to discover whether we could come to an anchor; but no bottom could be found, though we joined several lead-lines together, amounting to above one hundred and fifty fathoms.

The mouth of the SELINGA is surrounded with tall reeds, and contains several islands. The entry into it is very difficult, except the wind be fair, because of many flats and sand-banks, thrown up by the current of the river. Here we found great flocks of all kinds of water-fowl, particularly snipes.

The wind continuing fair, we sailed up the river to a small oratory, dedicated also to ST. NICOLAS, where all hands went ashore to return thanks for their safe passage.

passage. The prior of the POSSOLSKY monastery came to this place to salute the ambassador; and brought a present of fish, and such other provisions as these religious houses afford.

In the evening we proceeded up the river, till night overtook us, when we hauled our boats close to the bank, and lay till next morning, which was the 20th of May. This day being calm, the barques were towed up the river; and we walked along the banks, hunting all the way in a very pleasant country. At night we lay by, as formerly.

The 21st, the weather was very hot. We continued our voyage in the same manner as before.

The 22d, the wind being fair, we hoisted sails, and, in the evening, arrived at a large village, well built and peopled, called KABBANSKY OSTROGUE. This place is pleasantly situated, on a rising ground upon the west bank of the river, surrounded with many corn-fields and much pasturage. Here we took new hands on board our barques, and dismissed the former to return in open boats to IRKUTSKY.

The 25th, we reached another large village, called BOLSHOY ZAIMKA, situated in a fertile country. In the neighbourhood is a small monastery, and many lesser villa-

villages. Many of the BURATY were encamped, with their flocks and herds, on both sides of the river.

The climate on this side of the BAYKALL lake is much more temperate than on the north side. The land produces rich crops of wheat, rye, barley, oats, buck-wheat, and peafe; besides kitchen roots, and other garden stuff. The inhabitants have not yet begun to plant any kind of fruit-trees; which, I am persuaded, would thrive exceedingly; as the winters are short, and the snow does not ly above six weeks or two months. The banks of the river appeared very pleasant; being finely varied with plains and woods.

The 26th, we came to a large town, called UDINSKY, from the rivulet UDA, which runs into the SELINGA, on the east bank. This place also stands in a fertile plain, having high hills covered with woods towards the east.

In these hills are found several rich ores, particularly of lead; in digging which many hands are now employed. The miners say it is of too hard a quality; however, they have extracted considerable quantities of silver from it; and I have been informed that they also found some veins of silver ore. As these works are but lately begun, it is not doubted that they are

capable

capable of great improvement, at an easy charge, as the metal lies so near the surface. Samples of these ores have been sent to ST. PETERSBURG; and, I am informed, his majesty has engaged some GERMAN miners to make experiments upon them.

Both here and on the ANGARA, iron is to be found, in great abundance, at the very surface. But, as the distance is too great for exportation, it is not worth the labour. To supply the common consumption of the country, the smith takes his bellows, goes to the mine, and smelts and works as much iron as he needs. I have seen some of this iron of an excellent, soft, and pliable quality.

Besides the above mentioned, there are at this place very rich mines of copper. I have seen some of the ore with large veins of pure copper running through it. I make no doubt but time and future discoveries will bring these mines to perfection, to the great emolument of the RUSSIAN empire.

All this country is under the jurisdiction of the commandant of IRKUTSKY, who sends deputies to all the towns of this extensive province, to administer justice, and take care of his majesty's revenues. The power of nominating sub-governors and commandants, is vested, by his majesty, in the governor of SIBERIA; which gives him an authority equal to a sovereign prince.

The ambassador, finding the progress of the boats, against the stream, very slow and tedious; being besides much pestered with gnats and muskitoes; resolved to go by land, the rest of the way, to SELINGINSKY. For which purpose, the superintendant of this place ordered horses, and a proper escort, to be got ready against next morning, on the other side of the river; the road on this side being interrupted by thick woods and deep rivers.

The 27th, having sent off our barques, we crossed the river; and, having no baggage, we soon mounted. The road lay through a fine plain, covered with excellent grass. In the evening we came to a fountain of pure water, where we lodged in the tents of the BURATY, and slept on bull-hides.

The 28th, early, we proceeded; travelling over some pretty high hills overgrown with wood. About noon we came to a river called ORONGOY, which we crossed on a tall camel; it being too deep for horses. At this place we found a number of the BURATY encamped, with their flocks grazing in the neighbourhood.

Our

Our horses having swom the river, we went into one of the BURATSKY tents, till they were dried. The hospitable landlady immediately set her kettle on the fire, to make us some tea; the extraordinary cookery of which I cannot omit describing. After placing a large iron-kettle over the fire, she took care to wipe it very clean with a horse's tail, that hung in a corner of the tent for that purpose; then the water was put into it, and, soon after, some coarse bohea tea, which is got from CHINA, and a little salt. When near boiling, she took a large brass-ladle and tossed the tea, till the liquor turned very brown. It was now taken off the fire, and, after subsiding a little, was poured clear into another vessel. The kettle being wiped clean with the horse's tail, as before, was again set upon the fire. The mistress now prepared a paste, of meal and fresh butter, that hung in a skin near the horse's tail, which was put into the tea-kettle and fried. Upon this paste the tea was again poured; to which was added some good thick cream, taken out of a clean sheep's skin, which hung upon a peg among the other things. The ladle was again employed, for the space of six minutes, when the tea, being removed from the fire, was allowed to stand a while in order

der to cool. The landlady now took some wooden cups, which held about half a pint each, and served her tea to all the company. The principal advantage of this tea is, that it both satisfies hunger and quenches thirst. I thought it not disagreeable; but should have liked it much better had it been prepared in a manner a little more cleanly. Our bountiful hostess, however, gave us a hearty welcome; and, as these people know not the use of money, there was nothing to pay for our entertainment. We only made her a present of a little tobacco to smoke, of which these people are very fond. I have given this receipt with a view that some EUROPEAN ladies may improve upon it.

After this short repast, we mounted again; and, in the evening, came to a neat RUSSIAN village, on the front of a pleasant hill covered with wood. This place is surrounded with extensive valleys, and fine pasturage; and our accommodation was better than the preceeding night. Here we met Mr. FIRSOFF, colonel of the cossacks, or militia of SELINGINSKY, with a squadron of horse, armed with bows and arrows, and some firelocks, who came to escort the ambassador to that place.

The 29th of May, we mounted early, and, by means of

of our coffacks, hunted and ranged the woods, as we went along, in the manner of this country, called ob-lave in the RUSSIAN language. Their method is to form a femicircle of horfemen, armed with bows and arrows, in order to inclofe the game. Within the femicircle a few young men are placed, who give notice when the game is fprung; thefe only are permitted to purfue, the others being confined to keep their ranks. Our coffacks, with their arrows, killed three deer, and feveral hares. And, if killing harmlefs animals can be called diverfion, this may properly be reckoned one of the fineft. After this fafhion they hunt bears, wolves, foxes, and wild boars.

About noon we came to a village on the SELINGA, where we halted a few hours, and then croffed the river in boats; which was near a mile broad at this place. Our coffacks, however, fought no boats, except one to tranfport their arms, cloaths, and faddles; which being done, all of them mounted their horfes, and plunged into the river without the leaft concern. As foon as the horfes were fet a fwimming, for eafe to them the men difmounted, and, laying hold of the mane with one hand, guided them gently by the bridle with the other. This is the common method in this coun-

country of transporting men and horses; which I look upon to be both safe and easy, provided the horse is managed with a gentle hand, without checking him with sudden jerks of the bridle.

We halted a little, after crossing the river, till the horses were dried; after which we mounted, and, in the evening, arrived at the town of SELINGINSKY; where we intended to wait for our barques, and the rest of our people.

SELINGINSKY is situated on the east bank of the noble river SELINGA, in a deep, barren, sandy soil, that produces almost nothing. The choice of this situation was extremely injudicious; for, had the founders gone but half a mile further down, to the place where now the inhabitants have their gardens, they would have had a situation, in every respect, preferable to the present.

This place consists of about two hundred houses, and two churches, which are all of them built with wood. It is defended by a fortification of strong palisades, on which are mounted some cannon.

About a mile eastward of the town is a ridge of high hills, quite covered with wood. On the other side of the river, the country is open, dry, and somewhat barren; but affords excellent pasture, particularly for

for sheep, whereof the BURATY, the inhabitants, have large flocks. They are of that kind which hath broad tails, and their mutton is very good. These people have, besides, a large sort of horned cattle, and abundance of horses and camels, wherein all their riches consist. Here ends the tribe of the BURATY, and the nation of the MONGALLS begins.

The MONGALLS are a numerous people, and occupy a large extent of country, from this place to the KALL-GAN, which signifies the Everlasting Wall, or the great wall of CHINA. From this wall they stretch themselves northward as far as the river AMOOR; and from the AMOOR, westward, to the BAYKALL sea; where they border with the territories of the Kontaysha, or prince of the BLACK KALMUCKS. On the south, they are bounded by a nation called TONGUTS, among whom the Delay-Lama has his residence. One may easily imagine, from the vast track of land which the MONGALLS occupy, that they must be very numerous; especially, when it is considered, that they live in a healthy climate, and have been engaged in no wars, since they were conquered, partly by the RUSSIANS on the west, and partly by the CHINESE on the east; to whom all these people are now tributaries. In former times the

CHAP. V.
1720.

MONGALLS were troublesome neighbours to the CHI‑NESE, against whose incursions the great wall was built.

KAMHI, the present Emperor of CHINA, was the first who subdued these hardy TARTARS; which he effected more by kind usage and humanity than by his sword; for these people are great lovers of liberty. The same gentle treatment hath been observed by the RUSSIANS, towards those of them who are their subjects. And they themselves confess, that, under the protection of these two mighty Emperors, they enjoy more liberty, and live more at ease, than they formerly did under their own princes.

The present Prince of MONGALIA is called Tush-du-Chan, and resides about six days journey, to the south-east, from SELINGINSKY. The place is called URGA, and is near to where the Kutuchtu, or high priest, inhabits. When the MONGALLS submitted themselves to the Emperor of CHINA, it was agreed, that the Tush-du-Chan should still maintain the name and authority of a prince over his people; but undertake no war, nor expedition, without consent of the Emperor; which has strictly been observed ever since.

It is very remarkable, that, in all the vast dominions

of MONGALIA, there is not so much as a single house to be seen. All the people, even the prince and high priest, live constantly in tents; and remove, with their cattle, from place to place, as conveniency requires.

These people do not trouble themselves with ploughing, or digging the ground in any fashion; but are content with the produce of their flocks. Satisfied with necessaries, without aiming at superfluities, they pursue the most ancient and simple manner of life; which, I must confess, I think very pleasant in such a mild and dry climate.

From the river VOLGA, to the wall of CHINA, there are three great TARTAR princes; the Ayuka-Chan, the Kontaysha, and the Tush-du-Chan. These three mighty nations have almost the same features, religion, and language; and live in the same manner. It will easily be perceived, by casting an eye on the map, what an extent of territory these princes possess, whose subjects go by the general name of KALMUKS. Few languages can carry a traveller over a greater extent of country than that of the KALMUKS. With the ARABIC, indeed, a person may travel, through many places of the east, from EGYPT to the court of the Great Mogul; but, with the ILLYRIC, he can travel much further than

than with either of the former; viz. from the GULF of VENICE to the outmost boundaries of KAMTZATSKY; for the RUSSIAN is a dialect of the ILLYRIC.

The greatest part of MONGALIA is one continued waste; except the places along the AMOOR, and towards the RUSSIAN borders on the west. The soil also, to the south, from SELINGINSKY, is exceedingly fine; and capable, by proper culture, of producing grain of several sorts.

Since I have mentioned the AMOOR, I presume this will be no improper place to give some account of that river. It is called by the TARTARS SHAGGALYN-OULLA, or the BLACK DRAGON, I suppose from the colour of its waters, and the windings of its course. It is formed of two large rivers, whose sources are in the desert, far to the eastward of this place. One is called ARGUN, which issues from a lake named DELAY; the other is INCODA, on the north bank of which stands the famous RUSSIAN town NERTZINSKY. The conflux of these rivers produces the AMOOR, which runs towards the east, augmenting daily by means of the many great and small streams it receives, till it becomes one of the largest rivers in this part of the word; and, after a long course, discharges itself into the EASTERN or CHI-

NESE.

nese ocean. It is remarkable, that, from CAZAN to these parts, the AMOOR is the only river that runs eastward. Most, if not all, of the great rivers in SIBERIA have their courses to the north, and north-west.

Our barques arrived at SELINGINSKY on the 4th of June. After we had taken out of them what necessaries we wanted, they were dispatched with the rest of the baggage, for the greater security, to his Majesty's store-houses at STREALKA, about four miles up the river, where the caravan for CHINA then lay.

In the mean time, the ambassador writ a letter to the Allegada, or prime minister, at the imperial court of PEKIN, to notify his arrival; and desire his excellency would give orders for his reception on the borders. This letter was sent to the prince of MONGALIA, to be by him forwarded to court; for no strangers are allowed to travel through his territories to CHINA, without his permission. The officer, who carried the letter to the prince, was treated with great civility; and his letter immediately sent to court by an express. A few days after, the prince sent two gentlemen, one of whom was a lama, to congratulate the ambassador on his arrival in these parts. They were invited to dine with the ambassador, and behaved very decently.

The

CHAP. V.
1720.

The same officer, who carried the ambassador's letter to the prince of MONGALIA at URGA, was ordered to present his compliments to the Kutuchtu, or high priest, who is a near relation of the prince. He received the officer in a very friendly manner, desired him to sit down in his presence; an honour granted to very few, except ambassadors, and pilgrims from remote countries; and, at his departure, gave him a present of some inconsiderable things; particularly, a few pieces of CHINESE silks.

I cannot leave this venerable personage, without taking some notice of him. I shall therefore relate a few things concerning him, among thousands more ridiculous, which the people in this country tell and believe.

This extraordinary man assumes to himself the character of omniscience, which is the interpretation of the word Kutuchtu; and the people are taught to believe that he really knows all things, past, present, and future. As his intelligence, by means of his lamas, is very extensive, he is easily able to impose on the vulgar in this particular. They also believe that he is immortal; not that his body lives always; but that his soul, upon the decay of an old one, immediately transmigrates

into

into some young human body; which, by certain marks, the lamas discover to be animated by the soul of the Kutuchtu, and he is accordingly treated as high priest.

When the spirit of the Kutuchtu has taken possession of a new body, that is, in plain ENGLISH, when he is dead, the lamas are immediately employed to discover in what part of the world this wonderful person is regenerated, or born again, as they express it. They need, however, go to no great distance to find him; for, the affair being previously concerted among the chief lamas, they soon determine the choice of a successor; who generally happens to be a young boy, that has been well instructed how to behave on that occasion. When a successor is pretended to be found, a company of lamas are sent to examine the matter, who carry along with them many toys, such as small silver bells, and things of that nature, which belonged to the former Kutuchtu, intermixed with others that did not. All these are laid before the child, who picks out such things as belonged to his predecessor, and discovers the greatest fondness for them; but rejects, with disgust, whatever is not genuine. Besides this trial, some questions are put to him, relative to wars, or remarkable events, in his former state; all which are answered

answered to the satisfaction of the conclave. Whereupon he is unanimously declared to be the self-same Kutuchtu, is conducted with great pomp and ceremony to URGA, and lodged in the tent of the high priest.

Till the new Kutuchtu arrives at a certain age, he is entirely under the government of the lamas; and few are permitted to see him, except at a great distance, and even then it is not easy to get access to him. It may seem surprising, that, in so numerous an assembly of lamas, no intrigues should be carried on, nor disputes arise, among the electors. All is conducted without noise or contention. It is however imagined, that the authority of the prince greatly contributes to their unanimity.

The MONGALLS relate, that their Kutuchtu has now lived fourteen generations, and renews his age every moon; for, at the new moon, he appears like a youth; when she is full, like a full-grown man; but, when near the change, he is an old man with grey hairs.

What they call the URGA is the court, or the place where the prince and high priest reside; who are always encamped at no great distance from one another. They have several thousand tents about them, which

are

are removed from time to time. The URGA is much frequented by merchants, from CHINA, and RUSSIA, and other places; where all trade is carried on by barter, without money of any kind. The CHINESE bring hither ingots of gold, damasks, and other silk and cotton stuffs, tea, and some porcelain; which are generally of an inferior quality, and proper for such a market. The RUSSIAN commodities are chiefly furs of all sorts. Rhubarb is the principal article which is exchanged for these goods, great quantities whereof are produced in this country, without any culture. The MONGALLS gather and dry it in autumn; and bring it to this market, where it is bought up, at an easy rate, both by the RUSSIAN and CHINESE merchants.

The Kutuchtu and his lamas are all clothed in yellow, and no layman is allowed to wear this colour, except the Prince. This mark of distinction makes them known and respected every where. They also wear about their necks a string of beads, which are used in saying their prayers. The MONGALLS believe in, and worship, one Almighty Creator of all things. They hold that the Kutuchtu is GOD's vicegerent on earth; and that there will be a state of future rewards and punishments.

CHAP. V.
1720.

The following relation, which I had from a RUSSIAN merchant, to whom the thing happened, will show the methods taken by these lamas, to maintain the dignity and character of their mighty high-priest. This merchant had gone to the URGA, with an intention to trade with the CHINESE. While he was at this place, some pieces of damask were stollen out of his tent. He made a complaint to some of the lamas, with whom he was acquainted; and the matter was soon brought before the Kutuchtu, who immediately ordered proper steps to be taken with a view to find out the thief. The affair was conducted in this uncommon manner; one of the lamas took a bench with four feet, which seems to have been of the conjuring kind; after turning it, several times, in different directions, at last it pointed directly to the tent where the stollen goods lay concealed. The lama now mounted astride on the bench, and soon carried it, or, as was commonly believed, it carried him to the very tent; where he ordered the damask to be produced. The demand was directly complied with; for it is in vain, in such cases, to offer any excuse.

I shall now subjoin a few observations on the Delay-Lama, or priest of the desert, who is reckoned still

supe-

superior to the Kutuchtu. He lives about a month's journey to the south-east of this place, among a people called the TONGUTS, who use a different language from the KALMUCKS. I am informed that the religion of the TONGUTS is the same with that of the MONGALLS: that they hold the same opinions with respect to the transmigration of the Delay-Lama, as the MONGALLS do about the Kutuchtu, and that he is elected in the same manner. What appears most surprising is, that these two mighty Lamas keep a good correspondence, and never encroach on one another's priviledges. The word *delay* signifies either the sea, or a great plain, such as this priest inhabits.

CHAPTER VI.

Occurrences at SELINGINSKY; *Several parties of hunting; and journey continued to* SARATZYN, *the boundary between the* RUSSIAN *and* CHINESE *territories.*

THE TONGUTS are a separate people, governed by a Prince whom they call Lazin-Chan. One of their princes was lately killed, in an engagement with the Kontaysha, king of the BLACK KALMUCKS. The Delay-Lama himself narrowly escaped being taken prisoner, notwithstanding all his foresight. The Lama threatened the Kontaysha with many disasters, as the consequences of such proceedings. The Kontaysha, however, regarded them very little, till he had attained his ends; after which, he generously reinstated both the Prince and the Delay-Lama in their former dignity. The Kontaysha is of the same profession with the Delay-Lama, and acknowledges his authority in religious matters.

I am informed there is a third Lama, called Bogdu-Pantzin, of still greater authority than either of the former. But, as he lives at a great distance, near the frontiers of the Great Mogul, he is little known in these parts. Though I am unwilling to throw the least reflection on any society of men instituted for the promotion of religion and virtue, from all I can collect concerning these Lamas, they are little better than shamans of superior dignity.

The answer to the letter, which the ambassador had written to PEKIN, was not yet arrived. In the mean time we were obliged to remain at SELINGINSKY, where we entertained ourselves in the best manner we could.

June the 12th, walking along the bank of the river, I was

I was a little surprised at the figure and dress of a man standing among a number of boys who were angling for small fishes. The person bought all the fishes alive, and immediately let them go again into the river, which he did very gently one by one. The boys were very civil to him, though they looked upon him as distracted on account of his behaviour. During this ceremony he took little notice of me, though I spoke to him several times. I soon perceived, by his dress, and the streak of saffron on his fore-head, that he was one of the Brachmans from INDIA.

After setting all the fish a-swimming, he seemed much pleased; and, having learned a little of the RUSSIAN language, and a smattering of the PORTUGUESE, began to converse with me. I carried him to my lodgings, and offered to entertain him with a dram; but he would taste nothing; for he said, it was against the rules of his religion to eat or drink with strangers.

I asked him the reason why he bought the fish to let them go again. He told me, that, perhaps the souls of some of his deceased friends, or relations, had taken possession of these fishes; and, upon that supposition, it was his duty to relieve them: that, according to their

their law, no animal whatever ought to be killed or eaten; and they always lived on vegetables.

After this interview, we became so familiar that he came every day to visit me. He was a chearful man, about seventy years of age. He had a bush of hair growing on his fore-head, very much matted, and, at least, six feet in length; when it hung loose, it trailed upon the ground behind him; but he commonly wore it wrapped about his head, in form of a turban. The hair was not all his own; but collected as relicks of his friends, and others of his profession, reputed saints; all which he had intermixed, and matted, with his natural hair. Persons of this character are called Faquers, and esteemed sacred every where.

He told me he was a native of INDOSTAN, and had often been at MADRASS, which he called CHINPATAN, and said it belonged to the ENGLISH. This circumstance, added to several others, made me believe he was no impostor, but an innocent kind of creature, as are most of that sect. He came to this country, in company with some others of his countrymen, on a pilgrimage, in order to pay their devotions to the Kutuchtu and Delay-Lama. They had been twelve months on their journey, and had travelled all the way

on

on foot, over many high mountains and waste deserts, where they were obliged to carry their provisions, and even water, on their backs. I showed him a map of ASIA, whereon he pointed out the course of his journey; but found many errors in the geography; and no wonder; since few EUROPEANS would have had the resolution to undertake such a journey as this man had done.

The 14th, a chief named Taysha, of those MONGALLS who are subjects of his majesty, came to pay his respects to the ambassador, who gave him a friendly reception, and kept him to dinner. He was a merry old man, near fourscore, but so vigorous, that he could mount a horse, with as much agility as many young men. He was accompanied with five sons, and many attendants, who treated him with equal respect as a king; and even his sons would not sit down in his presence, till he desired them. I confess it gave me great pleasure to see the decency with which they behaved. One of our company, a pretty fat man, asked the Taysha what he should do in order to be as lean as he was. The old man replied in these few words, 'Eat less, 'and work more:' a saying worthy of HIPPOCRATES himself. In his youth he had been engaged in many

battles

battles with the CHINESE, whom he held in great contempt. As he was a keen sportsman, the ambassador made an appointment with him for a grand hunting match. After which he and his retinue returned to their tents.

The 15th, we dined at STREALKA with the commissary, Mr. STEPNIKOFF, of the caravan going to CHINA. STREALKA is situated, as I formerly observed, about three or four miles up the river from SELINGINSKY, in a fruitful plain of a triangular figure, formed by the conflux of two fine rivers; the STREALKA running from the east, and the SELINGA from the south. This would have been the strongest and most beautiful situation, of any in this province, for the town of SELINGINSKY. I am informed that the founders had a view to this delightful place; but the choice was determined against them by superstitious lots, to which it was referred. This method of chusing situations by lot, has hurt many noble cities, and rendered the work of ages ineffectual to remedy the error.

The same evening we returned, by water, to SELINGINSKY; and, next day, went a hunting to the west of the SELINGA. We had about two hundred cossacks along with us, who followed the common method of

rang-

ranging the woods, mentioned above. We killed six roe-bucks, and many hares. In the evening, we pitched our tents about a fountain, and feasted on venison.

The 16th, early, we left the woods to our right, and descended into a barren plain, where we found great flocks of antelopes. Our people killed about twenty of them. These animals avoid the woods, and frequent the open plains and deserts. They are exceedingly swift and watchful. And so far resemble sheep, that, if one breaks through the circle, the whole flock follows, though an hundred horsemen were in the way; which proves the destruction of many of these creatures. The noise of the arrows, with which they are hunted, contributes much to their confusion. The heads of these arrows are broad, and fixed in a round bit of bone, with two holes in it; which make them whistle as they fly through the air.

At noon, we set up our tents near a lake of brackish water, called SOLONOY-OSERA, or the salt lake. Round the edges lies a thick scurf of salt, as white as snow, which the inhabitants gather for use. Here we found great flocks of water-fowl; such as, swans, geese, ducks. The weather being very hot, we remained till next day.

The 17th, we hunted along the same waste plain, directing our course to the south, towards the river SELINGA. This day also we had very good sport. In the afternoon, we pitched our tents near a spring of fresh water, which is no small rarity in these parched deserts; and is as much regarded here, as a good inn would be in other parts of the world. I found, at this place, a prickly shrub, about three feet high, with a beautiful smooth bark as yellow as gold.

The 18th, in the morning, we had terrible flashes of lightning, accompanied with thunder, and heavy showers of hail and rain; which determined us to leave the plains, and return, by the shortest road, to SELINGINSKY. Besides the game already mentioned, we found many large bustards, which haunt the open country. As it is a very large bird, and rises slowly, our light horsemen killed several of them with their arrows.

The 24th, arrived an officer from the court of PEKIN, sent on purpose to discover the number and quality of the embassy. This gentleman, whose name was TULISHIN, was a MANTSHU TARTAR by birth, and a member of the tribunal for western affairs, with which he was very well acquainted. These officers are called

led Surgutsky by the MONGALLS, and by the EUROPE-
ANS Mandarin, a PORTUGUESE word derived from *man-
do*. He had formerly been in this country, and had
learned the RUSSIAN language. He pretended to have
been employed on some business with the Tush-du-
Chan at URGA; and, hearing of the ambassador's arrival, had come to pay his respects to him. It was however well known, that he was sent to enquire whether
the ambassador came on a friendly errand. He was
received very kindly; and, after he had stayed three days,
and made his observations, returned very well satisfied. At his departure, he told the ambassador, that
orders would soon be given for his reception on the
frontiers; but these could not be issued till his arrival at court, because on his report the whole affair
depended. This wise and cautious nation, jealous of
all the world, suffer none to enter their territories, but
such as bring friendly messages. By this circumstance
we were confined some time longer at SELINGINSKY.

I shall now give a description of the course of the
SELINGA, according to the best information I could
procure from those who had been at its source. The
SELINGA is formed of two other rivers, called the IDYR
and the TZOLATO, coming from the mountains of

KUN-

KUNGAY, far to the southward of this place. It is afterwards joined by two inconsiderable rivers, the ORCHON from the south-east, and the TZIDA from the south-west; and, lastly, by the STREALKA from the east, a little above the town of SELINGINSKY. At this place it is, at least, twice the breadth of the river THAMES; and is navigable a great way above it. The course now is due north, till it discharges itself into the BAYKALL lake. The source of this river is estimated at the distance of ten or twelve days journey above SELINGINSKY, which is the common method of computation in this country. It is plentifully furnished with variety of excellent fish. The omuly, which I formerly described, come in vast shoals from the BAYKALL, in autumn, up this river, to spawn; after which, they return to the sea; so weak, that many of them are carried down floating on the surface of the stream. During the progress of the omuly up the river, the inhabitants of the adjacent villages assemble, with their nets, and catch as many of them as they please. On this occasion the poor take what they can use, and the rest are left upon the banks. These fishes advance, up the river, about ten miles a-day. On their first appearance, the report is soon spread over the country; and, in two or three hours,

hours, the people catch as many as they need, either for present use, or winter provisions. This fish is very agreeable food, either fresh or salted. It is observed, they are much better and fatter, the nearer they are caught to the sea; a plain argument, that, were they caught in the sea, they would still be preferable to any caught in the river. I have often thought, what inestimable treasure these omuly would produce, in other parts of the world; whereas, here, the consumption being small, they are little valued. It is remarkable, that the omuly are not to be found, at any season, in the ANGARA, or other rivers to the north of the BAY-KALL.

July 5th, the Taysha-Batyr arrived, in consequence of his appointment with the ambassador, and brought along with him three hundred men, well mounted, for the chace. This old gentleman had the appellation of Batyr; a title of great respect among the MON-GALLS. It signifies a hero; and is conferred only on those who have signalized themselves, by their courage and conduct, in the field of battle. Besides these MON-GALLS, we carried with us fifty of our cossacks, and our tents, as we proposed to be abroad some days.

Early on the 6th, we took our way to the eastward,

over

CHAP. VI. over high hills, and through tall woods, having almoſt
1720. no underwood to incommode the horſes, or interrupt
our view; which made it very pleaſant. After riding
a few miles, the Tayſha, being maſter of the chace,
ordered his men to extend their lines. The Tayſha
and we were in the center; and often ſaw the game
paſs us, purſued by the horſemen, at full ſpeed, without the leaſt noiſe, but the whiſtling of arrows. The
horſes, being accuſtomed to this kind of ſport, follow
the game as a greyhound does a hare; ſo that the riders lay the bridles on their necks, and attend to nothing but their bows and arrows. One may eaſily imagine the exquiſite entertainment, in ſeeing ſeveral of
theſe horſemen in purſuit of an elk or ſtag through the
valleys. When the animal is driven from the woods,
it flies, for ſafety, to the neareſt rocks. Some of theſe
creatures are nearly as large, and ſtrong, as the horſes
that hunt them. The ſtags are of two kinds; one
called zuber, the ſame with the GERMAN crownhirſh,
but ſomewhat larger. The zuber is large and beautiful, and carries its head almoſt upright, as it runs;
which prevents its horns being entangled with branches
of trees. There are none of them in RUSSIA, nor
even in SIBERIA, except about the BAYKALL lake, and

caſt-eaſtward from it; the places farther to the north being too cold for them. The elk is larger than the ſtag, and ſtronger made; having alſo long branchy horns, but a little flat.

Tired with ſport, we left the hills in the afternoon, and came down into a fine valley, where we pitched our tents, near a pure brook. The Tayſha then ordered all the dead game to be brought before him, and ranged in proper order. We found, that, this day, we had killed no leſs than five large elks, four ſtags, a dozen roe-bucks, ſeveral wolves and foxes, beſides fawns and hares.

The Tayſha cauſed the game to be divided among the huntſmen; who began immediately to dreſs it, ſome of them by boiling, others by broiling, and eat it without either bread, or ſalt. The tails of the ſtags, which, by theſe people, are reckoned very delicate, fell to the Tayſha's ſhare. He cut them into ſlices, and eat them raw. I eat a bit of one of them, and thought it very palatable. The taſte reſembled nothing ſo much as that of freſh caviare. After we had feaſted on variety of excellent veniſon, for we had no other proviſions, we went to reſt, well ſatisfied with the diverſion of the day.

July

CHAP. VI.
1720.

July 7th, early in the morning, we left the plains, and directed our courfe eaftward, in the fame order we obferved the preceeding day. As our fport was much the fame, I need not mention the particulars. About noon we pitched our tents, near a fpring of frefh water, in a valley where the grafs was about two feet long. This circumftance is a proof of the goodnefs of the foil; which, in my opinion, cannot fail, if properly cultivated, to produce any kind of grain. As the weather was exceffively hot, we ftaid in this place till next day.

July 8th, we continued our fport in the woods till noon; when we came into an extenfive plain, in which we fet up our tents, near a fpring of brackifh water. In this place we obferved feveral flocks of antelopes, which we referved for next day's hunting.

In the morning, our Tayfha difpatched fome of his horfemen to the tops of the hills, in order to difcover where the antelopes were feeding; which, as I formerly obferved, are the moft watchful, and, at the fame time, the fwifteft animals in the world. When they returned, we extended our wings to a great diftance, that we might furround thefe creatures with the greater eafe; and, before noon, our people killed above

twenty

twenty of them. After which we returned to our tents, that were left standing in the morning.

July 10th, we took leave of the Tayſha, whoſe tents were to the eaſt of this place, and returned next day to SELINGINSKY.

During this ſhort excurſion, I could not enough admire the beauty of the country through which we paſſed. The gentle riſing of the hills, many of which have their tops only covered with wood, and the fertility of the vales, contribute to form one of the moſt delightful landſkips the world can afford. To this may be added the temperature, and dryneſs, of the climate; in which reſpects this far exceeds any country with which I am acquainted. After mid-ſummer there is almoſt no rain till December, when the ſnow falls; and in ſuch moderate quantities that it does not hinder the cattle from lying abroad all the winter.

In ſurveying theſe fertile plains and pleaſant woods, I have often entertained myſelf with painting, in my own imagination, the neat villages, country ſeats, and farm-houſes, which, in proceſs of time, may be erected on the banks of the rivers, and brows of the hills. There is here waſte land enough to maintain, with eaſy labour, ſeveral EUROPEAN nations, who are, at pre-

CHAP. VI.
1720.

sent, confined to barren and ungrateful soils: and, with regard to the MONGALLS, whose honesty and simplicity of manners are not unamiable, I should like them very well for neighbours.

From what I have read of NORTH AMERICA, I am of opinion, that this country resembles none so much as some of our colonies in that quarter of the world; particularly the inland parts of PENSYLVANIA and MARYLAND. Both countries ly nearly in the same latitude; in the one we find great lakes and mighty rivers; in the other, the BAYKALL sea, and rivers, which, for the length of their course and quantity of water, may be ranked with any in the western world.

Having rested ourselves a few days after our fatigue, on the 16th of July, we set out on another hunting-match, attended by our own cossacks, and a few of the neighbouring MONGALLS. We went, on this occasion, farther northward, and nearer to the BAYKALL lake, than in our former expedition. Our sport was almost of the same kind as already described. I shall only add, that both the stag and elk shed their horns once a year; at which time they retire to thickets, and solitary places, till their horns begin to spring again. It is surprising that animals so large, with such prodigious

gious weight of branchy horns, should run, with almost incredible speed, through the thickest woods, without entangling themselves; but, to avoid this misfortune, they point their noses always parallel to the horizon. When either the elk or stag are closely attacked, they make a vigorous defence both with horns and hoofs. At rutting time, especially, these creatures are so very furious, that it is extremely dangerous for any person to approach their haunts; they will then run at a man full speed, and, if he escapes being wounded by their horns, will trample him to death with their sharp hoofs. As the weather was excessively hot, we kept the field only two days; and then returned to SELIN-GINSKY.

July 20th, another Mandarin arrived from PEKIN, accompanied by an officer from ARGA; who brought a letter to the ambassador from the Tush-du-chan, acquainting him, that he might soon expect a person, properly authorised, to conduct him to the imperial city. No news could be more agreeable. We hoped now to be soon released from this solitary place, and arrive at the end of our journey. We were indeed well enough lodged, and wanted neither the necessaries nor conveniencies of life. The abundance of rural diversions, which this place afforded, coinciding happily with the genius of most of our gentlemen; and the harmony that subsisted among the retinue, though composed of people from most nations in EUROPE, and some from ASIA, contributed not a little to our passing the time very agreeably. Notwithstanding these advantages, and the affability and courteous behaviour of the ambassador, which heightened them all, we were uneasy at being detained so long on the frontiers. We were apprehensive that some accident might happen to prevent our journey; especially, as it was reported among the MONGALLS, that, the Emperor of CHINA, being far advanced in years, was sometimes sick, and not disposed to receive foreign ministers.

The 24th, there fell such a shower of hail-stones as no man then alive had ever seen. It was happy for us we were not then abroad, as the open field affords no kind of shelter. The hail lay some days in the woods, and cooled the air; which, before that time, had been excessively hot. This day the Kutuchtu sent two lamas to compliment the ambassador, to wish him a good journey, and a happy sight of the Emperor, or Boghdoy-chan, as he is called by these people.

August 9th, a courier arrived from PEKIN, who told the

the ambaffador, that he had paffed our conductor on the road; and that we fhould now prepare for our journey to the capital, as that gentleman would arrive in a few days.

On the 24th, our conductor, called LOMY, at laft arrived. He was, by birth, a MANTSHU TARTAR, and a member of the court for the weftern department. After remaining with us for fome days, he returned to YOLLA, a place upon the border, in order to procure horfes and camels for our journey.

September 8th, we fent our baggage by water to STREALKA, and next day we followed it. We lived in tents, while we ftaid at this place, till horfes and camels were got ready. In the mean time, our people were employed in packing up the baggage into proper loads for camels. STREALKA, I formerly obferved, is the place where his majefty's commiffary of the caravan has his abode, and the government of SIBERIA their ftore-houfes. I imagine, therefore, it will not be improper, before we proceed, to give fome account of the trade carried on from this place.

Formerly the fur trade was free to all his majefty's fubjects, both RUSSIANS and TARTARS. The merchants repaired to SIBERIA at the proper feafons, where they
bought

bought, at cheap rates, all the rich furs they could find; and disposed of them in PERSIA, TURKEY, and POLAND, at a price much below the real value. The government of SIBERIA perceived a very considerable diminution of the revenue in that country, and soon discovered the true cause of it; which was, that, a great part of the furs belonging to his majesty remained unsold. Upon inquiry, it appeared that this was owing to the foreign markets being supplied with these commodities, at low rates, by the subjects, before the goods belonging to the government could be exposed to sale. The government of SIBERIA represented to his majesty the loss of so considerable a branch of his revenue; in consequence of which, an order was immediately issued, prohibiting all private persons, for the future, to export sables in particular. Since this regulation took place, the government have sent their own furs, generally once in three years, by caravans, to CHINA. The value of one of these caravans is reckoned to amount to four or five thousand roubles, and yields a return of, at least, double that sum. The Emperor of CHINA, from regard to the friendship and good neighbourhood of his majesty, gives the caravans free quarters, and liberty to dispose of their goods, and buy others, without

out exacting any impoft. At firft the Emperor not
only gave the caravan free quarters, but alfo maintained, at his own charge, both men and horfes, during
their ftay in PEKIN. This laft expreffion of his majefty's bounty is, however, now withdrawn.

September 15th, our conductor having acquainted
the ambaffador that the horfes and camels were ready,
our baggage was difpatched to the frontiers, efcorted
by our own foldiers and fome coffacks; though, indeed,
there was no great occafion for any guard, as the MON-
GALLS feem to have little ufe for any thing that belonged to us.

After dining with the commiffary of the caravan,
at STREALKA, on the 18th, we left that place in the
evening, accompanied with the commiffary and moft
of the officers at SELINGINSKY. After we had travelled about twenty ENGLISH miles to the fouth-eaft,
through fine plains covered with exceeding long grafs,
we arrived at the end of the firft ftage, called KOLLUD-
TZY; where we found our tents, which had been fent off
in the morning, ready for our reception. This day
we faw fome fcattered tents of MONGALIANS, with their
flocks.

Next day, we travelled about twenty miles farther

to a single house, built by the commissary for a shade to his cattle in winter. We hunted all the way through a pleasant country, interspersed with little hills covered with wood; but saw as few inhabitants as the day before.

The 20th, about noon, we reached a place called SARATZYN, or the NEW MOON, situated on the bank of a rivulet of the same name. This rivulet is the boundary between the RUSSIAN and CHINESE territories, and separates two of the most mighty monarchies in the world. The distance between SELINGINSKY and this place is computed to be about one hundred and four verst, nearly seventy ENGLISH miles.

The conductor was encamped on the east side of the rivulet, and we pitched our tents on the other. The ground, on both sides, rises a little, and the soil seems to be extremely good. The grass is rank and thick, and, as the season is very dry, would, with little labour, make excellent hay. This grass is often set on fire, by the MONGALLS, in the spring, during high winds. At such times it burns most furiously, running like wild-fire, and spreading its flames to the distance of perhaps ten or twenty miles, till its progress is interrupted by some river or barren hill. The impe-

impetuofity of thefe flames, their fmoke and crackling noife, cannot eafily be conceived by thofe who have not feen them. When any perfon finds himfelf to the leeward of them, the only method, by which he can fave himfelf from their fury, is to kindle immediately the grafs where he ftands, and follow his own fire. For this purpofe, every perfon is provided with flints, fteel, and tinder. The reafon why the MONGALLS fet fire to the grafs is to procure early pafture for their cattle. The afhes, left upon the ground, fink into the earth at the melting of the fnow, and prove an excellent manure; fo that the grafs, in the spring, rifes on the lands, which have been prepared in this manner, as thick as a field of wheat. Caravans, travellers with merchandife, but efpecially armies, never encamp upon this rank grafs. And there are feveral inftances of confiderable bodies of men being put in confufion, and even defeated, by the enemy's fetting fire to the grafs.

Before I leave the RUSSIAN territories, I fhall give fome account of the marches between thefe two famous empires. The frontier, according to the beft information I could procure, begins, a great way weftward of this place, near the fource of the river DZIDA;

from thence it proceeds to the east, crossing the SE-LINGA, and runs along the tops of the hills, inclining sometimes to the north, and sometimes to the south, till it meets with the rivulet SARATZYN. It runs then in a very irregular line, varying its direction according to the course of the rivers and brooks; or, from the top of one hill to some other remarkable point in view; pointing, in general, towards the north-east, till it ends at the river ARGUN; which, together with the INGODA, forms the AMOOR. This boundary includes a vast tract of excellent land on the RUSSIAN side; and that part of the MONGALLS who inhabit it, being stout men, and living much at ease, will, in time, become a numerous people.

The marches were settled upon the present footing about twenty-five years ago, on the following occasion. The MONGALLS, on the CHINESE side, alledged, that their countrymen, subjects of RUSSIA, encroached on their borders; which created some disputes between the two nations. The causes of this misunderstanding being represented to the two courts, it was agreed to send ministers, with full powers to terminate the affair in an amicable manner. His Majesty's minister, THEODORE ALEXIOVITZ GOLOVIN, met the CHI-

NESE plenipotentiaries, on the frontiers, in the neighbourhood of NERTSHINSKY, a confiderable town, belonging to RUSSIA, near the river AMOOR. All matters were foon accommodated, to the mutual fatisfaction of both parties, on the footing of *uti poffidetis*; i. e. each of the parties retaining the people and territories that then belonged to them.

This determination kept all quiet for fome time. The CHINESE, however, foon appeared to be diffatisfied with the decifion; and want to have the marches reviewed; to which, in my opinion, the RUSSIANS will not eafily affent.

The 21ft, the conductor came to congratulate the ambaffador on his arrival at the borders; and acquainted him, that, the horfes and camels being ready, he might proceed when he pleafed. I cannot omit an inconfiderable circumftance, that happened at this place, as it ftrongly reprefents the caution and prudence of the CHINESE. Our conductor, having feen fome women walking in the fields, asked the ambaffador, who they were? and whither they were going? He was told, they belonged to the retinue, and were going along with it to CHINA.

He replied, they had women enough in PEKIN already;

ready; and, as there never had been an EUROPEAN woman in CHINA, he could not be anfwerable for introducing the firft, without a fpecial order from the Emperor. But, if his excellency would wait for an anfwer, he would difpatch a courier to court for that purpofe. The return of this meffenger could not be fooner than fix weeks; it was therefore thought more expedient to fend back the women to SELINGINSKY, with the waggons that brought our baggage to this place.

CHAPTER VII.

From paffing the SARATZYN, *and entering the* CHINESE *territories, to our arrival at the wall of* CHINA.

THE 22d of September, having loaded the camels with our baggage, and procured carriages for the boxes that contained his Majefty's prefents to the Emperor, which were too large for camels to bear, we mounted, and paffed the SARATZYN, and foon entered the CHINESE territories. We travelled fifteen miles, when we arrived, about evening, at the river ORCHON, running with a fmooth ftream to the north. The carriages

riages retarded our progress greatly, as the horses were sprightly, and unaccustomed to draught.

This day we commenced guests of the Emperor of CHINA, who entertains all ambassadors, and bears their expences, from the day they enter his dominions, till the time they quit them again. Our retinue consisted of about one hundred persons, who were allowed fifteen sheep every day. The overplus of this large allowance was given to the MONGALLS who drove the camels. Besides mutton and beef, there is no other kind of provision to be found, till you come within the wall of CHINA. The mutton is of a middle size; but, I must confess, exceeding fine. The conductor was attended by an officer from the Tush-du-Chan, who procured, from the MONGALLS encamped nearest our road, what sheep we wanted. The camels were very tractable, and stooped to take on their loads. But the horses were, at first, very unmanageable. Many of them had never before been employed for any use; and were saddled with great difficulty, but mounted with much more; for the very smell of our cloaths, which they perceived to be different from that of the MONGALLS, their masters, made them snort and spring with great

great fury. They were easily managed, notwithstanding, when we got upon their backs.

Our road, this day, lay through fine plains and vallies, covered with rank grafs; but not a single tent was to be seen. I inquired why such a fine soil was without inhabitants; and was told, that the CHINESE had forbid the MONGALLS to encamp so near the RUSSIAN borders, for fear of being allured to pass over to their territories, as many had formerly done. These fruitful vallies are surrounded with pleasant hills, of easy ascent, whose summits are covered with tufts of trees. Many of these tufts, being of a circular figure, and having no under-wood, appear as if they had been planted and pruned by art; others are irregular; and, sometimes, a ridge of trees runs from one hill to another. These objects afford a prospect so pleasing to the eye, and so seldom to be found, that one cannot help being charmed. And this pleasure is still heightened by the gentle-flowing rivulets; abounding with fish, and plenty of game, in the vallies, and among the trees.

The 23d, we set out early, and came to a rivulet, called IRA, running to the north-west, till it falls into the ORCHON; which we passed, and pitched our tents

on

on the other side. The rank grass, by accident, took fire; and, had not water been at hand to extinguish it, and the weather very calm, the consequences might have been fatal. We travelled farther this day than the former, as fewer inconveniencies arose from the restifness of the horses.

The 24th, we continued our journey towards the south-east, along smooth roads, through a pleasant country; and, at evening, reached a rivulet called SHARA, or the yellow rivulet, on the banks of which we set up our tents. The vallies now were more contracted; and less wood upon the hills, than formerly.

The 25th, we came to a rivulet called KARA, or the black rivulet, from the colour of the water, which is tinged by the richness of the soil.

The 26th, we proceeded. The country retained much the same appearance, and the weather was very fine; but not a single inhabitant was yet to be seen. In the evening, I walked from our tents, with some of our company, to the top of a neighbouring hill, where I found many plants of excellent rhubarb; and, by the help of a stick, dug up as much of it as I wanted.

On these hills are a great number of animals called marmots, of a brownish colour, having feet like a badger,

badger; and nearly of the same size. They make deep burrows on the declivities of the hills; and, it is said, that, in winter, they continue in these holes, for a certain time, even without food. At this season, however, they sit or ly near their burrows, keeping a strict watch; and, at the approach of danger, rear themselves upon their hind-feet, giving a loud whistle, like a man, to call in the stragglers; and then drop into their holes in a moment.

I should not have mentioned an animal so well known as the marmot, had it not been on account of the rhubarb. Wherever you see ten or twenty plants growing, you are sure of finding several burrows under the shades of their broad spreading leaves. Perhaps they may some times eat the leaves and roots of this plant. However, it is probable, the manure they leave about the roots, contributes not a little to its increase; and their casting up the earth makes it shoot out young buds, and multiply. This plant does not run, and spread itself, like docks, and others of the same species; but grows in tufts, at uncertain distances, as if the seeds had been dropped with design. It appears that the MONGALLS never accounted it worth cultivating; but that the world is obliged to the marmots for the quantities

scat-

scattered, at random, in many parts of this country. For whatever part of the ripe seed happens to be blown among the thick grass, can very seldom reach the ground, but must there wither and die; whereas, should it fall among the loose earth, thrown up by the marmots, it immediately takes root, and produces a new plant.

After digging and gathering the rhubarb, the MON-GALLS cut the large roots into small pieces, in order to make them dry more readily. In the middle of every piece they scoop a hole, through which a cord is drawn, in order to suspend them in any convenient place. They hang them, for most part, about their tents, and sometimes on the horns of their sheep. This is a most pernicious custom, as it destroys some of the best part of the root; for all about the hole is rotten and useless; whereas, were people rightly informed how to dig and dry this plant, there would not be one pound of refuse in an hundred; which would save a great deal of trouble and expence, that much diminish the profits on this commodity. At present, the dealers in this article think these improvments not worthy of their attention, as their gains are more considerable on this than on any other branch of trade. Perhaps the government may hereafter think it proper to make some regulations with regard to this matter.

I have been more particular in describing the growth and management of the rhubarb; because I never met with an author, or person, who could give a satisfactory account where, or how, it grows. I am persuaded, that, in such a dry climate as this, it might easily be so cultivated as to produce any quantity that could be wanted.

I omit any computation of the distances of places, along this road, as the whole of it, from the borders to PEKIN, has been measured by a wheel, or machine, given to the caravan, by the governor of SIBERIA, for that purpose. I shall afterwards subjoin the exact distances taken from this measurement.

The 27th, and 28th, we pursued the same road, over hills and through vallies. For, though few travel this way, the caravans, with their heavy carriages, leave such marks as are not soon effaced. It is only of late that the caravans travelled this road. Formerly they went farther to the north, by a RUSSIAN town called NERTZINSKY, and thence to a CHINESE city called NAUN. That road is more convenient than the present

present, as it lies through places better inhabited; but the present is shorter, and therefore taken by most travellers.

The 29th, we reached a river called BUROY, where we lodged. At this dry season all these rivers are fordable; and they abound with sturgeon, and other fish. Next morning, Mr. VENANT, our chief cook, dropped down, as he was coming out of his tent, and immediately expired, notwithstanding all possible care was taken for his recovery. We interred him as decently as time and circumstances would admit; and proceeded to a river called BOR-GUALTY, where we pitched our tents for this night.

October 1st, after a long day's journey, we reached a rivulet called KOYRA. The face of the country appeared nearly the same as formerly.

The 2d, after another long march, we came to the banks of the river TOLA, the largest we had seen since we left the SELINGA.

Next day, we crossed the TOLA at a pretty deep ford, where the river was in breadth about the flight of an arrow at point blank. It was noon before our camels got over, and too late to proceed. We were therefore obliged to set up our tents on the east bank of the river, which was overgrown with tall oziers.

Here our conductor furnished us with fresh horses and camels. From the borders to this place, our stages were regulated by brooks and rivers; for the conveniency of getting water. And, for the same reason, as there are no rivers nor brooks, from hence to the wall of CHINA, fountains and springs will be our only stages.

On the banks of the TOLA we found many MONGALLS encamped, with numerous flocks of cattle, being the first inhabitants we had seen since our leaving the border. The RUSSIANS, and the MONGALLS who are subjects of RUSSIA, claim all the country westward from the TOLA; which, they say, is the natural boundary between the two empires. This would indeed be a considerable addition to the dominions of RUSSIA. But, as both these mighty monarchs are abundantly provided with a vast extent of territory, neither party think it worth while to dispute about a few hundred miles of property, which, obtained, would perhaps not balance the cost, or contribute but little to the advantage of either.

The appearance of the country was now greatly altered to the worse. We saw no more pleasant hills and

and woods; neither could I find one single plant of rhubarb. The soil was dry and barren; and the grass not to be compared to what we had already passed over.

The 4th, after every man had drunk his fill of the pure and wholesome water of TOLA, and filled his bottle with it, we departed with some regret, as we could hope for no more rivers, or brooks, till we came to the wall of CHINA. We soon entered the desert commonly named, by the MONGALLS, the HUNGRY DESERT. How far it deserves that title, will be seen as we advance.

In the evening, we reached some pits, called TOLA-TOLOGOY, of brackish water, where we pitched our tents. The road still pointed to the south-east, with little variation, over grounds that rose a little at first, but afterwards gradually declined. We saw many MONGALIAN tents, and cattle, dispersed along the desert.

The 5th, we set out again, and, in the evening came to some fountains, called CHELO-TOLOGOY, of pretty fresh water. The country was quite level, and appeared to the eye as plain as the sea. The soil was dry,

dry, barren, and gravelly; and neither tree nor bush to be seen; a prospect not very agreeable.

The 6th, early in the morning, we proceeded eastward, through the same sort of flat country. The weather was very fine, and the roads excellent. In the evening, we arrived at a pool, called TYLACK, of brackish water, where we remained the following night. This day we saw several large flocks of antelopes, and some MONGALLS in their tents; which was no disagreeable object in this continued plain. We passed few of these tents without visiting them, where we always found an hospitable reception, and were entertained with some zaturan, a kind of tea which I formerly described. And, if we happened to stay till our baggage was gone out of sight, the landlord conducted us, by the shortest way, to the springs that terminated the next stage.

The next day, we came to the wells called GACHUN. Our bisket being now spent, we were reduced to live on mutton only, during the rest of our journey through this desert; which we accounted no great hardship, as it was extremely fine. It is not a little surprising, that, notwithstanding the barren appearance of this unsheltered plain, the cattle are in good condition, but particularly

ticularly the sheep. The short grafs, though in many places thinly scattered, must be of a very nourishing quality. This will naturally proceed from the climate, and the soil, which every where partakes of a nitrous quality, as plainly appears from the scurf of salt round the edges of the lakes and ponds, and the taste of the water, generally brackish in the springs and pits.

The 8th, our conductor furnished us with a fresh set of cattle, which detained us latter than our usual time of setting out. This day, the soil was very much inclined to gravel, containing a number of red and yellow pebbles, many of which, being transparent, made a fine appearance while the sun shone. We were informed there were sometimes stones of value found here; which so much excited our curiosity, that each of us, every day, picked up a considerable quantity. On examination, most of them were thrown away, as altogether useless; the few we thought proper to retain were wrought into very good seals. A man might gather a bushel of such stones every day in this desert. One of our people, a GRECIAN by birth, who understood something of the nature of stones, found one that he called a yellow sapphire, and valued it at fifty crowns. Perhaps these pebbles might be of that kind
which

which the lapidaries call cornelian; for they are sufficiently hard, and take a fine polish.

The 9th, we set out early, and travelled to a pool named OKO-TOULGU. This day, a lama from the Kutuchtu, going to PEKIN, joined our company, who, by his habit and equipage, seemed to be a person of eminence. In marching along the tedious desert, the conversation turned on a terrible earthquake which happened, during the month of July last, in CHINA, between the long wall and PEKIN; and had laid in ruins several villages, and walled towns, and buried many people in their ruins. The lama inquired what was the opinion of the learned men in EUROPE concerning the cause of this phaenomenon. We told him, it was commonly reckoned to be subterraneous fire; and then asked, in our turn, to what cause such extraordinary appearances were imputed by his countrymen? He replied, that some of their learned lamas had written, that GOD, after he had formed the earth, placed it on a golden frog; and, whenever this prodigious frog had occasion to scratch its head, or stretch out its foot, that part of the earth, immediately above, was shaken. There was no reasoning on a notion so fantastical; we therefore left the lama to please himself with his hypothesis

pothesis, and turned the discourse to some other subject.

The 10th, we came to the springs called KORPARTU. The appearances of things this day were almost the same as on the preceding days. The soil appeared so barren, that none of the common methods of improvement could make it bear any kind of grain, or even alter its present condition. The dispositions of its inhabitants, the MONGALLS, seem wonderfully suited to their situation; as they appear more contented with their condition than those who possess the most fruitful countries.

In the evening of the 11th, we arrived at KHODODU; where we found the water clear, and pretty fresh, bursting, in a strong spring, from the gravelly earth, and running, in a stream, to a considerable distance, till it loses itself in the sand. This was the first running water we had seen since we left the TOLA. And we were as happy, while sitting round this fountain, and broiling our mutton chops, as others at a table plentifully furnished with BURGUNDY and CHAMPAIGN. Our appetites were, indeed, very keen; to which daily exercise, the coldness of the air, and drinking nothing but water, greatly contributed.

CHAP. VII.
1720.

Next morning, being the 12th, there was a little froft upon the ground. Several flocks of gray plovers came to drink at the spring; of which our people killed as many as our prefent circumftances required. Thefe poor harmlefs birds feemed infenfible of danger; and, perhaps, they had never before heard the report of a gun; for no fooner was the piece fired, than they took a fhort flight round the fountain, whiftling as they flew, and immediately alighted to drink again. The plover is a pretty bird, and pleafant to eat; and the foles of its feet are as hard as fo much horn, which prevent its being hurt by the ftones or gravel. In the evening, we came to the wells called BOUK-HOR-LIKE, without any thing material happening, or any difference on the face of the country.

The 13th, we continued our journey to the wells of BUDURUY; where we were again furnifhed with frefh horfes and camels.

The 14th, we came to a place, called KADAN-KACHU, where we were obliged to dig a pit, four feet deep, in order to procure water; which was very bad, having both a difagreeable fmell, and bitter tafte; but was drinkable, when boiled with fome tea. We could, however, get none for our cattle, as the high wind filled

the

the pits with sand as fast as we could dig them. This sand is of a whitish colour, and so light and dry, that it is driven, by the winds, into your face and eyes; and becomes very disagreeable. Most of our people, indeed, were provided with a piece of net-work, made of horse-hair, which covered their eyes; and is very useful in drifts, either of sand or snow.

The 15th, we travelled over deep sands; and, in the evening, arrived at other springs called TZAGAN-TEGGERICK. The wind continuing high, it was with much difficulty we set up our tents. It is to be observed, that, on these deep and light sands, our EUROPEAN tents are of little use, as there is no earth in which the tent-pins can be fastened. The TARTAR tents are much preferable; for, their figure being round and taper, like a bee-hive, the wind takes but little hold of them; and they stand, equally well, on a sandy, or on any other surface. They are, besides, warmer, more easily erected, taken down, and transported.

The 16th, we left the deep sand, and travelled along the same sort of dry gravelly ground as formerly. In the evening, we pitched our tents at the springs called SADJIN. The variety of objects, in this dreary waste,

waste, are so few, that, in this, as well as in other respects, it much resembles the sea. Here one can see no farther than if he was placed on the surface of the water, out of sight of land; the rounding of the globe, in both cases, being the same. Sometimes, in the morning, I have been agreeably surprized in fancying I saw, at a small distance, a fine river, having rows of trees growing upon it banks; but this was only a deception of the sight, proceeding from the vapours magnifying some scattered shrubs into great trees.

The 17th, we came to some wells of very bad water, called OUDEY, where we found fresh horses and camels waiting for us. Our conductor resolved to lose no time, being apprehensive that we might be overtaken in the desert by the frost and deep snow, which usually happen at this season. Such an event would have retarded our march, and incommoded us not a little in many respects. We therefore travelled as long stages as the convenience of water, and the strength of our cattle would permit.

The 18th, after a long day's journey, we came to the wells called ULAN-KALA. We found, almost every day, MONGALLS in their tents, which stood like so many hives, dispersed through this solitary plain.

The

The 19th, we mounted again, and travelled to the springs named TZILAN-TEGGERICK. This day we saw several flocks of antelopes; and, indeed, few days passed in which we did not see some of these animals.

The 20th, we came to a place called OURANDABU. The weather still continued fair, the sky clear, and the mornings frosty. The water, at this place, was tolerable; but we were obliged to dig for it. When it happened that we had a long stage from one spring to another, for fear of coming too late, we usually sent a couple of men before us, in order to gather fewel, and to dig pits, that the water might have time to settle before our arrival.

The 21st, we proceeded; and, in the evening, arrived at a lake of salt water. After digging, however, we found some fresher. Were it not that these lakes and pits are scattered through this desert, it must have been altogether uninhabited, either by man or beast. This consideration, among many others, has often led me to admire the infinite wisdom of almighty God, in the dispensations of his providence, for the support of all his creatures.

In my opinion, these springs are produced by the rains and melted snow in the spring; for the water sinking in the sand, is thereby prevented from being exhaled, in summer, by the heat of the sun; which must be very scorching in this desert, in which there is not the least shade to be found.

The 22d, we quitted the salt lake, in a cold frosty morning, and a strong northerly wind; which was very disagreeable. At evening we reached the wells of KU-LAT. These pits take their names from the quality of the water, as salt, sour, sweet, bitter; or from the different tribes of people who inhabit the country in the neighbourhood.

In the midst of our fatigues, we had the satisfaction to be among a friendly people, who did every thing in their power to lessen our wants.

Next day, we reached the wells of MINGAT. The weather, though cold, was not unpleasant. And, the 24th, having got fresh horses and camels, we came, in the evening, to a pond of brackish water, called KO-RUNTEER, upon the extremity of a dismal bank of sand, running a-cross our road.

The day following, we entered on the sand-bank, along a narrow and crooked passage between two hillocks. Every one prayed for calm weather while we travelled over the sand; which put me in mind of being

at

at sea. We continued our journey, through deep sand, till about noon; when, all our horses and camels being tired, we halted in a hollow place; where we dug, and found very bad water. We remained here till next morning.

Our cattle being a little refreshed, though they had been very indifferently fed among the sand, where nothing was to be seen but some tufts of withered grass, we set out again. Along this bank there is not the least tract, or path of any kind; for the smallest blast of wind immediately effaces it, and renders all the surface smooth.

We had gone but a few miles when most of our people were obliged to alight, and walk on foot, the horses being quite tired with the deepness of the sand; which made our progress extremely slow. The weather, fortunately, was still very calm. About noon, we pitched our tents in a hollow place, encompassed with high hillocks of sand. I observed, that, in the open desert we had already passed, the prospect was much confined; but here it was quite straitened; for, if you ascended one of these mounts, you could see nothing but mount rising above mount, like so many sugar-loaves, or rather like so many cupolas.

In

In the evening it began to blow a little at northeast, which drove about the light sand like snow; but, about midnight, the wind rose to such an height, that all our tents were overset at once, and our beds filled with sand. As it was near morning, we thought it not worth while to pitch them again. We therefore prepared ourselves to set out at the dawn, in hopes of getting over the sand-bank before night; which, by riding and walking by turns, in order to hasten our progress, we happily effected. And, in the evening, reached the springs of KOCHATU.

At the place where we passed the sand, it was not above twenty ENGLISH miles in breadth, which took us up three days. We could have travelled four times that distance on the plain, with more ease both to ourselves and cattle. I am informed this bank of sand runs a great way southward; and, in some places, is above thirty leagues broad. They, whose business calls them often to cross the sands, have thin leather coats, made on purpose, and round pieces of glass tied before their eyes.

This sand-bank appears like the waves of the sea; for the hillocks, some of which are about twenty feet of perpendicular height, are of so light a nature, that the wind

wind carries them from place to place; levelling one, and forming another. And hence it is eafy to conceive, that, a weary traveller, lying down on the lee-fide of one of thefe hillocks, might, in a few hours, be buried in the fand; which is reported to have often happened in this and other fandy deferts.

The 28th, we proceeded along the plain to the fprings called CHABERTU. I cannot but take notice of the uncommon manner the people here have of killing their fheep. They make a flit with a knife between two ribs, through which they put their hand, and fqueeze the heart till the creature expire; by this method all the blood remains in the carcafs. When the fheep is dead, and hungry people cannot wait till the flefh is regularly dreffed, they generally cut out the bisket and rump, wool and all, and broil them on the coals; then fcrape off the finged wool, and eat them. This I have found, by experience, to be no difagreeable morfel, even without any kind of fauce.

The next day, we travelled another ftage to the wells of SAMINSA; where we found better water than ufual. The length and thicknefs of the grafs fhowed that the foil now began to mend. This day there fell fome fnow, and the wind was cold and northerly.

The 30th, we got fresh horses, and proceeded to the springs of KREMA. From the appearance of the grafs one would conclude, that the soil, at this place, was very fine. We saw great numbers of horses, belonging to the Emperor, turned out to graze. Notwithstanding all the haste we had hitherto made, we were, this day, overtaken by a fall of snow, which proved very inconvenient; not so much on account of the cold, but it covered all fewel, so that we could find none to dress our victuals.

The 31st, we came to a place called NARINGKARUSSU, where, to our great satisfaction, we found a small brook of fresh water, and some MONGALIAN huts. I observed, that, from the sand-bank eastward, the soil becomes gradually better every day. This was now the fortieth day, since we left the border; during which time we had not halted one day, nor seen a single house; and the twentieth and eight, from the time we quitted the river TOLA, and entered the desert, in which we had neither seen river, tree, bush, nor mountain. Though we were obliged now and then to fetch a compass, on account of the watering places, yet, in general, our course deviated but little from the south-east point.

The 1st of November, we halted at this place, that we might have time to put things in order before we passed the long wall, which was now at no great distance.

Next day we proceeded, and about noon we could perceive the famous wall, running along the tops of the mountains, towards the north-east. One of our people cried out LAND, as if we had been all this while at sea. It was now, as nearly as I can compute, about forty ENGLISH miles from us, and appeared white at this distance. We could not, this night, reach the passage through the mountains; and, therefore, pitched our tents in the open plain as usual. We now began to feel the effects of the cold; for the snow, continuing to ly upon the desert, proved very inconvenient on many accounts; but particularly by retarding the progress of our heavy and cumbersome baggage. But we comforted ourselves with the hopes of soon seeing an end of all our toils, and arriving in a rich and inhabited country; for, though all of our people were in good health, they began to be very weary of the desert; and no wonder, as many of them had lain in the open field ever since we left SELINGINSKY.

November 3d, after travelling about an hour, we passed

passed the vestiges of a camp, which seemed to have been regularly designed. I was informed that the Emperor encamped here, when he led his troops against the MONGALLS, called, by the missionaries in CHINA, the WESTERN TARTARS.

The nearer we came to the mountains, we were the more surprised at the sight of the so much celebrated wall of CHINA, commonly called, for its length, the endless wall. The appearance of it, running from one high rock to another, with square towers at certain intervals, even at this distance, is most magnificent.

About noon, we quitted the plain, and entered an opening between two mountains. To the left, the mountains are very high. On the right, they decline as far as they are within view; but, I am told, they rise again to a great height.

We descended by a narrow path, about eight feet broad, between the mountains, till we came to a small CHINESE monastery, situated on the declivity of a steep rock. Curiosity led us to visit this solitary place. But, the road being impassable to horses, we alighted and walked thither. On our arriving near the place, the monks came out to meet us, with the usual friendly salutation of the country; which is performed by lay-

ing

ing one of their hands on the other, and then shaking them, and pronouncing these words *Cho-loy-cho*. The compliment being returned, they conducted us into the apartments of their little chapel, and treated us with a dish of green tea; which was very agreeable. In the chapel was a sort of altar-piece, on which were placed several small brass images; and, in one of the corners, I observed a sack filled with wheat. The habit of the monks, was a long gown with wide sleeves. On their heads was a small cap, and their long lank hair hung down over their shoulders. They had very few hairs in their beards. This being the first CHINESE house we met with, I have, on that account, been more particular in describing it. Every thing now appeared to us as if we had arrived in another world. We felt, especially, a sensible alteration in the weather; for, instead of the cold bleak wind in the desert, we had here a warm and pleasant air.

We again proceeded along the narrow path; but of breadth sufficient for a wheel-carriage. The road being steep, and in many places rugged, we walked down the hill; and, in half an hour, came to the foot of it, where we found ourselves surrounded, on all sides, by high rocky mountains. Our route now lay along the
south

south side of a rivulet, full of great stones, which had fallen from the rocks in rainy weather. In the cliffs of the rocks you see little scattered cottages, with spots of cultivated ground, much resembling those romantick figures of landskips which are painted on the CHINA-ware and other manufactures of this country. These are accounted fanciful by most EUROPEANS, but are really natural.

After we had travelled about seven or eight miles, along the bank of the brook, we came, in the evening, to a CHINESE village, at the foot of a high mountain, where we lodged in clean rooms with warm fires of charcoal. There were no chimneys in the rooms; but, instead of these, the charcoal was put into a portable grate of brass or iron, and allowed to burn clear in the open air; after which it was brought into the apartment. Though the desert is one continued plain, it lies much higher than the plains and villages of CHINA; for, when we entered the defile, the ascent was very inconsiderable when compared with the descent on the other side.

Here we began to taste of the fine fruits of CHINA; for, soon after our arrival in the village, our conductor sent a present to the ambassador of some baskets of of fruits; confifting of water-melons, musk-melons, fweet and bitter oranges, peaches, apples, wall-nuts, chefs-nuts, and feveral other forts which I never faw before; together with a jar of CHINESE arrack, provifions of feveral forts, and fome CHINESE bread, called bobon, made of wheaten flour, and baked over a pot with the fteam of boiling-water. It is very light, and not difagreeable in tafte; at leaft it feemed fo to us, who had feen no bread for a month before.

Next day, we halted to refrefh ourfelves after our long fatigue. I took this opportunity to walk up to the top of the mountain, in order to view the adjacent country; but could only fee a continuation of the chain of mountains, rifing one above another, and, to the northward, fome glimpfes of the long wall, as it runs along them.

The 5th, we proceeded eaftward, down the fouth bank of a river, whofe channel was covered with great ftones. The road is cut out of the rock, for a confiderable length, at thofe places where there is no natural paffage between the rocks and the river; which muft have been a work of great labour. This river cannot fail to be a complete torrent in time of great rains.

Having

A JOURNEY

CHAP. VII.
1720.

Having travelled about six or eight miles, we arrived at the famous wall of CHINA. We entered at a great gate, which is shut every night, and always guarded by a thousand men, under the command of two officers of distinction, one a CHINESE, and the other a MANTZUR TARTAR; for, it is an established custom in CHINA, and has prevailed ever since the conquest of the TARTARS, that, in all places of publick trust, there must be a CHINESE and a TARTAR invested with equal power. This rule is observed both in civil and military affairs. The CHINESE pretend, that, two in an office are a sort of spies upon one another's actions, and thereby many fraudulent practices are either prevented or detected.

CHAPTER VIII.

From the wall of CHINA *to* PEKIN; *Our entry into that city.*

AS soon as we had entered the gate, these two officers, and many subalterns, came to compliment the ambassador on his safe arrival; and asked the favour of him to walk into the guard-room and drink a dish of tea. We accordingly dismounted, and went

into

into a spacious hall on the south side of the gate. This apartment was very clean, having benches all around; and is kept on purpose for the reception of persons of distinction. We were entertained with variety of fruits and confections, and several sorts of tea. After staying about half an hour, the ambassador took leave of the gentlemen, and we proceeded on our journey. We travelled about four miles farther, and came to a considerable town named KALGAN. At some distance from the place, we were met by the commandant, and the Mandarin TULISHIN, who had paid us a visit at SELINGINSKY. They accompanied the ambassador to his lodgings; which were in houses a-part from the rest of the town; and provisions were sent us in great plenty.

From the wall to this place, the country, to the north, begins to open; and contains some villages, corn-fields, and gardens.

The same evening, the ambassador and the gentlemen of the retinue were invited to sup at the commandant's house; and horses were sent to carry us thither. We alighted in the outer-court, where the commandant in person waited for us; and conducted us, through a neat inner-court, into a hall, in the middle

middle of which stood a large brass chaffing-dish, in shape of an urn, with a fire of charcoal in it. The floor was covered with mats, and the room quite set round with chairs, and little square japanned tables. The ambassador sat at a table by himself, and the rest of the company at separate tables, by two and two. We were first entertained with tea, and a dram of hot arrack; after which supper was brought, and placed on the tables, without either table-cloth, napkins, knives, or forks. Instead of forks, were laid down, to every person, a couple of ivory-pins, with which the CHINESE take up their meat. The dishes were small, and placed upon the table in the most regular manner; the vacancies being filled with saucers, containing pickles and bitter herbs. The entertainment consisted of pork, mutton, fowls, and two roasted pigs. The carver sits upon the floor, and executes his office with great dexterity. He cuts the flesh into such small bits, as may easily be taken up by the guests, without further trouble. The meat being cut up, is given to the footmen, who supply the empty dishes on the tables. The whole is served in CHINA-ware; and neither gold nor silver is to be seen. All the servants perform their duty with the utmost regularity, and without the least noise.

noife. I muft confefs, I was never better pleafed with any entertainment.

The victuals being removed, the defert was placed on the tables in the fame order; and confifted of a variety of fruits and confections. In the mean time a band of mufick was called in, which confifted of ten or twelve performers, on various, but chiefly wind-inftruments, fo different from thofe of that clafs in EUROPE, that I fhall not pretend to defcribe them. The mufick was accompanied with dancing, which was very entertaining. The dancers were nearly as numerous as the muficians. Their performances were only a kind of gefticulation, confifting of many ridiculous poftures; for they feldom moved from the fame place. The evening being pretty far fpent, we took leave, and returned to our lodgings.

The 6th, a great fall of fnow, and a cold frofty wind, obliged us to halt at this place.

Next day, the froft and fnow ftill continued; notwithftanding, we fet out, and paffed over a ftone-bridge, near this place, paved, not with fmall ftones, but, with large, fquare, free ftones, neatly joined. After travelling eaftward about thirty ENGLISH miles, we reached a large and populous city called SIANG-FU. We were

were met, without the gate, by some of the principal inhabitants, and conducted to our lodgings.

When we arrived, the governor was out a-hunting with one of the Emperor's sons. As soon as he returned in the evening, he waited on the ambassador, and complimented him in a very polite manner; excusing himself for not waiting on him sooner. At the same time, he gave his excellency a formal invitation to supper; for it is appointed, by the court, that foreign ambassadors should be magnificently entertained in all the towns through which they pass. But the ambassador, being somewhat indisposed, desired to be excused.

Our route, this day, was through a fine champaign country, well cultivated, but containing very few trees. We passed several small towns, and many villages, well built, and inclosed with walls. The roads were well made, and in good order; running always in straight lines, where the ground will allow. I had heard a great deal of the order and oeconomy of these people; but found my information far short of what I daily saw in all their works and actions. The streets of every village run in straight lines.

Upon the road we met with many turrets, called

post-

post-houses, erected at certain distances from one another, with a flag-staff, on which is hoisted the imperial pendant. These places are guarded by a few soldiers, who run a-foot, from one post to another, with great speed; carrying letters or dispatches that concern the Emperor. The turrets are so contrived, as to be in sight of one another; and, by signals, they can convey intelligence of any remarkable event. By this means the court is informed, in the speediest manner imaginable, of whatever disturbance may happen in the most remote provinces of the empire. These posts are also very useful, by keeping the country free from highwaymen; for should a person escape at one house, on a signal being made, he would certainly be stopped at the next. The distance of one post-house from another is usually five CHINESE li, or miles; each li consisting of five hundred bow-lengths. I compute five of their miles to be about two and an half ENGLISH.

The 8th, we halted at this place. As we could not be present at the entertainment to which we were invited, last night, by the governor, he had resolved that the delicacies, prepared on that occasion, should not be lost; and therefore sent into our court twelve tables, whereon were placed, by a number of people, all the

victuals

victuals that were dressed the preceding night, with the desert, and several sorts of tea. The whole was afterwards brought into the hall; and there placed, in form, upon the tables. When this was done, an officer of distinction came to desire the ambassador to taste of his Imperial Majesty's bounty. We accordingly sat down at the tables in great order. Every thing was very good, but mostly cold; having been carried through the streets to some distance. After we had removed from the table, the person, who had the direction of the entertainment, called our servants, and ordered them to sit down at the tables, and eat. This produced a very diverting scene; but, had it not been complied with, the governor would have thought himself highly affronted.

In the evening, the Emperor's third son went through this city, on his way towards the capital. He was carried, upon men's shoulders, in a palankin; a vehicle very easy for the traveller, and well known in EUROPEAN settlements in INDIA. The Emperor's sons have no other names than those of first, second, third, &c. This prince had only a small retinue of a few horsemen.

Our new conductor, TULISHIN, invited the ambassador

fador and his retinue to pass the evening at his lodgings. His excellency excused himself, as he had not been at the governor's. All the gentlemen, however, accepted the invitation. The entertainment was elegant, and something like that I formerly described, accompanied with dancing and musick, and quail-fighting. It is surprising to see how these little birds fly at one another, as soon as they are set upon the table; and fight, like game-cocks, to death. The CHINESE are very fond of this diversion; and bet as high on their quails, as the ENGLISH do on cocks. They are also great lovers of cock-fighting; but it is reckoned among the vulgar sports. The quails are generally parted before they hurt one another too much; and reserved, in cages, till another occasion.

The 9th, having sent off the baggage in the morning, the ambassador returned the governor's visit. We only staid to drink tea; after which we immediately mounted, and pursued our journey to a small town called JUNY; where we arrived in the evening. Near this place is a steep rock, standing on a plain, inaccessible on all sides, except to the west; where a narrow winding path is cut in the rock, which leads to a PAGAN temple and nunnery, built upon the top of it.

These

CHAP. VIII.
1720.

These edifices make a pretty appearance from the plain; and, as the story goes, were built, from the foundation, in one night, by a lady, on the following occasion. This lady was very beautiful, virtuous, and rich; and had many powerful princes for her suitors. She told them, she intended to build a temple and a monastery, of certain dimensions, with her own hands, in one night, on the top of this rock; and whoever would undertake to build a stone-bridge, over a river in the neighbourhood, in the same space of time, him she promised to accept for a husband. All the lovers, having heard the difficult task imposed on them, returned to their respective dominions; except one stranger, who undertook to perform the hard condition. The lover and the lady began their labour at the same time; and the lady completed her part before the light appeared; but, as soon as the sun was risen, she saw, from the top of the rock, that her lover had not half-finished his bridge; having raised only the pillars for the arches. Failing, therefore, in his part of the performance, he also was obliged to depart to his own country; and the lady passed the remainder of her days in her own monastery.

The river is about a quarter of a mile from the rock,

rock, and the pillars still remain about five or six feet above the water; they are six or eight in number, and good substantial work. This tale I relate as a specimen of many fabulous stories, which I heard every day, and the people firmly believe. In the monastery there are, at present, many monks and nuns.

The chain of mountains running to the north, which bound this plain to the west, are very high, rugged, and barren. Their breadth, from the desert to the plain habitable country of CHINA, I compute not to exceed fifteen or twenty miles, and in many places it is much less. But their length, I am informed, is above one thousand ENGLISH miles. They encompass all, or the greatest part of the empire of CHINA, to the north and west. These impregnable bulwarks, together with the almost impassable deserts, have, in my opinion, so long preserved this nation from being over-run by the western heroes. One would imagine, that a country, so fortified by nature, had little need of such a strong wall for its defence; for, if all the passes of the mountains are as narrow and difficult as that where we entered, a small number of men might defend it against a mighty army.

JUNY is but a small place; it suffered greatly by the earth-

CHAP. VIII. earthquake that happened in the month of July the
1720. preceding year; above one half of it being thereby
laid in ruins. Indeed more than one half of the towns
and villages, through which we travelled this day, had
suffered much on the same occasion; and vast numbers
of people had been buried in the ruins. I must confess, it was a dismal scene to see, every where, such
heaps of rubbish.

All the best houses being thrown down by the earthquake, we were lodged in the priests apartments of a
temple, which had escaped the general devastation.
Our conductor treated the monks with very little ceremony, and desired them to seek other lodgings for
themselves. These priests were not at all superstitious, as appeared sufficiently from the little reverence
they paid to their idols, and statues of reputed saints.
They conducted us into the temple, and several apartments adjoining, where stood many images of saints,
some of which were monstrous figures of stone and plaister. One of the priests gave us the history of some of
them; which I thought too absurd to be inserted. We
then returned into the temple, which was a small but
neat building. In one end of it we saw an altar, rising by steps to the cieling, on which were placed a

number

number of small images, cast chiefly in brass, resembling men and women, birds and beasts. We were entertained in the temple with tea, till the priests had removed their beds. At the entrance is hung a large bell, attended by a priest, who tolls it on seeing passengers, in order to invite them to say their prayers; which having done, they generally leave a small gratuity to the temple.

In the night, we were a little alarmed with the shock of an earthquake, which awakened all our people, but did no damage.

Next day, our conductor notified to the ambassador, that he could proceed no farther till he received an answer to some dispatches he had sent to court. These news were not altogether agreeable, as we apprehended another shock of an earthquake. Nothing, however, of that kind happened during the two days we were obliged to remain at this place.

The 12th, we continued our journey to a little town, where we lodged. This, and most of the towns, and villages, through which we passed to day, had suffered greatly by the earthquake; particularly one considerable walled town, where very few houses remained, and the walls were levelled with the ground.

CHAP. VIII.
1720.

About noon, next day, we came to a large, populous, and well built city, with broad streets, as straight as a line. Near this place runs a fine river, which appears navigable; having a-crofs it a noble ftone bridge, of several arches, and paved with large square ftones. In the evening, we arrived at a fmall town, after paffing through a very pleafant and fruitful country.

On the 14th, we halted at this little town. But our baggage, and his majefty's prefents, advanced a ftage farther. Thefe, by order of the Mandarin, our conductor, were carried on mens fhoulders, covered with pieces of yellow filk; as every thing is which hath any connexion with the court. Whatever is diftinguifhed by this badge is looked on as facred. And he who has the care of any thing belonging to the Emperor needs no other protection: fuch is the reverence paid him all over the empire. The yellow colour is chofen by the Emperor, becaufe, among the CHINESE, it is the emblem of the fun, to which he is compared.

The following day, our road, lying over fome rocks, was very rugged. In fome places it was cut, for a confiderable length, above twenty feet deep, through the folid rock; which appears to have been a work of great labour and expence. But no people, I ever faw, take fuch such pains to make their streets, and high-ways, easy to travellers, as the CHINESE. In some places of the rocks were cut out images of CHINESE saints; but the workmanship very mean.

Near this place, we passed through six or eight strong semicircular walls, within one another, which have the endless wall for their common diameter, and take in a great compass. In all these walls there are large well built gates, guarded by a constant watch, both in times of peace and war. At one of them, the ambassador was saluted with three great guns, from a tower over the gate-way. These walls seem to be of the same materials and architecture with the long wall; having square towers at the distance of a bow-shot from each other. While we stopped at one of the gates to refresh ourselves, I took the opportunity to walk into one of these towers, where I saw some hundreds of old iron cannon thrown together as useless. On examination, I found them to be composed of three or four pieces of hammered iron, joined, and fastened together with hoops of the same metal. The CHINESE have, however, now learned to cast as fine brass cannon as are any where to be found. From this tower I was led, by a broad stone-stair, to the top of the

the wall, which is above twenty feet in breadth, and paved with large square stones, closely joined, and cemented with strong mortar. I walked along this flat, till I came to a rock, where I found a high stair of above a thousand steps, the whole breadth of the wall, which led to a tower on the summit, from whence I could see a like stair, on the other side, forming a descent to a narrow passage between two rocks. I observed also, that the wall was neither so high nor broad where it was carried over another rock, to the south-west, as at the place where I stood. But time not allowing me to go farther, I returned, by the same way, to our company; and, after staying a few hours, we proceeded, this afternoon, to the town of ZULINGUANG, where we lodged.

The next day, after travelling about two hours, we came to the last semicircular wall. Here ended all the hills and mountains. Our road now lay through a fine champaign country, interspersed with many small towns and villages. In the evening, we reached a large neat city called ZANG-PING-JEW. In the market place, stood a triumphal arch, whereon were hung a number of streamers, and silken pendants, of various colours. The streets were clean, straight, and broad; in some places

places covered with gravel, in others paved with flat square stones.

As soon as we had reached our lodgings, the governor of the place came to salute the ambassador, and invited him to an entertainment, prepared by order of his majesty.

The invitation was accepted, and we immediately went to the governor's palace. The entertainment was very magnificent, somewhat of the same kind with that I formerly described, and accompanied with musick and dancing. This place is situated in a fruitful plain, about thirty ENGLISH miles northward of PEKIN.

The 17th, after travelling about a dozen of miles, we came to a small town called SHACH. The weather being very fine and warm, the governor came to meet the ambassador, and desired him to refresh himself a little by drinking tea. Here we halted about an hour, and then proceeded six or eight miles farther, to a small village, about four miles from the capital; where we lodged.

Next morning, two Mandarins came from court to congratulate the ambassador on his arrival, and brought some horses, on which he and his retinue were to make their entry. The furniture of the horses

ses was very simple, and far inferior to the costly trappings of the PERSIANS.

My lodgings, in this village, happened to be at a cook's house; which gave me an opportunity of observing the ingenuity of these people, even on trifling occasions. My landlord being in his shop, I paid him a visit; where I found six kettles, placed in a row on furnaces, having a separate opening under each of them, for receiving the fewel, which consisted of a few small sticks and straw. On his pulling a thong, he blew a pair of bellows, which made all his kettles boil in a very short time. They are indeed very thin, and made of cast iron, being extremely smooth both within and without. The scarcity of fewel, near such a populous city, prompts people to contrive the easiest methods of dressing their victuals, and keeping themselves warm during the winter, which is severe for two months.

About ten of the clock, we mounted, and proceeded towards the city, in the following order.

An officer, with his sword drawn.
Three soldiers.
One kettle-drummer.
Twenty four soldiers, three in a rank.

The

TO PEKIN.

The steward.
Twelve footmen.
Two pages.
Three interpreters.
The ambassador, and a Mandarin of distinction.
Two secretaries.
Six gentlemen, two and two.
Servants and attendants.

The whole retinue was drest in their best apparel. The soldiers in uniform, carrying their muskets like horsemen standing centry; drawn swords being refused by our conductor, the officer only had that priviledge.

We travelled from the village, along a fine road, through a cloud of dust and multitudes of spectators; and, in two hours, entered the city at the great north gate; which opened into a spacious street, perfectly straight, as far as the eye-sight could reach. We found it all sprinkled with water, which was very refreshing after the dust we had passed through.

A guard of five hundred CHINESE horsemen was appointed to clear the way; notwithstanding which, we found it very difficult to get through the crowd. One would have imagined all the people in PEKIN were assembled to see us; though I was informed that only a

small

CHAP. VIII. small part of the inhabitants of the city were present.
1720. I observed also great crowds of women unveiled; but they kept in the windows, doors, and in corners of the street. The soldiers did not behave with roughness to the people, as in some other places of the east; but treated them with great mildness and humanity. Indeed the people, of themselves, made as much way as was possible for them, considering their numbers. After a march of two hours from the gate where we entered; we, at last, came to our lodgings, in that part of the city called the TARTAR's town; which is near the center of PEKIN, and not far from the Emperor's palace.

We lodged in what is called the RUSSIA-house. It was allotted, by the present Emperor, for the accommodation of the caravans from MOSCOVY; and is surrounded with a high wall of brick, which incloses three courts. The first, from the street, is appointed for the guard of CHINESE soldiers. The second is a spacious square, on the sides whereof are apartments for servants. The third is divided from the second by a high brick-wall, through which you enter by a great gate. Opposite to this gate is the great hall, which rises a few steps above the level of the court. The floor

floor is neatly paved with white and black marble; and, on the same floor, to the right and left of the hall, are two small bed-chambers. This hall was occupied by the ambassador. In the same court are two large houses, divided into apartments, in which the retinue was lodged. All these structures are but of one story, with large windows of lettice-work, on which is pasted white paper. The cielings are very flight and airy; consisting only of strong laths, with reeds laid a-cross them, and done over on the in-side with paper. The roofs project considerably over the walls, and are covered with fine, light, glazed tiles; which, as far as I could learn, are of a quality to last ages. The bed-chambers only of the hall are neatly finished with lath and plaister.

The same evening, the master of the ceremonies came to compliment the ambassador. He, in the Emperor's name, enquired into the chief subject of his commission; and, having received a satisfactory answer, retired.

This gentleman, named ALOY, was, by birth, a MONGALL TARTAR; and a great favourite of the Emperor. He was a person of great politeness; and a good friend to the CHRISTIANS, especially the missionaries, who received fresh marks of his kindness every day. In his youth he conversed much with the JESUITS, who taught him geography, and some other branches of science; which contributed not a little to raise his character among the CHINESE, and recommend him to the notice and favour of the Emperor.

Thus we happily arrived at the famous and long wished for city of PEKIN, the capital of this mighty empire, after a tedious journey of exactly sixteen months. It is, indeed, very long; yet may be performed in much less time. I am of opinion that travellers might go from ST. PETERSBURG to PEKIN, and return, in the space of six months; which, were it necessary, I think I could easily demonstrate.

After the departure of the master of the ceremonies, the aleggada, or prime minister, sent an officer to salute the ambassador, and excuse himself for not paying him a visit immediately, as it was then late in the night; but promised to see him next day. At the same time he sent great variety of fruits and provisions, as a mark of respect, notwithstanding we were abundantly supplied with these things by those appointed for that purpose.

At ten of the clock at night, the officer on guard, in

in the outer-court, locked our gate, and sealed it with the Emperor's seal; that no person might go out, or come in, during the night. The ambassador, not approving of this proceeding, as soon as the gate was opened in the morning, sent his secretary, and an interpreter, to the prime minister, to complain of his being confined. The aleggada said he was altogether ignorant of what had happened; but expressly forbid any such behaviour for the future. In PERSIA, indeed, and some other nations of the east, it is the custom to restrain foreign ministers from conversing with the inhabitants, till they have had an audience of the prince.

THE END OF THE FIRST VOLUME.

www.ingramcontent.com/pod-product-compliance
Lightning Source LLC
Chambersburg PA
CBHW030407230426
43664CB00007BB/788